OUR VISIT

TO

HINDOSTÁN, KASHMIR, AND LADAKH.

BY

MRS J. C. MURRAY AYNSLEY.

GYAN

Published by

Gyan Publishing House
5, Ansari Road
Daryaganj, New Delhi-110002
Phone: 011-47034999, 9811692060
E-mail: books@gyanbooks.com

Distribution Network
gyanbooks.com
India, USA, Canada, UK, Australia, France

ISBN: 978-81-212-7779-2 (PB)
First Published, 1879

2nd Impression 2023

Printed at: Gyan Press, Delhi.

OUR VISIT TO HINDOSTÁN, KASHMIR, AND LADAKH
Author: J. C. MURRAY AYNSLEY

OUR VISIT

TO

HINDOSTÁN, KASHMIR, AND LADAKH

OUR VISIT

TO

HINDOSTÁN, KASHMIR, AND LADAKH

Plate 4.

Vincent Brooks Day & Son lith

THE GUN CUSTOM.

OUR VISIT

TO

HINDOSTÁN, KASHMIR, AND LADAKH.

BY

MRS J. C. MURRAY AYNSLEY.

LONDON:
WM. H. ALLEN & CO., 13 WATERLOO PLACE, S.W.
Publishers to the India Office.
1879.

PREFACE.

COMING to India as simple travellers, we were able to go wherever fancy led us—so that, at the expiration of nearly three years, we have perhaps seen much more of that country than many who have passed half their lives there. A friend in England seemed pleased with some letters I wrote to him, giving descriptions of places we had visited; and thus arose the idea of a continued series of papers, which I thought might possibly interest other friends at home at some future period. The idea of publication was an after-thought; and this must be my excuse for the almost colloquial style in which they are written. Those who know me will, I trust, excuse the many imperfections incidental to a first attempt at coming before the public; and I crave the indulgence of strangers also for the same reason. I am much indebted to various friends in India for the loan of some rare and valuable books; also of departmental works belonging to their offices, by means of which I have obtained information on many subjects of interest.

Amongst the former may be classed Ferishta's 'History of Hindostán,' translated by Dow, from the original Persian, more than one hundred years ago; and the travels of Fa Hiang and Hionen Thsang, the Chinese pilgrims, who visited India, the former in the fifth, and the latter in the seventh, century of our era. Other works I have also consulted and compared with each other, as opportunity occurred; but many months spent in camp, with, at times, an almost daily removal to a fresh spot, has prevented much study for want of the necessary time and materials. I only wish I could insure my friends as much pleasure in reading our travels as I have felt in writing about them.

H. G. M. M. A.

KULU VALLEY, *Oct.* 4, 1878.

CONTENTS.

CHAPTER V.

CHAPTER VI.

CHAPTER VII.

CHAPTER VIII.

CHAPTER IX.

CHAPTER X.

CHAPTER XI.

CHAPTER XII.

CHAPTER XIII.

CHAPTER XIV.

CHAPTER XV.

CHAPTER XVI.

CHAPTER XVII.

CHAPTER XVIII.

CHAPTER XIX.

CHAPTER XX.

CHAPTER XXI.

CHAPTER XXII.

OUR VISIT TO HINDOSTAN, KASHMIR, AND LADAKH.

CHAPTER I.

ARRIVAL AT BOMBAY—THE PARSÍS—BOMBAY—ITS PUBLIC BUILDINGS—SAUGOR—FESTIVAL OF THE MOHURRUM—AGRA—SLIGHT SKETCH OF THE HISTORY OF THE MOGHUL EMPIRE IN INDIA FROM TAMERLANE TO AURUNGZEBE.

HAVING for some years had a great desire to visit our Indian possessions, at length one or two circumstances combined made my husband and myself resolve to put this long-cherished plan in execution; and, accordingly, we left England early in October 1875, and after the usual uneventful journey through France, embarked at Genoa, in the Rubattino s.s. Arabia, on the 24th of that month. We reached Bombay at an early hour on 18th November, and landed at once. On our way into the harbour we passed close to the Serapis and the Osborne, and the other vessels escorting the Prince of Wales; this was all we saw of H.R.H., as that evening he and his suite left Bombay to go down the coast.

The view of Bombay, as seen on entering the harbour,

is not very striking, for one of its great features, the cocoa-nut palms, only appear a confused mass from thence; but once landed, everything is so new to one fresh from Europe, natives from all parts of Hindostán being seen in their various distinctive costumes: amongst these, however, the Parsís, with their quaint head-gear, form by far the largest proportion.

The Parsís, including those of Yezd and Kirman in Persia, number about 105,500 souls. Their numbers have dwindled in an extraordinary manner; the cause has not been ascertained. It is not that many converts have been made from amongst them either to Christianity or Mohammedanism, though many of the more enlightened members seem deeply impressed with the excellence of the Christian religion and our general civilisation; but some who have gone into the subject consider that their rapid diminution is owing to their mode of life, which is so sedentary: they occupy themselves solely with desk-work, or become shopkeepers, and never invest in land, or become cultivators of the soil. I have been told, too, that they live almost entirely upon farinaceous food, and use much oil and *ghi* (or clarified butter) in their cooking; but, however this may be, I have rarely, if ever, seen a muscular-looking Parsí, or one with well-knit limbs. Both men and women have, as a rule, a shuffling rolling gait, and badly-proportioned figures.

In Western India the Parsís number about 100,000, and are divided into two parties—Conservatives and Liberals—who are both equally attached to the old faith, but differ in their modes of life. The Conservatives adhere to the good old mode of eating seated on the floor, and use their fingers instead of knives and forks;

whilst the Liberals have adopted European customs and appliances.

According to the Parsís, the world is to last 12,000 years, which they divide into four periods. During the first 3000 years the world was created; during the second, man lived by himself without suffering from attacks of evil; during the third, war began between good and evil—between Ormuzd and Ahriman—and raged with the utmost fierceness; this will gradually abate during the fourth period, which must be completed before the final victory of good over evil. They say they do not *worship* fire, and much object to be called "fire-worshippers," but admit that they are taught from their youth to face some luminous object whilst praying to God, and that they look upon *fire*, as upon other natural phenomena, as an emblem of divine power, but never ask assistance or blessings from it.

The Parsís abstain from smoking, and will not blow out a candle if they can help it; thus they would appear to look upon fire with great reverence, much as we Christians regard the symbol of the Cross. All their prayers and services are in the old Zend language, which none understand, not even their priests. They have a most imperfect translation of the Zend Avesta, which was not made from the original, but from a Pehlvi paraphrase; they do not recognise this as an authorised version. Thus, owing to this repetition of the words of their sacred writings without any attempt at understanding their meaning, each one is left to pick up his religion as best he may. They believe in one God, and address their prayers to Him. A priest must be the son of a priest, but all priests' sons need not necessarily follow their father's profession.

There are possibly other reasons why they should be unwilling to change their faith; but the three given by Professor Max Müller seem at least plausible ones: 1st, The conciseness of their belief; 2d, The great antiquity and former glory of their religion; 3d, The feeling that, in relinquishing this, they would be giving up the heirloom they have received from their remote ancestors and their own fathers, thus showing a want of filial piety to those whose memory they cherish as precious and sacred. They teach that morality consists of three things—pure thoughts, pure words, and pure deeds.

The European part of the town of Bombay contains some very fine public buildings, for the most part designed by an officer in the Royal Engineers; and these combine excellence of form and design with the necessary requirements of arrangement for a hot climate. One of the native quarters is most curious and interesting to a stranger—the fronts of most of the principal shops being carved in the style of the well-known Bombay black-wood furniture, and for the most part coloured in green, red, and yellow. Byculla is separated from Bombay by the Chinese quarter. The Celestials are the great workers in bamboo, and make chairs, couches, baskets, and boxes of this material.

The climate of Bombay is said to be at all times of the year hot and unpleasant; and even at that season we were glad to leave it after two or three days' stay, and started off up country by rail to Kureli, a distance of 550 miles, where we were met by relatives.

From this point began our first experience of Indian palanquin travelling, as our destination was Saugor, in the Central Provinces, distant about 75 miles from the railway, and possessing no regular service for the conveyance of travellers to and fro. We went chiefly by night, resting during the day. Each palanquin had twelve bearers, or *kahars* as they are called, and an additional man to act as torch-bearer, who ran alongside all the way. Early in the morning of the second day we reached our relations' house in Saugor, and saw the mode of life pursued in an Indian station, which has been so often described that it is unnecessary to detail it here.

Our stay at Saugor was limited to about three months, which enabled us to pick up a few words of the language, and also in some degree to realise how vast the country was which we had come to visit, and to learn what inexhaustible subjects of interest it contained, whether as regards its various peoples or its ancient monuments and history.

During our stay in Saugor the Mohammedan festival of the Mohurrum occurred. It is celebrated every year in memory of the first alleged martyred Shiahs, Hassan and Hussain, who were the sons of Ali the cousin, and Fatima the daughter, of Mohammed. These men, after the murder of their father Ali, moved from Kufah, the capital, to Medina. Hassan, the elder, abdicated voluntarily, but was afterwards poisoned. After some years' interval his brother Hussain was invited to return, the government having been seized in the meanwhile by Abi Safr, the first of the Omniades, and his son Yesid, who succeeded him; but on Hussain's arrival he was murdered, and his eldest son alone escaped of all his retinue. The murder of these two brothers is the subject of the ten days' wailing.

The Mohurrum begins when the moon of the first month becomes visible. Each family, according to their means, makes or provides themselves with what is called a *tarboot*, or representation of their tombs, which is more or less ornamented. Some of the best we saw were covered with thin sheets of talc, sprinkled over with gold leaf, which gave them a brilliant and dazzling appearance. At the expiration of twelve days (though the fast lasts ten days only) these *tarboots* are all carried in procession through the bazaar; and if, as in the case at Saugor, there is a lake, or large piece of water, the *tarboots*, after being stripped of the best of their decorations, are carried out in a boat some little distance and cast into the water; or, where no water is at hand, a large pit is dug, we were told, in which they are placed, and then burned.

On 1st March 1876 we again set forth on our travels, accompanied by our nephew J., who was thenceforward our companion for some months; and in due course we visited Jubbulpore and its marble rocks, with which we were disappointed, as we had expected grander scenery; but on a second visit to them by moonlight, more than a year later, I much changed my opinion, and should probably have admired them much more the first time had my expectations not been too highly raised by previous descriptions of them.

We passed hurriedly through Allahabad (so I will reserve all description of that place till after our second visit), and went on to Agra. Before proceeding to give a description of the buildings at Agra, it will be necessary, in a short historical sketch, to trace the rise of the so-called Moghul dynasty in Hindostán.

The empire of Persia was governed by petty princes till Timur-Bec, commonly known as Tamerlane, obtained possession of the kingdoms of Zagatay, which comprehended Transoxiana, and the provinces of Cabul, Zabulistán, and others towards the Indus. After conquering Northern Tartary, Timur turned his arms against Persia, and entered Khorassan seven years before the death of Feroze, the Paṭán Emperor of Hindostán. He completed the conquest of Persia in less than five years, and when Feroze died was employed in subduing the provinces on the Euphrates. Timur-Bec, hearing of the commotions and civil wars in India consequent on the death of Feroze, began his expedition into that country A.D. 1397.

During the eight previous years, Timur had extended his conquests all over Western Asia, reduced Northern Tartary, and spread his ravages into Siberia as far as the Arctic Circle. He now advanced southwards, plundering towns and villages, and massacring their inhabitants, burning what supplies of grain he found after reserving sufficient to feed his army. On reaching Delhi, he divided his forces; and himself, at the head of 700 men only, crossed the river to reconnoitre the citadel

Mahmood III., the then King of Delhi, and his minister Eckbal, seeing such a small force opposed to them, issued forth with 5000 men and 27 elephants. Sillif, an *omrah* (or noble) of repute, led on the attack, was repulsed, and taken prisoner. Timur, having made the observations he intended, repassed the river and rejoined his army. He found that his generals and princes had taken upwards of 100,000 people captive, whom he caused to be put to death with great barbarity; and this act gained for him the name of *Hillak Chan*, or the destroying prince. He shortly afterwards again forded the river with his whole army, and not encountering any opposition, Timur encamped on the plains of Feroze, near Delhi; gave battle to its king, Mahmood III., and Eckbal, routed them with great slaughter up to the very gates of Delhi, and there fixed his quarters.

Disturbances in Persia, and his ardent desire to extend his conquests to the extremities of Asia on the north and west, deterred Timur from making further progress in India, which he felt he could at any time reduce. On his return from Hindostán he settled the affairs of Persia, and reduced Syria, Egypt, and Asia Minor. When planning the conquest of China he died A.D. 1405, on his march thither, and was succeeded by his son Sharoch.

Mahmood III. died A.D. 1413, and Delhi was ruled in succession by six different princes; under the last of whom, Ibrahim II., the country was invaded by Baber the Tartar, who overthrew Ibrahim in a battle at Panniput, and thus transferred the empire to the family of Tamerlane, Baber himself being the fourth in descent from Timur.

In A.D. 1531 Baber was succeeded by his son Humaion, whose tomb will be mentioned in the description of the monuments at Delhi. The kingdom during Humaion's reign was convulsed by insurrections, and in 1541 he was obliged to fly, being defeated by Shere Shah, a native of India, of Patán descent, the word Patán signifying a highlander from beyond the Indus.

Shere's father had been governor of Jounpore. On the death of Shere in 1545, his eldest son, Adil, being absent, the government was usurped by the younger, named Jellal, generally known as Selim.

Selim dying in 1552, was succeeded by his son Feroze, a lad of 12. He had only reigned three days when he was assassinated by a nephew of the late

Emperor Shere, who mounted the throne under the name of Mahomed VI.

The following year the king's cousin and brother-in-law raised an army, possessed himself of the city of Delhi, mounted the throne, marched to Agra, and reduced the adjoining provinces. Mahomed, finding himself not strong enough to oppose him, fled towards Chinar, and contented himself with retaining the eastern provinces.

Humaion, since his deposition from the throne—viz., from the year 1544 to this period—had retired to Persia, where Tamasp was the reigning emperor. His sister, the Sultana Begum, favoured Humaion, and pleaded his cause with Tamasp, who told her that if Humaion were to become a Shiah, and enforce that doctrine in India, he would assist him to recover his empire.

The Shiahs hold Ali to be the only successor to Mohammed in his apostolic functions; but the Sunnis hold that there were four, adding Osman, Omar, and Abubeker to Ali.

Humaion, accompanied by his son, the young Prince Akbar, marched through Peshawur, caused the Patán governor to evacuate the new fort of Rhotas, and pursued the Patán troops as far as Lahore, from whence they also retreated, and the king peaceably entered it.

One final decisive battle was fought before Sirhind, in which Humaion was victorious, and this finally decided the fate of the empire, which for ever fell from the Patáns; and thus Humaion found himself reinstated on his throne after an interval of ten years.

A year later Humaion was killed by a fall, and in 1556 he was succeeded by his son, the afterwards renowned Akbar, who may be called a child of the desert, having been born on its confines in the year 1542.

Before he was a year old he became a captive in the hands of an uncle with whom his father was at war, and when a mere child was barbarously exposed on the ramparts of Cábul, when it was besieged, in order that the besiegers' cannon might kill him. After many hair-breadth escapes he was sent into the Punjaub in command of an army, at which time he could have been but a mere boy, as he was already in command when at the age of fourteen he lost his father.

He was at once proclaimed successor to the throne. He had very formidable enemies in Sikunder Sur, in the Punjaub, who tried to seize Delhi; in Mirzà Soliman of Budukshan, who made a sudden irruption and seized Cábul; and also in the minister of the pretender Adil, who was advancing towards Agra.

His officers advised him to retreat in face of the superior force opposing him, but he resolved to risk an encounter, and fought a battle at Panniput, a place where the fate of India has more than once hung in the balance—Akbar's grandfather, as we have already seen, having gained an important victory there. Akbar then marched on to Delhi, and entered it without opposition. He erected buildings at Allahabad, Agra, Secundra, Futtehpore, Sikri, and Delhi.

Akbar had been bred up in all the strictness of the Mohammedan faith, but either with a design to choose his own religion, or perhaps from curiosity, he made it his business to inquire into most of the various systems of divinity. He caused himself to be instructed in Christian tenets by missionaries from Portugal, and was anxious also to inquire into the Hindú religion, and tried to conciliate them in many ways.

The Hindús, unlike any other religious sect, say that every one can get to heaven in their own way, at the same time maintaining that theirs is the most expeditious method.

In the time of Akbar their Vedas, or sacred writings, had not been translated from the Sanscrit; accordingly, Akbar's secretary and great friend, Abul Fusl, the historian, tried by a *ruse* to investigate the principles of their faith, and sent his young brother Feizi, then a mere boy, to Benares to the Brahmins, in the character of a poor orphan of their tribe. This fraud was practised upon a learned Brahmin, who received him into his house, and brought him up as his own son.

When, after ten years of study, Feizi had perfected himself in Sanscrit, Akbar took measures to ensure his safe return. Feizi, it seems, on attaining manhood, had fallen in love with the Brahmin's only daughter, and her father, seeing the mutual affection of the young pair, offered him his daughter in marriage. Feizi, perplexed between love and gratitude, discovered himself to the old man, fell down at his feet, and with many tears entreated his forgiveness for the deceit which he had put upon him. The Brahmin did not reproach him, but drew a dagger and prepared to stab himself; but Feizi seized his hand and conjured him to say if he could make any atonement for the fraud. The Brahmin answered that he would forgive him, and consent to live, if Feizi would grant him two requests—viz., that he would never translate the Vedas, nor repeat the creed of the Hindús.

Akbar died in 1605, and was succeeded by his son

Jehangir, who erected a tomb to his father's memory at Secundra, near Agra, which will presently be described; but he made Lahore his chief capital, where his palace in the fort is still to be seen.

Jehangir's name has principally come down to us in connection with his wife, the celebrated Nur-Mehal, whose romantic early history is worth relating. About twenty years before the accession of Jehangir, her father, Chiaja Aiass (or Ghias-od-deen, as he is sometimes called), a native of Western Tartary, started from thence for India. He belonged to a noble family fallen into decay, and his wife was as poor as himself. His whole wealth was one sorry steed on which she rode; but she could at that time ill endure any fatigue.

For some time they subsisted on charity; to return to their own country was misery, to advance destruction. To complete their distress, a daughter was born to them. The mother was too weak to hold the child in her arms, and the father was exhausted with fatigue and privations. They saw no alternative but to expose the child on the highway, so they placed her under a tree and went on their way, but had only proceeded a short distance when the mother could no longer contain herself, and cried out to bring her the child. Chiaja Aiass returned to the spot to fetch it, and, some say, found a black snake coiled round the infant; but when he called out the serpent retired, and he took the child up unharmed, and proceeded, by slow marches, to Lahore, where Akbar at that time held his court.

One of the chief *omrahs* (or nobles) being a relation of Chiaja Aiass, he protected him, and in course of time this poor adventurer rose to be Master of the Household, and his daughter received the name of Mher-ul-Nissa, or the

Sun of Women; but on her marriage with Jehangir her name was changed to Nur-Mehal, or the Light of the Seraglio. In beauty she excelled all, and had no equal in the accomplishments of music, painting, and dancing.

Jehangir (who, till he became emperor, was called Prince Selim) paid a visit to her father, and she, aspiring to the conquest of the prince, showed off all her acquirements, and he was captivated by her charms. This syren, however, had been already betrothed to Shere Afkun, a Turcoman nobleman, whose wife she became; and when Selim ascended the throne and moved to Delhi, his great desire was to remove this man out of the way, and he tried and adopted all sorts of expedients to accomplish this.

Sometimes Shere Afkun himself seems to have tempted fate, for on one occasion, when a tiger had been heard of in the forest of Nidarbani, the emperor went out, and with his principal officers surrounded the ground for many miles. When at length the tiger was roused, Shere Afkun, to show his prowess, begged to be allowed to attack the beast unarmed, which he did, and prevailed, though himself mangled with wounds. He is said to have applied for permission to do so in the following words: "I think it a shame so many hundreds of armed men should be set to attack a tiger; I would, therefore, like to meet him in fair fight without arms. To attack an animal with weapons is both unmanly and unfair: God has given limbs and sinews to *men* as well as to tigers, and he has given *reason* to the former to aid his strength."

He then, in accordance with the emperor's commands, presented himself at Court, where a snare, however, had been prepared for him, as Jehangir had given orders to the driver of one of his largest and fiercest elephants to waylay him the next time he came, and tread him to death. The occasion thus arrived, the elephant met him in a narrow spot; he had just time to rise from his palanquin, draw a short dagger, and cut off the elephant's trunk. The animal roared, turned from him, and expired.

Another time his life was attempted by assassins, who got at night into his house, but he attacked and dispersed them. He then retired to Burdwan, where he hoped to live in obscurity with his beloved one, but the *suba* (or Governor) of Bengal had received orders to kill him. On some purposed insult from the pikemen of the *suba,* Shere Afkun set upon him as he was mounted upon his elephant, and cut him in two. Shere was now thoroughly roused, and dealt his blows around; but at length some of the officers of the *suba* formed a circle round him, and began to gall him with arrows; his horse was shot under him, and seeing plainly his approaching fate he turned towards Mecca, and threw some dust on his head instead of water for his ablutions. Six balls entered his body before he fell.

His widow, Mher-ul-Nissa, was then sent with all care and respect to Delhi. She was fired with ambition to become the emperor's favourite sultana. Jehangir at first refused to see her,—as some say, stricken with remorse, or else being in much grief on account of the death of his friend the *suba.*

Mher-ul-Nissa, ill brooking such neglect, gave herself up to apparent grief for the death of her husband, but still trusted that her beauty would in time cause the renewal of the emperor's former affection for her—a very small pittance only being allowed her for her maintenance. To augment this, she worked pieces of tapestry and embroidery, and made paintings on silk; these being so exquisite were bought up with great avidity, and she thus accumulated a large sum of money, and clothed her slaves with great magnificence, whilst she herself affected a plain and simple mode of dress.

She remained thus four years in retirement, when at length Jehangir's resolution to avoid her presence being vanquished by his curiosity, he determined to see for himself the truth of all he had heard, and sought an interview with her. His first glance caused all his former love to return, and the emperor, remarking the splendour of the dress of the slaves, and the rigid simplicity of their mistress's dress, inquired the reason; when the lady replied, that she *liked* to see her slaves richly attired, but that his Majesty was clearly of a different opinion, or the pension which he had presented to her, the humblest of his slaves, would have been a larger one. The emperor, charmed both with her wit and beauty, married her immediately, and gave her the name of Nur-Mehal, or the Light of the Seraglio; and during the rest of his reign she bore the chief sway in the affairs of the empire.

Jehangir dying in 1627, he was succeeded by his third son, Prince Kurrum, who took the name of Shah Jehan during his father's lifetime. His mother was Jodh-Bai, a Hindú of Rajput descent. Before Jehangir's death, the succession had been contested by several of his family.

His eldest son had failed in an attempt to seize the kingdom on the death of his grandfather, Akbar. Jehangir's second son then naturally looked forward to the succession, but proving himself incompetent to rule when intrusted with a nominal command in the Dekhan, where war was then raging between the Mohammedans and Hindús, Shah Jehan eventually came to the throne, though his stepmother, Nur-Mehal, whose early history was so romantic, intrigued to try and gain the kingdom for Sheriar, another son of Jehangir's, who had married her daughter by her first husband, Shere Afkun.

Sheriar assembled troops, gave battle, and was defeated; and at the end of a year, all opposition being at an end, Kurrum mounted the throne.

In 1657, when all his sons were of mature age, Shah Jehan being then in bad health, his fourth son, Aurungzebe, revolted against him, and, after several minor victories, he and his brother Murád gained a final battle and took possession of the capital, A. D. 1658, Shah Jehan being allowed to remain in his palace—deprived of all power, however. He became then almost forgotten, though his public buildings still speak for him, and prove him to have been, if not the wisest, at least the most magnificent, prince who ever ruled in India. The Taj alone, erected to the memory of his wife, Mumtaz Mehal, the niece of Nur-Mehal, will carry down his name to posterity as a great, if not the greatest, patron of the arts in Hindostán.

On the celebrated peacock throne he is said to have spent more than six millions sterling, chiefly in diamonds and other precious stones. He also built the then new city of Delhi, called after him Shahjehanabad. His son Aurungzebe, whose reign was the longest of any of the descendants of Timur, and in some respects a very brilliant one, has left no important buildings behind him, though one mosque at Benares bears his name.

CHAPTER II.

BUILDINGS AT AGRA—THOSE IN THE FORT SUCCESSIVELY THE WORK OF AKBAR, JEHANGIR, AND SHAH JEHAN—JUMMA MUSJID—TAJ MEHAL—TOMBS AT SECUNDRA, ETC.

ON arriving at Agra by the railroad, a distant view of the Taj is obtained; but the fort is the principal object which strikes the eye, with its great extent of red walls, and round towers at various distances. The greater part of, if not all, the walls of the fort are said to have been built by Akbar. The palace, which is within it, bears the name of Jehangir, Akbar's son and successor, though a good deal of it was probably erected by his father, as it is in Akbar's style, which was very much more Hindú than Mohammedan. The palace is entirely of red sandstone, and the principal front is covered with delicate lace-like carving, disposed in geometric patterns. None of this is deeply cut. It contains many courtyards. The number of rooms is so great, and the ground-plan so intricate, that people might easily lose themselves.

Jehangir's work, as seen in this palace (which, if not Akbar's work, is believed to have been built by Jehangir immediately after his father's death), is distinct in character from the later Moghul style, and resembles Hindú architecture, inasmuch as it avoids the use of the arch, is much more massive, and also that the construction is always obvious. These things combined lend it a peculiar charm and interest. In some respects this building gives one the idea of a highly carved and finished wooden one, which a magician's wand had turned to stone; and one cannot but think that Hindú architects and artists must have been employed to build the greater part of it, as much of the ornamentation, but more especially that of the central court, is decidedly Hindú in all its parts and details. In this courtyard are two lofty halls, opposite to each other. The larger and more highly-decorated one is 62 feet long by 37 wide, and has a flat stone ceiling. In the interior of this hall, a space about 45 feet by 20 is divided off in the centre by massive square pillars, reaching the whole height of the hall; on three sides there is a gallery at about half-way up the pillars; on the fourth side, towards the courtyard, instead of a gallery there is a passage, formed in and by the thickness of the pillars. From the pillars, at the level of the gallery, start eight stone struts, four on each side, and these assist the pillars to support the ceiling. In a line with the river front is a lovely little sandstone pavilion, reached by a steep staircase, and perched on the roof of one of the lower buildings of the palace. It is about 28 feet by 18, and open all round, being supported by square pillars. The great peculiarity of this, and of all the buildings in the fort of the same period, is, that no wood seems ever to have been employed in any part of them; and yet the style of the carving is much more like what would be made in wood than in stone, both in character and in execution.

Jehangir's son, Shah Jehan, much enlarged the original palace: the Angoorie Bagh (a square court with a garden), and the buildings in and immediately round it, are said to be his work. The Angoorie Bagh formed the small court of the zenana or women's apartments; and in the little chambers on three sides of this were lodged our officers and their families during the dreadful summer of 1857, at the end of which the then Lieutenant - Governor, Mr Colvin, succumbed from fatigue and anxiety, and his tomb is within the fort. The fourth side of this garden fronts the river Jumna, and has three several pavilions in it, all of white marble. The centre one is called the Khas Mehal, and there the sultana gave her receptions. To the left of this is another pavilion, within a small court. On the side where this court is entered, there is the most exquisite lattice-work, carved out of a solid block of white marble.

At the further end of this court is the so-called *pucheese* board, on the pavement. *Pucheese* is an Indian game. On this pavement the pieces played with were living female slaves, who became the property of the winner. This little court is the entrance to the so-called Jasmine Tower, or boudoir of the chief sultana. There are two apartments, each decorated with inlaid work of precious stones, in the same style as the Taj Mehal, and in the first of these there is a fountain. The whole forms a lovely little retreat,—the view facing the river is most striking and extensive. Over each doorway is a bunch of iris with its leaves; these have been carved out of a solid block of marble, of considerable thickness.

The pavilion to the right of the Khas Mehal consists of three chambers, which were formerly the apartments of the emperor's children, and is now converted into a museum. It contains two prettily-carved marble chairs, and a couch of the same material. The collection of objects is small, and consists mainly of fragments of Buddhist and Jain sculptures. In the verandah belonging to these rooms are the celebrated gates called of Somnath, though it is doubtful if they ever came from thence. They formed the doors of Mahmood's sepulchre at Ghuznee when the English forces took that place. There is a Cufic inscription on the framework, which some believe was a later addition: many and various have been the opinions concerning them. Lord Ellenborough caused them to be transported to Agra; and his object in doing this would seem to have been, that he wished to show that as Mohammedanism had once triumphed over Hindúism, so we had then become the first power in Asia. Besides the buildings already described as opening out of this garden, there is also the Shish-Mehal, or palace of glass, consisting of two rooms, in each of which is an eastern bath. These rooms are decorated with thousands of small mirrors, worked in round a lovely flower tracery, which is painted white. The effect, as may be imagined, is most silvery and lovely. The lower panels all round these rooms have had groups of flowers in brilliant colours painted on them.

At right angles to the Jasmine Tower is the *Dewan-i-Khas*, which was the emperor's small hall of audience, and also built by Shah Jehan. This is likewise entirely made of white marble, and has double twelve-sided pillars, which support an open hall raised on a marble platform about three feet high. It is also very highly decorated: the pillars and the rest of the structure are all inlaid with various patterns in cornelians, agates, &c. Behind this open hall, and entered from it by three archways, is a second enclosed one, lighted from the back by three windows of lovely lace-like marble tracery. Both these halls have their walls panelled with marble, each panel being encircled with inlaid work in coloured stones, and having in the centre a group of flowers in *bas-relief.*

Shah Jehan's throne, which is of black basalt, is in the centre of the terrace of the same courtyard. When seated on it, the emperor had his back to the river. A smaller throne opposite to this is said to have been for the use of his ministers. Taken as a whole, all Shah Jehan's buildings have a decided Italian character: the *bas-reliefs* and other decorations, wherever they occur, are perfectly lovely, and of infinite variety. Looking down from the Dewan-i-Khas, the spectator can see into the court called the Muchee Bowan, which was formerly a tank filled with fish, but is now entirely filled up. Round this court are two-storied colonnades, whence the ladies and children in Moghul times could watch the fish disporting themselves. Opening out of the upper colonnade, at the north-west corner, is the Nagina Musjid, a little gem in white marble, about 30 feet long by 18 wide. It is not unlike the Moti Musjid, the description of which is to follow, and was built by Shah Jehan as a private mosque for the royal ladies of his Court.

The Moti Musjid, or Pearl Mosque, was also built by Shah Jehan, A.D. 1654, as stated in the inscription upon its front. It is placed on a three-storied platform of red sandstone; but when seen, as it can be from most parts of the town without, only its three domes are visible above the walls of the fort. Bishop Heber says of the Taj, that it looks as if it had been built by Titans and finished by jewellers; and of the fort it may likewise be said, that the walls are the work of a Titan; while these domes may be likened to soap bubbles blown by the giant's children, and arrested half-way in their fall to earth.

A high and steep flight of steps leads up to the top of the platform whereon is the mosque, which is made of pure white marble. It is very lovely; though, when one is standing on this platform, the building seems to want height, as from no part of this court can the bases of the domes be seen, for the parapet hides them. This mosque is purely Saracenic in style, with horse-shoe engrailed arches; and it has a triple row of columns.

The Dewan-i-Am, or large hall of audience, is the only other important building within the fort. It is all of red sandstone, but has been painted white, picked out with red and gold. Like the Khas Mehal, and the Dewan-i-Khas, it is an open hall supported on many pillars. The back or eastern wall forms one side of the court of the Muchee Bowan; and in this wall is an enclosed gallery, or rather recess, to which a small side staircase gives access from the hall. This recess is about 20 feet long by 14 wide; and its roof, walls, and pillars are all cased with marble, richly inlaid with precious stones. In detail and execution this is quite equal, if not superior, to the work I have before described of the same nature.

The Dewan-i-Am, on the contrary, is so inferior to the other halls of audience, both in architecture and material, that there are good grounds for imagining, as has been thought by many, that this hall was not the work of Shah Jehan at all, but was built by his son, Aurungzebe, who, from an anecdote which is told of him, which I will here relate, must have possessed a certain amount of dry humour.

Aurungzebe had issued edicts against the fine arts, as tending to frivolity and irreligion, and on one occasion the singers, actors, and dancers, gave him a singular rebuke. In one part of the palace there was a balcony where he daily sat at a certain hour. One day, seeing a funeral going on upon the glacis, he inquired whose it was. On being informed that they were proceeding to bury Music, who was dead, he answered, "Do so by all means, and mind you bury her deep enough, so that no sound may ever come to me from her grave." The sultan then went away, and from that day forth never again resumed the practice of showing himself thus publicly to his subjects.

All the red sandstone buildings of Akbar have a massive boldness about them, whereas those erected only in the second generation later have an effeminate look: the grandfather's buildings are typical of a warrior, and his grandson's of a man of peace and lover of ease.

The Jumma Musjid, or large Mosque of Agra, is situated immediately opposite the Delhi gate of the fort. It was the work of Shah Jehan, who built it in the name of his daughter, Jehanara, whose name has come down to us associated with her devotion to her father, whose long captivity she shared when he was deposed by his son Aurungzebe. This mosque is all of red sandstone, and has three large domes, which have a zigzag pattern in white marble running round them. The entrance is by a flight of steps to a large square platform, with colonnades on two sides of it, surmounted by tiny domed pinnacles running the whole length of them, each supported on four slender shafts, and there is a larger pinnacle of the same shape at each corner. The mosque itself has five entrances or arched doorways: these open into the same number of halls, which all communicate with each other by lateral doorways. All lead into the mosque proper beyond, which has five domed halls of the same form, though the centre one only seemed to have the Kiblah, and the steps used by the moolahs when they are preaching. The outside of this mosque is decorated with small domed cupolas along the top, and a larger one of the same kind at each corner. The central archway, which is much larger than the others, has two pillar-like minarets built on to it, and dividing it from the other lateral entrances.

The Taj Mehal is nowhere seen to greater advantage, as a whole, than from one place inside the walls of the fort, the river Jumna there making a great bend, so that this exquisite creation of mason-work appears almost opposite to the spectator, though it may be nearly a three-miles' drive from the fort to the Taj, which is approached through a large court with recesses in it on two sides: these were probably originally intended for and used, as at present, as a *durrumsala*, or place to lodge travellers. This court, again, has beyond it a large garden surrounded on all sides by high walls, and entered by a grand gateway of red sandstone, inlaid with white and coloured stones and marbles. Within this gateway is a large octagonal domed chamber; and passing through this the garden is entered, where, at the end of a long vista, the Taj itself bursts upon the view, which is a *coup-d'œil* never to be forgotten. It is as though a heap of snow had fallen from heaven, and there become crystallised for ever, the whole effect of the building being so light looking, and yet it has an enduring appearance.

The garden and the approach to this tomb are on the same plan as all those built by the Moghul emperors —viz., that from the central gateway radiated a broad avenue, generally paved with marble and adorned with fountains; another avenue intersected this in the middle, thus forming a cross. The avenue leading direct from the principal entrance is bordered on either side with a symmetrical garden; grand and lofty palms and flowering shrubs overhang this, and lend still greater enchantment to the whole scene. At the upper end of the principal avenue is the tomb itself, placed on a large terrace or platform. In this instance Shah Jehan built the tomb after his wife's death, in order to place her remains there; but more generally a tomb was built during the lifetime of the intended occupant, and used first as a *barra-durrie*, or hall of feasting: but once used as a tomb, from thenceforth the building was never applied to festal purposes.

The Taj can be compared to no other building in the world, either in form or decoration, as it has a beauty of its own, both in the design of the whole and in the extraordinary minuteness and delicacy of its ornamentation without and within. The material (white marble) of which it is composed is almost unique in a building of that size: the whole of the exterior is inlaid in the style of the Florentine mosaic-work, with precious or semi-precious stones, such as agates, cornelians, bloodstones, lapis lazuli, &c., every detail of which will bear minute examination, though the finer and more elaborate work is reserved for the interior of the building.

A low red-sandstone terrace rises at the upper end of this avenue, and from this rises a smaller white marble platform about 18 feet high, with a tall minaret at each of the four corners, and in the centre is the Taj itself, which is, exteriorly, a square with the four corners which face the minarets cut off. A grand dome rises from the centre, and at each corner of the roof there is a cupola supported on four pillars, and having a small dome. The whole of the outside of the building is inlaid with bold designs in coloured stones, and passages from the Koran in black marble. It has only one entrance, leading into a large chamber. There are four such rooms of equal size, connected by a corridor, which goes right round the interior of the building. In the chamber by which the visitor enters there is a staircase leading down to a large square hall, in the centre of which are the tombs containing the remains of Shah Jehan and his wife Mumtaz Mehal. The inlaid work, even on these, is a masterpiece of art; but the most elaborate and highly-finished work is to be seen on their cenotaphs, which are in a large octagonal domed chamber over this. Mumtaz Mehal's cenotaph is in the centre, and Shah Jehan's is on the left side of hers. Round the cenotaphs is an octagonal screen of white marble, about six feet high, which, in its perfect finish and lovely patterns, resembles old point lace turned to stone. In this octagonal chamber there is a wonderfully quick echo, and the chord of the seventh is said to produce a beautiful effect.

I have already spoken of the low red-sandstone terrace which forms the base of the Taj as being of a considerable size. On the western side of this, or to the left of the Taj, there is a mosque built of red sandstone also, and decorated with coloured stones and black and white marble, in the same style as the principal gateway. This mosque differs much from the usual form of such buildings belonging to the Moghul period. It has a double row of chambers, six in all, each communicating with the other by arched doorways. Each of the three hinder halls has a domed ceiling, and its Kiblah in a recess. Externally there are three large domes; and projecting from the building on either side is a colonnade terminating in an octagonal pavilion of two storeys, surmounted by a domed cupola which rests on pillars, giving the whole a light and graceful appearance.

At the other or east side of this terrace, and exactly similar in size and form to the mosque, is another building, called the *Jawab,* which means answer or reply; and this was placed there, as it would appear, simply for the sake of uniformity, in respect of the whole. This circumstance alone gives us some idea of the grand conceptions which were not only imagined, but executed, in those days—as the entrance gateway, the mosque, or the *Jawab,* would either of them singly, anywhere but in Agra (where there is such a wealth of fine buildings), have been cited as singularly worthy of remark and admiration.

On the opposite side of the river to Agra is a tomb called *Itmad-ud-dowlah,* which signifies, we were told, "feasting-place of the rich." It is said to be the tomb of Chiaja Aiass, sometimes called Ghaias-ud-dín, who was the father of Jehangir's wife, Nur-Mehal, and of Asuf Khan, who was the father of Mumtaz Mehal, the wife of Shah Jehan. Thus aunt and niece were both renowned, —the former for her talents and beauty, and early adventures; while her splendid tomb, the Taj, will for all time perpetuate the name of the niece.

After crossing the bridge over the river Jumna, a few yards to the left, is the entrance to the tomb of Chiaja Aiass, which stands, like all of that period, in the centre of a garden. It is of white marble, supported on a platform of red sandstone. The whole of the exterior is very rich in decoration, being inlaid with coloured marbles. The style of this work differs much from that of other tombs in and near Agra, inasmuch as, besides geometrical patterns, are also trees, vases, water-vessels, &c., among the designs, which would go some way to prove that this, if not any of the others, was used as a place of feasting and recreation previous to its being made into a mausoleum. It is two-storied, and has domed turrets at each of the four corners of the roof of the first storey. The upper storey, which is smaller than the lower one, has in this instance no dome, but a steep coved roof forms the summit of the whole. The entrance doorways, and all the openings for admitting light into the building, are of pierced white marble. The interior has a central hall containing the principal tomb, and a wide passage which runs all round this has mortuary chambers opening out of it at the four corners.

The Taj is embellished with mosaics made of cornelians, jaspers, &c.; the tomb of Itmad-ud-dowlah is covered with designs in coloured marbles.

A few minutes' walk from this tomb is another called the Chini-ka-Roza, which is said to be that of Ufzul Khan, a literary adventurer of the seventeenth century, who was one of the ministers of Shah Jehan. This beautiful and, I believe, unique specimen, is quite past restoration, chiefly because the art of producing this style of decoration is lost. At first sight it would appear to have been covered with glazed tiles disposed in conventional flower patterns; but this is not the case, as further examination proves that it has really been enamelled—that is to say, a coat of plaster of a certain thickness was laid on and then enamelled; though how this process was conducted, or how it was managed that no seams or joins should appear—at least at the end of each day's work—is unknown. The centre dome was intact when we saw it, though the rest of the roof was in a very ruinous condition.

Akbar's tomb at Secundra was built by his son Jehangir, who, in his autobiography, mentions that in the third year of his reign, being dissatisfied with the work then done, he ordered it to be rebuilt. The enclosure is approached by a grand three-chambered gateway; the central hall of this is domed, and the side chambers are each flanked by two tall minarets. This gateway is of red sandstone, and is decorated with inlaid work of coloured stones and white marble, disposed for the most part in geometrical patterns. The garden, which is surrounded by high walls, is nearly as large in extent as a moderate-sized English park, and the approach to the tomb is by a causeway of stone with fountains at distances. As seen from the gateway, the tomb gives one an idea of incompleteness. According to the opinion of Fergusson, it was originally intended to have surmounted it with a dome. Possibly Jehangir may, at the end of seven years' labour and expense, have become tired of it, and therefore finished it off without carrying out his original plan, especially as Agra is known not to have been his favourite residence.

In the centre of this garden is a red-sandstone platform, from which rises a building composed of four terraces, three of red sandstone, and the fourth of white marble. Each terrace has numerous pinnacles, with domed roofs resting on four slender shafts: some of these domes are roofed with coloured tiles. Each terrace is smaller than the one below it: the topmost of all, in white marble, is about 70 feet square, exclusive of a colonnade which runs all round it, and is latticed with pierced white marble in lace-like tracery of an infinite variety of designs. Here, open to the sky, is placed the cenotaph, in the purest white marble, richly carved. The lowest of these terraces has a massive arched colonnade, some part of which has been divided off into separate mortuary chambers, and the rest so arranged as to have been capable of being divided in the same manner, should occasion have required it. The grand portal is of pierced white marble, and leads into a domed hall 38 feet square, painted in rich designs: the colours are chiefly dark blue and gold. From this, a short incline and a long vaulted passage lead down to a vast domed hall, where, in a square tomb of plain white marble, lie the remains of the great Akbar. The whole building, when we saw it, was in process of being carefully and thoroughly restored.

Akbar's tomb is situated about six miles from Agra; and though it appears a very magnificent structure at a certain distance, yet, on closer inspection, the masonry of the lower terraces is seen to be much wanting in finish, and very inferior in all its details to the work of the great hero to whose memory it was erected.

CHAPTER III.

DELHI—ITS EARLY HISTORY—SOME ACCOUNT OF THE SLAVE, KHILGI, AND TOGHLAK DYNASTIES—JAIN TEMPLES AT DELHI—THE JAINS AND THEIR RELIGIOUS TENETS—JUMMA MUSJID—OTHER MOSQUES—THE FORT—ASOKA'S LÁTS, OR PILLARS—THE RIDGE, ITS CONNECTION WITH THE MUTINY OF 1857.

OUR next move was to Delhi, which has been the site of a city for more than three thousand years, though the earliest monument now existing is the iron column at the Kutb, erected about A.D. 500. There are two stone *láts*, or pillars, of the time of Asoka, which date much earlier—about 250 B.C.—but these were brought to Delhi from a distance; yet it is mentioned in the Mahabarata that, about fifteen centuries before the Christian era, Yudish Thira founded the great Pandava empire, built his capital upon the left bank of the Jumna, and called it Indraprastha. Tradition, and the ruins which still remain, indicate the existence of thirteen capital cities at different periods within a space of forty-five square miles; and within a distance of eleven miles the remains of five cities can even now be seen—viz., Toghlakabad, the Hindú fort called Raj Pithara, within which the Kutb now stands, and the cities of Feroz-Shah, Shir Shah, and Shahjehanabad, or the present Delhi.

Three distinct styles of architecture strike the eye in and about Delhi—viz., the Hindú, the Patán, and the

Moghul. The first style may be seen in parts of the mosque near the Kutb; the best specimens of Patán work are in the tomb of Ala-ud-din Khilgi, also near the Kutb, and the fine mosque inside the Purana Keela, or old fort on the road to Humaion's tomb; while the last named exists within the walls of the present Delhi. In addition to these three styles, there are also some most interesting buildings forming an intermediate link between the Hindú and the Patán periods, in which the delicacy and elegance of the former are combined with the grandeur of the latter.

The Mohammedan reign in India, and, consequently, their rule at Delhi, dates from the time when the last of the Rajput sovereigns was dethroned, about A.D. 1190—Delhi and Kanouj having been governed up to that time by rival dynasties of this race, who then, as ever since, though a brave and gallant people, have shown throughout an utter incapacity to combine together against a common enemy.

The first sovereign of any note was Kutb-ud-dín Eibak, the first of the so-called slave kings, who began to reign A.D. 1206. He had been brought up by Shahab-ud-dín, the last but one of the Ghori dynasty (who, having no son, was fond of bringing up Turki slaves), became his minister, and was eventually left in charge, as Shahab's representative in India when he returned to Ghusnee after taking Ajmere. Kutb also took possession of Delhi for his master, and of the district called Coél, between the Jumna and the Ganges, and likewise proceeded to Guzerat and ravaged that province. On the death of Shahab-ud-dín, India became an independent province, as, though his nephew Mahmood was proclaimed in all his dominions, yet the kingdom at once broke up into many separate states, hardly united even in name by his general supremacy. Kutb thus became king over the provinces where he had till then only ruled as governor.

Kutb was succeeded by Shams-ud-dín Altumsh, of whom it is related that he was really of a good family, but was sold, like Joseph, by his envious brethren. Anyhow, Kutb-ud-dín is said to have bought him for fifty thousand pieces of silver.

Gheias-ud-dín Bulbun, another of the slave kings, had been brought up at the Court of Altumsh, and, on the death of that sovereign's grandson, usurped the title in 1266, having already before had all the power. Gheias-ud-dín's grandson was the last of this dynasty; on his death there were two competing parties—the Tartar chiefs, and the chiefs of the old kingdom of Ghusnee. The Khilgis of the last named race prevailed over the Tartars, and their reign began in 1288, in the person of Jelál-ud-dín Khilgi. This dynasty came to an end in 1321, when the last of the race, a usurper named Mobarick, was killed in a conflict before Delhi, with some of the nobles who had risen against his tyrannies and exactions, amongst whom was Juna Khan, son of Ghásí Khan Toghlak, the then Governor of the Punjaub.

On entering Delhi, Ghásí Khan gave out that he was willing to place any of the royal line upon the throne, his only object being to deliver the country from oppression, but no member of the Khilgi family was found to have survived, and Toghlak was himself proclaimed king in 1321, under the title of Gheias-ud-dín Toghlak, being the son of a Turki slave of Gheias-ud-dín Bulbun by an Indian mother. His son Muhammad bin-Toghlak succeeded him in 1325, of whom Elphinstone in his history of India says, "He was the most accomplished prince, and the most furious tyrant, that ever lived."

Muhammad dying in 1351, Firoz Shah came to the throne: his name is associated with the now ruined city of Firozabad just outside the gates of the present Delhi, and he also built the fort at Jounpore.

Though Delhi has been for so long a time a stronghold of the Mohammedan religion, and for many centuries under Mohammedan rule, yet we found there two very highly decorated small temples belonging to the Jainas, or Jains—a religious sect of the Hindús, who are most numerous in Western Hindustán, and are principally engaged in commerce. Their name is derived from the Sanscrit word *jini*—victorious—which is the generic term for the deified saints of their sect. Their doctrines and opinions are interesting, from their striking similarity to the chief peculiarities of the religion of Buddha. The Brahmins consider that they form no part of the Hindú body. The principal points in which they differ from these are: Firstly, denial of the divine origin of the Vedas; secondly, the worship of certain holy mortals who have acquired, by self-mortification and penance, a power which renders them superior to the gods; and thirdly, extreme tenderness for animal life. Their doctrines and customs are similar to those of the Buddhists. They do not entirely reject the gods of the Hindú mythology, but consider them inferior to their holy mortals, who, they say, are 72 in number, of whom 24 belong to the former age, 24 to the present, and 24 to the age to come. The statues of all, or a part of these, are sculptured in black or white marble, and placed in their temples. The most celebrated of these holy mortals are Pársvanátha and Mahavira, who alone can be said to have had any historical existence. Some state that the last Jina died B.C. 500.

General Cunningham found some Jain statues at Muttra, with the dates 99 and 177 A.D. upon them. The origin of this sect has been much disputed, some saying that both Buddhism and Jainism are older than Brahminism, or modern Hindúism—that is to say, the worship of Shiva and the incarnations of Vishnu.

In the eleventh and twelfth centuries Jainism appears to have been more widely diffused than at any other period. The strange resemblance between the Buddhist and the Jain religions renders it probable that they had one and the same origin. Though the Jains of Southern India preserve the distinction of castes, many things would lead to the supposition that originally caste did not exist among them. The Jains are divided into two classes—clerical and lay; the former subsist upon the alms of the latter. The two classes are called Yatis and Srávakas. Their religious ritual is very simple: the former can dispense with acts of devotion at their pleasure, and the Srávakas are only bound to visit a temple daily wherein some of the images of the Jinas are erected, and make an offering of flowers, accompanied by a short prayer. They insist upon five great duties—viz., refraining from injury to animal life, truth, honesty, chastity, and freedom from worldly desires.

Apropos of the first of these duties, it is said of them that in one part of Guzerát, where they are numerous and influential, they are in the habit of persuading the cultivators to bring them their surplus male kids instead of destroying them, as would otherwise be done: these they place in a shed, putting pans of milk near them; but these little creatures, being too young to drink the milk, speedily die of hunger; thus no one has actually killed them, so they are considered to have died by the dispensation of Providence.

Of the two Jain temples at Delhi, one is about fifty years old, and the other was built ten years later. They are quite near each other, being situated in a labyrinth of small streets not far from the Chandni Chowk (or great bazaar of the city). They are both alike in style and arrangement; but one, they told us, had been much injured at the time of the Mutiny in 1857, and has been restored in a plain manner, so I shall describe the first I visited, which I believe did not suffer at that time.

Some steps in a small back street lead to a gateway of finely carved white stone; a passage then takes one to a staircase going up to the temple itself—to reach which a porch and a courtyard are passed through. The courtyard is paved with white marble, and surrounded on three sides with a colonnade, the pillars of which are of the same material. The walls and ceiling of this colonnade are of white stucco, which has been painted all over with very pretty flower designs, with much gold intermixed: this ornamentation has been a good deal injured by time and weather, though, from the comparatively recent date of the building, one would hardly expect it could have suffered so much.

The temple itself occupies the fourth side of the courtyard, is raised about four feet from its level, and consists of a large chamber divided into three parts by double marble columns. The centre, which is the largest compartment, holds the shrine of the idol Pársvanátha, standing in an enclosed marble erection of many tiers, one above the other, resembling very much a large wedding-cake, the god being the ornament at the top; above the god is a domed canopy. The whole of this shrine is inlaid with very minute and delicate designs in coloured stones, and looks much like a finely-wrought piece of jewellery. The centre compartment of this, the principal chamber, has a steep coved roof; both it and the walls are covered with gold-leaf, having flowers painted upon it in various brilliant colours, much in the style of the Kashmir *papier-maché* work. Hanging from the roof, at a little distance in front of the idol, are two bells, with several smaller ones between them; on either side of these are brass stands about five feet high, with large trays on the top of them to receive offerings of flowers, grain, &c. These chambers are capable of being entirely shut off from the courtyard by wooden doors.

At no great distance from these temples is the Jumma Musjid, or large mosque, which is placed in a most commanding situation on a natural platform of rock; and immediately in front of it is a large open space, or *maidán*, as it is called in India. The three gateways are each of them approached by high flights of steps; the principal door facing the mosque is generally kept closed, and the usual entrances are by the north and south gateways. The whole is built of red sandstone, but a good deal of white marble is used in its ornamentation. The domes of the mosque—of the four cupolas at the corners of the courtyard, and of the numerous little kiosques—are veneered with it. The courtyard is of considerable size, and has an open colonnade running all round it, supported on slender shafts: near one of the small corner cupolas there is a space partitioned off, and closed by a padlocked door, which they opened for us, and then exhibited some most curious old Arabic manuscripts: two of these, they said, had been written by their prophet Mohammed's son-in-law Ali, and the third by Ali's son. They also show the prophet's slipper in a glass case, and a piece of white marble with, as they tell you, the impression of his foot upon it, and say it came from Medina.

In the centre of the courtyard of the mosque is the tank where the faithful perform their ablutions, and, as is usual, the whole of the western side of the square is occupied with the mosque proper, which has three domes, the centre one having in front of it (but not concealing the dome, as in some of the Patán mosques) an arched doorway, or *propylon,* as it is called, with a minar on either side of it. At each end of the building there is also a very high minaret: these towering up to a great height make the whole building a most imposing pile as seen at a distance, but on a close inspection it can bear no comparison with the finest examples of Patán architecture. Its general effect, however, is so grand that this mosque is considered by some the finest in the East. That it should look well from a little distance was probably what was aimed at by Shah Jehan when he built it, his palace in the fort being directly opposite.

The fort has a circuit of about a mile and a half, and has two entrances, called respectively the Lahore and the Delhi gates. Within the Lahore gate is a courtyard, containing what was once the Noubat-Khana, or music gallery; and further on is the Dewan-i-Khas, or small hall of audience. To the north of this are the royal baths; and on the south a suite of small rooms entirely composed of white marble, and more or less richly inlaid with mosaic-work, in coloured stones or marbles. These buildings are all placed on a marble platform, about four feet high.

The Dewan-i-Khas is open all round, and supported on solid-looking square pillars, with Moorish crenelated arches between them. The roof of this building is flat, with a domed kiosque at each corner, resting upon four small columns, and sloping eaves projecting all round. The whole of the interior is richly ornamented with paintings of flowers, and the ceiling is said to have been originally covered with silver filagree-work, which the Mahrattas melted down and carried away with them when they captured the city in 1759. The value of this has been estimated at £170,000 sterling.

The buildings to the right of the Dewan-i-Khas consist of a series of small chambers, exquisitely inlaid with flower patterns in coloured semi-precious stones. The fineness of the work is equal to that of a jewel casket; and such being the shrine, imagination can hardly picture what must have been the splendour of its contents.

The bathing apartments to the left of the Dewan-i-Khas consist of two rooms, each about 24 feet square, and lighted from above. The first has a square bath in the centre, and a large recess, which formed a dressing-room; in the second chamber the position of these is reversed. The pavement of both rooms is of inlaid work in coloured marbles, arranged in geometric patterns; the walls of each are also of white marble, inlaid with various designs up to a height of about four feet; above this they are of stucco, on which one can still trace remains of painting in some places.

The Dewan-i-Am, or large hall of audience, is about 200 feet long by 100 wide, and rests on rows of red sandstone pillars, the outer being double ones. The throne, which communicated with the emperor's apartments, and was reached by a staircase at the back, is raised about ten feet above the floor of this hall. The throne is surmounted by a canopy resting on four pillars; this and the wall behind the throne were originally beautifully inlaid with representations in precious stones of fruits, flowers, birds, and beasts, which have all disappeared, and have been replaced by very coarse paintings of similar subjects. The celebrated peacock throne stood in this place; it was carried off in 1739 by Nadir Shah, the then Emperor of Persia, together with nearly all the treasures of Delhi, when, after defeating Mahomed Shah at Kurnaul, he marched with his train into the city, and some of his followers being attacked and killed, he ordered a general massacre, and gave the city up to plunder.

The whole of these buildings are believed to be of a later date than those of Shah Jehan in the palace at Agra. Of his palace at Delhi, nothing now remains except those parts I have enumerated, which are all detached, so that one cannot understand their original position in the building. It is said, that immediately after the Mutiny in 1857, a great deal of wanton destruction took place consequent on the irritation of the public mind, which, in less thrilling times, and on sober reflection, would never have occurred.

The little Moti Musjid, or Pearl Mosque, still remains to be described. It was added by Aurungzebe, and is only about 60 feet square, but is much more highly finished than the one of the same name at Agra. Possibly, the Jumma Musjid being so near, this may have been intended for the use of the ladies of the royal family only. The small courtyard of this mosque is surrounded on three sides with a marble screen about 15 feet high, having little minars at distances along the top of it.

I will here note the difference in the decorations used by the Arab and the Indian Mussulmans. They both equally rejected any representation of the human figure. In India they destroyed or mutilated any Hindú statues they met with; but, unlike the Arabs, allowed and used both animals and flowers in their stone-work and paintings.

The Kalán Musjid, or chief mosque, is now within the walls of Shahjehanabad, or the modern Delhi; but it is only reasonable to suppose that formerly it was in a part or suburb of the city of Firozabad, having been built in 1387, in the reign of Firoz Shah Toghlak, and it is very characteristic of the style of that age. It much resembles a fortress, with its rough-hewn stone-work and bastions at the four outer corners of the courtyard; in fact, when looking at it from any point where the domes are not visible, you might almost imagine it to be some old Saxon or Norman castle, which likeness is still further carried out in the high battlemented walls which surround the whole. The entrance to it is by a high flight of steps; the gateway has a tall minar on either side of it, differing totally in form from any others we had seen, in that they are broad at the base, and taper almost to a point at the summit. The mosque itself, standing within this courtyard, is of the same solid construction, and consists of a series of arches and domes: these last number fifteen in all, there being three rows with five in each row; the centre dome is slightly larger than the rest. The cloisters, which form the other three sides of the interior of the courtyard, have also small domes and sloping eaves, supported on roughly finished brackets. The whole building has great simplicity and rudeness, and is not without a certain grandeur.

The two most interesting mosques in the city are the Jumma Musjid and the Zináth-ul-Musjid: the first I have already described; the latter was built much later, during the reign of Aurungzebe, by his daughter, Zináth-ul-Nissa Begum, A.D. 1700. It stands on the western bank of the Jumna, and is a very conspicuous object from the other side of the river. As seen from thence, it stands on an eminence; but inland its terrace is on a level with the city road. It is about 30 feet from the walls of the town; and its terrace, which is about 14 feet high, is built upon arches, which are used as shops or dwellings by the poorer classes of natives. On the north and south are two arched entrances, with steps leading up to the court of the mosque. In the centre of this court there is the usual tank, which has now, however, no water in it.

The tomb of Zináth stood originally on the north side of the mosque, but was destroyed immediately after the Mutiny of 1857: the mosque also was at that time much altered in the interior, when it was turned into an artillery barrack. There are three very bulbous domes to this mosque, striped longitudinally with black and white, and surmounted with gilt pinnacles. At both corners of the front of the mosque there are immense minars, towering high above the domes; these and the small pillars terminating either side of the central archway are crowned with small domed cupolas. There are seven archways forming entrances to this mosque, which are scolloped in the Moorish style; and another such row of archways running the whole length of the interior divides the building into fourteen chambers. Here too, as in most, if not all the mosques built by the Moghuls, the inside of the building is very plain, all the decoration being on the exterior, in this respect differing much from the architecture of the Hindús, who finished every part most carefully.

One of the pillars of Asoka, which was originally erected at Meerut in the third century B.C., was put up by Firoz Shah Toghlak on what is now called the "Ridge," to the north-west of the modern Delhi, near his hunting palace, where two half-dilapidated buildings may still be seen. This column was thrown down during the reign of Farokhsir, by the accidental explosion of a powder-magazine, which broke it into five pieces. These, after divers vicissitudes (the portion containing the inscription having been sawn off and sent to Calcutta), are now once more united, and the restored column again put up. This *lát* was never much more than 35 feet in height, though it is larger in diameter than the other outside the Delhi gate of the city, which last is upwards of 42 feet high, and is placed on a massive building of rubble stone, pierced below with numerous small chambers, and forming a terrace above, whereon the pillar rests.

A native contemporary writer gives the following curious account of how this pillar was removed, which, I think, is worth inserting, as we in these days are often puzzled to know how the people of early times, possessed of only the rudest appliances, could transport such columns from one place to another. He thus describes the process: "Kaizrabad is about 90 *kos* (or 135 miles) from Delhi, in the vicinity of the hills.

When the sultan visited that district, and saw the column in the village of Tobra, he resolved to remove it to Delhi, and there erect it as a memorial to future generations. After thinking over the best means of lowering the column, orders were issued, commanding the attendance of all the people dwelling in the neighbourhood, within and without the Doab, and all soldiers, both horse and foot. They were ordered to bring all implements and materials suitable for the work.

"Directions were issued for bringing parcels of the cotton of the *sembal* (or silk-cotton tree). Quantities of this silk cotton were placed round the column, and when the earth at its base was removed, it fell gently over on the bed prepared for it. The cotton was then removed by degrees, and after some days, the pillar lay safe upon the ground. When the foundations of the pillar were examined, a large square stone was found as a base, which also was taken out. The pillar was then encased from top to bottom in reeds and ram skins, so that no damage might accrue to it. A carriage with forty-two wheels was constructed, and ropes were attached to each wheel. Thousands of men hauled at every rope, and after great labour and difficulty, the pillar was raised on to the carriage. A strong rope was fastened to each wheel, and two hundred men pulled at each of these ropes. By the simultaneous exertions of so many thousand men the carriage was moved, and was brought to the banks of the Jumna. There the sultan went to meet it; a number of large boats had been collected, some of which would carry 5000 and 7000 maunds of grain (the maund is 80 lb.), and the least of them 2000 maunds. The column was very ingeniously transferred to these boats, and was then conducted to Firozabad, where it was landed with infinite labour and skill."

I have already alluded to "the Ridge" in speaking of one of Asoka's *láts*, and this spot has a peculiar though sad interest for all English people, in connection with the mutiny of 1857, as it was there, in the Flagstaff Tower, that many of the European residents took refuge; and this was also the main picket of our besieging force.

On this my first visit to Delhi, I could not help picturing the whole of these events so vividly to myself as to render it quite painful to me to look at any native of the place who might have been at that time of an age to have taken an active part in them; but after-reflection brought the thought that to the Mohammedans (whose tools the Hindús were to a great extent) the Mutiny was a religious war—almost the same as the Crusades were to Europe—and in their eyes the joining in it was as praiseworthy as an early Christian dying for his faith in the days of the Roman empire is in our opinion; so that one must not judge of their acts entirely from the standpoint of the nineteenth century.

CHAPTER IV.

LAHORE—EARLY HINDÚ TRADITIONS RESPECTING IT—AFGHAN INCURSIONS —INVASION BY MOHAMMEDAN FORCES—MAHMOOD OF GHUSNEE—HIS CAMPAIGNS IN HINDUSTÁN — COMPARISONS BETWEEN HINDÚS AND MOHAMMEDANS—TAMERLANE AND BABER, THEIR EXPEDITIONS TO INDIA —PALACE IN THE FORT AT LAHORE—KASHI WORK—HOW SUPPOSED TO HAVE BEEN MADE—JEHANGIR'S TOMB AT SHADERA—NUR-MEHAL'S TOMB — PERSIAN INVASION OF INDIA—LAHORE COMES UNDER SIKH RULE—TOMB OF RANJIT SINGH—MOSQUE OF WAZIR ALÍ KHAN.

OUR next move was to Lahore. Little is known of the pre-Mohammedan history of that city, except from casual notices in the histories of neighbouring states, and the glimpses given by early Mohammedan writers. Hindú tradition traces it to Rama, king of Ajudia (Oudh), who was the hero of the Rámayana, and I believe it is generally thought that its founders were of the Rajput race. The exact date of its foundation has not been ascertained, but it had already become the capital of a great kingdom before the end of the seventh century A.D. Perhaps owing to change of dynasty, or that it was on the high road between Afghanistan and India, and therefore subject to irruptions and invasions, Lahore was deserted about this period, and the seat of government removed to Sialkote, where it remained till the invasion of Mahmood of Ghusnee in the eleventh century, when the conqueror reoccupied the deserted city.

During the period from the seventh to the eleventh century, the Afghans from Kermán and Peshawur, who had even then embraced Mohammedanism, made various incursions into India, and Ferishta the historian states that in A.D. 682 they wrested certain possessions from the Hindú prince who then reigned in Lahore. In A.D. 977 a prince called Jeipal, of the Brahmin race, reigned over that country, and being much annoyed by the repeated invasions of the Mohammedans, he raised a great force, intending to invade them in their own country. Sabuktagin (of Tartar extraction), the then ruler of Ghusnee, on hearing of this, marched to meet him, and several skirmishes ensued. His son, the afterwards celebrated Mahmood, though then but a boy, gave great proofs of valour on these occasions. At length a very violent storm of hail and wind arose, from which the natives of India suffered much more severely than their more hardy adversaries of the north. This caused Jeipal to treat for peace—he offering the King of Ghusnee a certain tribute and large presents, also adding that whenever the Indian people are reduced to extremity, they murder their wives and children, and rush forward in despair amongst the enemy. Sabuktagin, on hearing this, consented to allow them to retreat, on the payment of a large sum of money, and a present of fifty elephants. Jeipal, stating that he could not pay this large sum on the spot, was allowed to return to Lahore, four trustworthy persons on the part of Sabuktagin being appointed to accompany him, to receive the balance, for whose safety he left hostages. But arrived at Lahore, he imprisoned the messengers, and refused to pay the money. On hearing of this treachery, Sabuktagin was in a furious rage, and hastened towards

Hindostán at the head of a great army. Jeipal also assembled his forces, and marched to meet him, being assisted with troops and money by the kings of Delhi, Ajmere, Callinger, and Kanouj; but the forces of Sabuktagin, though inferior in numbers, were much better organised and disciplined than those of the Hindú princes, who were defeated with great slaughter, and driven back to the banks of the Nilab (or blue river), the ancient Hydaspes, and their camp plundered by the enemy, who raised large contributions in the countries of Limgan and Peshawur, and annexed them to his own dominions.

Sabuktagin dying rather suddenly, in 997, and his eldest son, Mahmood, being then in Khorassan, a considerable distance off, the younger son, Ismaiel, usurped the supreme power, and collected an army; but Mahmood, hastening thither at the head of his troops, repulsed the forces of Ismaiel with such vigour that he was forced to retire and take refuge in the fort at Ghusnee, whither Mahmood pursued him, and invested the place. At length want of provisions obliged Ismaiel to treat for a surrender; and on condition of his personal safety being secured, he gave up the keys of the garrison and of the treasury to his brother. It is related of Mahmood, that he, having built a pleasure-house in a garden near the city of Ghusnee, when it was finished gave a magnificent entertainment, to which he invited his father, Sabuktagin. The son then asked his father's opinion respecting the house and garden, which had been much admired by others. The king, to Mahmood's great disappointment, told him that he looked upon the whole as a bauble, which any of his subjects might have erected if he had possessed the necessary funds, but "that a prince's business was to erect the more durable structure of good fame, which might stand for ever, to be imitated, but never to be equalled, by posterity." One of their poets, named Nizami, made the following reflection upon this: "Of all the magnificent palaces which we are told Mahmood built, we now find not one stone upon another; but the edifice of his fame, as he was told by his father, still triumphs over time, and seems established on a lasting foundation."

Mahmood having made a vow to heaven that, as soon as tranquillity prevailed in his own dominions, he would turn his arms against the idolaters of Hindostán, marched from Ghusnee, A.D. 1000, with 10,000 chosen horse, and came to Peshawur, where he was opposed by Jeipal, the Indian Prince of Lahore, who had brought a superior force into the field; but, after an obstinate battle, Mahmood was victorious, and Jeipal, with his principal friends, was taken prisoner. The sixteen strings of jewels round Jeipal's neck, each of which was valued at about £320,000 of our money, became, of course, the property of the conqueror. After this victory, the king marched from Peshawur and reduced the fort of Bitindi, releasing his prisoners upon the payment of a large ransom, and the promise of an annual tribute, and returned to Ghusnee. According to a Hindú custom which prevailed in those days, that any rajah who had been twice defeated by the Mussulmans should be considered unfit for further command, Jeipal performed the Hindú sacrifice of *johár*, or devotion, by burning himself to death outside the walls of his capital. Having first raised his son Anangpál to the throne, he ordered a funeral-pile to be prepared, on which he sacrificed himself to his gods. In the year 1005, Mahmood again left Ghusnee, with the intention of reconquering Moultán, which had revolted, and was met by Anang-pál, whom he defeated, and obliged to fly into Kashmir. Mahmood then entered Moultán by way of Bitindi, after which he was preparing to return to Ghusnee, when he heard that Elich, the Usbec king of Kashgar, in Tartary, had invaded his territories. A great friendship had previously subsisted between them, Mahmood having married Elich's daughter; but when Mahmood marched into Hindostán, Elich resolved to appropriate Khorassan, which had been left quite unprotected.

The armies met near the Oxus, and Mahmood's army had been thrown into disorder, when he leapt from his horse, and, kissing the ground, invoked the aid of the Almighty. Mounting a war-elephant, he then made a violent assault at the head of his troops, who seem to have derived fresh courage from the determination of their leader, on seeing him thus forcing his way alone through the ranks of the enemy, who were then driven back with great slaughter. Though Elich never more took the field against Mahmood, he was, however, anxious to pursue his flying enemy, though much dissuaded from it by his generals on account of the inclemency of the weather, it being then winter. But the king persisted in attempting it, and followed the retreating troops for two days. On the third night a severe storm overtook them in a desert district. The king's tents were pitched with great difficulty, but the army had all to lie down in the snow. Mahmood having ordered large fires to be lit near his tents, he and his courtiers soon became so warm that they began to throw off their upper garments; and when a chief, called Dilk, who was renowned for his witty sayings, came in, shivering with cold, the king turned to him and said, "Go out, Dilk, and tell Winter that he may burst his cheeks with blustering, as here we do not care for his resentment." Dilk accordingly went out, and returning in a short time, kissed the ground, and thus addressed the king: "I have delivered your Majesty's message to Winter, but the surly season replied, 'That if his hands cannot tear the skirts of royalty, and hurt the attendants of the king, yet he will so exercise his power to-night on the army, that to-morrow morning Mahmood will be obliged to saddle his own horses.'" The king smiled at this answer, and after reflecting a short time, determined to retrace his steps. The following morning some hundreds of men and horses were found to have perished with the cold.

Lahore remained intact thirteen years longer, and another Jeipal ascended the throne. In 1022 Mahmood suddenly marched down from Kashmir. Jeipal II. fled, and the reign of the Hindús was at an end in Lahore, though a final effort was made by them in 1045 to recover their lost sovereignty; but they retired, after a fruitless siege of six months. Lahore passed in succession under the Ghusnivide, Ghorian, Slave, Khilgi, and Toghlak dynastics, till, in 1397, it was conquered by Timur or Tamerlane, who left a viceroy to rule it.

Seen at a distance, the Mohammedan religion appears to be a much purer faith than Hindúism; but the results, as viewed in the present day, are decidedly in favour of the latter. The Hindús, according to almost all persons who have been long in India, are a much more industrious and contented people than the Mussulmans, and are, generally speaking, more honest and moral, and also more trustworthy in all their relations towards Europeans and towards each other.

In A.D. 1436 Lahore was seized by Beholi Khan Lodi, an Afghan chief, who eventually became emperor. In the reign of his grandson the Afghan governor of Lahore revolted, and invited Baber to help him. Baber took the city in 1524, conquered the Patán army sent against him, and plundered and partly burnt the place. He did not remain long there, but a few days later marched on towards Delhi.

This time, however, he only got as far as Sirhind, as intrigues had begun against him. He returned to Lahore, bestowed grants of the land which he had conquered on some of his nobles, and returned to Cábul. Two years later Baber again appeared. A feeble attempt was made to oppose him at the river Ravi, near Lahore; but the force dispersed itself without coming to any engagement, and Baber passed on into Hindostán. This expedition ended in 1526 in the victory Baber gained at Panniput over the Patán army, in the capture of Delhi, and the foundation of the Moghul empire.

The palace in the fort has a frontage of about 500 feet from east to west, and was the work of four successive emperors—viz., Akbar, Jehangir, and Shah Jehan, with additions by Aurungzebe, and later by the Sikhs. It is curious and interesting from the exterior, being richly ornamented with what is called *kashi* work. The composition of this has been analysed, and found to be a layer of glass spread on a hard kind of plaster, formed of a mixture of lime and silicious sand, which accounts for its bearing the heat necessary to fuse the glass. This art, as practised in India and Persia, is believed to have been derived from China at the end of the thirteenth century. The word *kashi* is said to be of Arabic origin. This substance was imported into Europe by the Arabians, and was imitated by the Italians in the fourteenth century in their *majolica* ware. In preparing the *kashi* work, certain different kinds of sand containing sulphuret of copper and magnetic iron were used. The oxides of these, and the lead which was mixed with the lime, gave the peculiar metallic lustre. Three distinct layers of material were laid on: the plaster called *khamir*, which was made of lime and pounded glass in certain proportions, formed into a paste with rice-water, then dried by a gentle heat, and afterwards covered with *asthar*, which was composed of lime and pounded glass containing a good deal of lead. This was rendered soluble, and painted on the plaster. The *kánch*, or glass of various colours, was then pounded and suspended in a viscid fluid made from certain plants, and the tile painted over with this. The whole was then placed in a furnace till all the glass on the surface was fused. We were told by a friend that some specimens of this work were made in Lahore about twenty years ago by a very old man, who then still practised this art, but would impart the process to no one. This old workman demanded 50 rupees, or £5, for a single tile. The *kashi* work may be called a species of mosaic rather than true tile-work, as each little leaf or separate piece of colour has been made in the requisite form, and then cemented into its place. On the walls of the palace at Lahore, in defiance of all ordinary Mohammedan rules, there are representations of men, horses, elephants, and tigers.

A gentle winding incline leads to the upper part of the fort, where it terminates in a large square containing many detached buildings now used as officers' and sergeants' quarters, &c. One building is set apart as a Roman Catholic chapel; and in another, which is entirely of white marble, the services of the Church of England are held.

The old work left in some of these buildings must be of the time of Akbar, I should imagine; the white marble one, however, would appear to be of a later date. All the columns are of red sandstone; some are highly ornamented in their whole height, with carving which is quite equal in execution to the finest work which we afterwards saw at Futtehpore Sikri, near Agra; and, therefore, I am inclined to attribute them to the same period. The spaces between the pillars have been filled up with masonry to convert the buildings into dwelling-houses: in many parts the sloping eaves, with Hindú brackets supporting them, still remain in their original places. These brackets, however, differ in one respect from all others we had seen, inasmuch as instead of the conventional elephant's head, the whole animal is sculptured, with the Hindú bell-ornament hanging from its trunk. Other brackets have well-executed lions or birds carved upon them. Some of these buildings have coved roofs, and small oriel balconies projecting on either side of the pillared colonnade. We entered one of these, now converted into the sergeant-major's quarters, which had evidently been a small dwelling-house. There was a room in the centre, and a colonnade had at one time existed all round; but this in modern days had been partitioned off into sleeping-rooms, and at present only one side of the old colonnade remains. This has been richly carved on the inner side, but when we saw it, it was thickly covered with whitewash; yet one can trace sufficiently clearly the presence of carving upon the walls to make one long to set to work and scrape off the disfiguring crust which covers them.

Jehangir, as I have before stated, made Lahore his capital. The tomb at Shadera was erected to his memory by his wife, the proud and ambitious Nur-Mehal, in connection with the wish he expressed to be buried at Lahore when he was dying at Rajauri in Kashmir in 1627. It is related that Jehangir left her an annuity equivalent to £250,000 of our money, and she is said from that time forward to have always dressed herself in white, as a token of inconsolable widowhood; but in spite of this she engaged in political intrigues, in order to try and secure the succession for Sheriar, a son of Jehangir by another wife, who had married her daughter by her first husband, Shere Afkun.

Jehangir's tomb is not on the same side of the river Ravi as Lahore, and is placed in a large garden, like all Moghul tombs of any importance. In the centre of this garden is a large square platform, about six feet high. The tomb itself, which rests upon this platform, is built of red sandstone inlaid with white marble. It has no dome, but the roof of the building forms a large terrace, which has a handsome tesselated pavement. At each corner of this terrace there is a minar, with a domed cupola. According to the *khadúns* (or hereditary keepers of this tomb), it had originally a central domed cupola on the roof, and over the whole terrace were spread magnificent awnings of silk and gold stuffs; but they say these were removed by Bahadur Shah, the son of Aurungzebe, and also that it was Ranjit Singh who carried off the marble latticed parapet which surrounded the roof and the galleries of the minars. A colonnade runs all round the interior of this tomb, and has small chambers opening out of it. The vault in the centre of the building is approached on all four sides by three small chambers opening out of each other; the walls of all these chambers are painted with various flower patterns, and they, as well as the central hall, have tesselated pavements composed of coloured stones and marbles. Three of these approaches terminate in pierced marble screens, through which the tomb is visible; the only entrance is on the fourth side. In the middle of the central hall is a square platform about eighteen inches high. This, and the sarcophagus which rests upon it, are both of white marble, inlaid with semi-precious stones in the style of the Taj at Agra. At the head of the sarcophagus is a Persian inscription, which has been translated as follows: "The illumined resting-place of his Majesty, the asylum of pardon, Nur-ud-dín Jehangir Bádshah," year of Hegira 1037 (A.D. 1628), which was the date of the erection of the sarcophagus; and adding, "Reason said Jehangir hath departed from the world," year of Hegira 1036 (A.D. 1627), being the date of the emperor's death.

Adjoining this garden there is another, containing the tomb of Asiph Chan, a relation of Nur-Mehal's. This tomb has a singular bulbous-shaped dome; in the centre of each of the four sides there is an arched recess filled up with flower patterns in true tile-work, each group of flowers having a different coloured groundwork. At a short distance from these tombs, but separated from them by the railway which goes to Jelum, are the remains of the tomb of Nur-Mehal, which is of a large size, and was originally very highly decorated, it is said, but now not a trace of ornamentation remains. The Sikhs are believed to have used it as a quarry, and to have built the Golden Temple at Amritsur with plunder from this source.

There is much food for reflection in contemplating the last resting-place of one who was so famed for her personal beauty, whose lovely embroideries and artistic talents were so renowned in her day, and who, from the time she became the wife of Jehangir, belonged to the most luxurious and splendid court of her time. And now to see her tomb! Divided from that of her husband by the prosaic railroad, and denuded of decoration both without and within, the sarcophagus is only of white stucco, and no inscription remains.

During the interval between the years A.D. 1628 and 1657, Lahore enjoyed a time of peace and prosperity; but during the latter part of the reign of Shah Jehan and the struggles between his sons, Lahore upheld the cause of Dara-Sheko, the oldest, and, according to our views, the rightful heir, who lived in that city, and took much interest in its welfare. In 1658, when he was pursued by his brother Aurungzebe, Lahore gave him men and money, but his cause was hopeless: he fled to Ahmedabad, and shortly after was betrayed and killed.

During the reign of Aurungzebe, Lahore was but little mixed up with political events, as that emperor chiefly directed his attention to obtaining possession of the Dekhan, and subduing certain rebellious tribes in Rajputana. From the time of Aurungzebe's death to the accession of Ranjit Singh, Lahore was a prey to Sikh insurrections, till, in 1712, Bahádur Shah, Aurungzebe's son and successor, marched from Delhi in order to try and crush the rebellion, but he died before gaining any very decisive success. On his death the usual contest took place between his two sons: the younger, being hotly pursued, was drowned in the river Ravi whilst attempting to cross it; the other, by name Jehándár, after a reign of seven months, was ousted by Farokshir, his brother's son, and by him put to death. Their struggles encouraged the Sikhs to more excesses, and Farokshir was obliged to take strong measures against them. He appointed Abdul Samad Khan, a man of known determination, as his viceroy, who gained brilliant successes, and sent the Sikh leader to Delhi as a captive.

Lahore had twenty-one years of peace under the rule of Abdul Samad Khan, and of his son, who succeeded him in the viceroyalty—viz., from 1717 till 1738, when the Persians swept down, in the reign of their emperor, Nadir Shah, the army being led by a great Turcoman warrior, Nadir Kúli Khan. A very faint show of resistance was made at Wasirabad, and again close to Lahore, but in vain. The conquering army encamped in the Shalimar gardens, and a month later marched on to Delhi, which city, as we have already seen, they sacked, and despoiled of all the wondrous jewels and treasures which had been in a great measure collected by Shah Jehan and his immediate predecessors.

One portion of the European part of Lahore is called Anárkali; and what is now St James's, or the Station Church, is a building which contained the tomb of Anárkali, a favourite slave girl of the emperor Akbar. It is related that Jehangir being one day in his father's apartments, he smiled upon the girl, and she returned it, on which the emperor ordered her to be buried alive. This tomb was erected by Jehangir in A.D. 1660, and was originally placed beneath the central dome, but is now in a side chamber; it has a Persian inscription to the following effect: "Ah, could I behold the face of my beloved once more, I would give thanks unto my God unto the day of resurrection."

Not far from St James's Church is the Museum, which was erected in 1864 as a temporary building only. Opposite the entrance is a famous piece of ordnance, called Zamzamah, one of the largest known specimens of native casting. It was made in 1760 by Shah Wali Khan, by whom it was used in a battle at Panniput. It afterwards came into the possession of the Sikh Sardárs, and was looked upon by them as a talisman of supremacy. Eventually this cannon came into the hands of Ranjit Singh, and was used by him at the siege of Moultán in 1818. From the time that Moultán was captured till the year 1860, this gun stood at the Delhi gate of Lahore city. Many Hindús regard it as an incarnation of Mahádéo, and almost invariably, whenever we have passed by, I have seen natives, to the number of a dozen and more occasionally, standing round it, regarding it with affectionate admiration, and rubbing or stroking it. To such an extent has this been done, that in one particular part the metal has a bright and polished appearance. The museum contains specimens of the antiquities, arts, and manufactures of the Punjaub; also a collection of native musical instruments, all in one large apartment; and a corresponding room on the other side of the entrance is filled with specimens of minerals, fossils, woods, timbers, grains, and raw silk; also models of various kinds of machinery, &c., &c. What most interested me were the old Buddhist sculptures, which were most, if not all of them, discovered and excavated by Dr Bellew, C.S.I., who is now the sanitary commissioner for the Punjaub. They were found in the province of Peshawar corresponding to the ancient Gandhara, in two principal groups of ruins—viz., Takht-i-Bahi, and Jumal Garhi, to the west of the Indus. Amongst these sculptures are two semi-colossal figures made of a dark-looking stone, which was capable of taking a high polish. One of these, supposed to be a king, represents a young man with long hair flowing down over his shoulders; he has a moustache, but no beard, and his countenance is grave and thoughtful. Drapery falls round the figure from the waist downwards, and covers the left arm. The left hand is perfect, but the right fore-arm and hand are wanting. Small curls cover the top of the head; part of the hair is drawn up into a knot on the crown, and helps to sustain a diadem which encircles the head. A necklace is clasped almost tight round the throat of this statue, a rope-like ornament hangs round the neck descending to the chest, and a number of talismans strung on a cord (much resembling those that many natives wear at the present day) depend from the left shoulder and rest upon the right hip. Another statue near this, and about the same size, is represented with a plaited muslin robe falling in graceful folds, and descending nearly to the feet. The left hand holds up the bottom of this robe; the right fore-arm and hand are missing. The hair is arranged in tight little curls, and a knot of hair covers the crown of the head. The statue of the king looks as if it were a portrait from life, the expression of the countenance is so animated; while the other has the peculiar Buddhist type of contemplation and repose, and is without ornaments of any kind. In another place there is the seated figure of a king, which was found at Takht; this is about one-third the size of life. This, I think, may also have been a portrait, and General Cunningham says of it, "I infer, with confidence, that this must have been a royal portrait from the description of Hiouen Thsang, the Chinese traveller, who says that an Indian king had no step to his throne, but used a footstool, which served the same purpose." There are four small figures belonging to this group, two on either side of the central one; three of these are in an attitude of supplication, the fourth holds a *chauri* (or fan made of a yak's tail) to fan away the flies.

There is also another statue about the same size as the last named, which may, too, be a king's portrait. The attitude is different: the left hand rests upon the hip in an easy and graceful manner, the right fore-arm is wanting, but from the position of the upper part of the arm, it would appear to have been raised, as if giving some command. Besides these, there are many small fragments of minute Buddhist sculpture, which have been considerably defaced and mutilated. In some of these the figures are very numerous, each being not more than four or five inches high. A long examination and study would be necessary to make out the subjects of them, were it even possible, for much must be left to conjecture only. On one fragment, two friends appear to be having a joyful meeting; on another, there was a seated figure in the midst, and other persons advancing on either side as petitioners for some favour; some stones also had on them processions of men with grotesque masks.

In the corridor which divides the two apartments there is an ancient Sikh gun, supposed to be of the time of Govind Singh, the last of their *gurus*, or teachers, who died A.D. 1708. In the centre of this gun are two lions, each bestridden by a warrior with a drawn sword in his hand.

In Anárkali there are small public gardens, where a band plays occasionally; these are very well kept, and at the time we were there the roses were in high beauty. The kinds which seem to succeed best in India are the tea varieties. The Maréchal Niel grows everywhere in great perfection, and all kinds of white and yellow roses appear to do much better than the pink or red ones: as a rule, these last seldom seem to produce what in England we should call completely perfect flowers; either the centres are defective, or the petals have not the entire regularity which is so much desired.

The Laurence gardens, containing the Laurence and Montgomerie halls, are situated not far from the residence of the Lieut.-Governor. These halls are used as places of public recreation, and a covered corridor unites them. The gardens, which cover an area of more than 100 acres, are very tastefully laid out on ground which, till 1860, was nothing but a wild jungle. Part of the land belongs to the Agri-Horticultural Society of the Punjaub, and is under the superintendence of a gardener sent out from Kew; the remainder belongs to the Municipality.

To Nur-Mehal is given the credit of inventing the manufacture of attar of roses. This industry is now prosecuted both at Lahore and Amritsar. The common country rose—the *rosa centifolia*—is used, as being found to yield a stronger essential oil than any foreign or hybrid variety. A very pretty kind of striped washing silk is also made in Lahore, chiefly in three colours only—blue and white, black and white, and violet and white—in longitudinal stripes of various widths. Ivory carving and turning is also carried on there. In the educational department for natives, Lahore has also made great advances. There is a Lahore Government College, where Arabic, Persian, and Sanscrit, the classical languages of the East, are compulsory subjects, but where English, which is in India the only door to European civilisation, is optional.

In Anárkali there is a high school for the children of Europeans and Eurasians, a clergyman of the Church of England being the headmaster. Besides these, there are also missionary establishments and a divinity school for training and preparing native Christians for ordination. Mission schools for girls, and zenana mission work, is also conducted by English ladies sent out for this purpose by some of our societies at home.

In the Hazuri Bagh, or garden, near the fort, there is a pretty kind of summer-house, standing on a platform about four feet high, the whole being of white marble. Much of the material is said to have been pilfered from older buildings in the neighbourhood of Lahore. The pavement of the platform is richly inlaid, and the building itself has flowers, butterflies, and peacocks, also water vessels carved in relief upon it. The roof is flat, and has a balcony all round projecting from it, which is supported on brackets. There is an open colonnade all round the building, and a square space in the centre, supported on pillars. The ceilings are composed of delicate tracery in stucco, with small convex mirrors in the intervening spaces. From the centre of the roof rises a small open pavilion, supported on slender pillars. From this garden a flight of steps, and an archway known as the Roshnai gateway, leads to the Jumma Musjid, which is a fair example of the latest style of Moghul work: Humaion's tomb at Delhi may be called a specimen of their earliest style. This gateway is of red sandstone; its recessed archways and windows are of stucco, painted in the brightest colours. A tall minar is built into it at either corner; and the courtyard of the mosque, which is of a large size, has minars at each of the four corners. The mosque, also of red sandstone, is carved, but not richly so, and has a certain amount of white marble inlaying, which is more elaborate in the central entrance than in any other part of the edifice. The three domes, made of white marble with gilt pinnacles, are all nearly of the same size, the centre one being considerably raised above the others in order to give it height. The inscription on the front of the mosque shows that it was built A.D. 1674, during the reign of Aurungzebe, by Fidæ Khan Khokah, who was the emperor's master of ordnance. Its general style and architectural details struck us as very inferior to many specimens of the Moghul work of that period which we had seen elsewhere: the minars no doubt have lost much of their original effect from the absence of their cupolas, which were so much shaken in 1840 by an earthquake that they had to be removed.

The tomb of Ranjit Singh, surnamed the Lion of the Punjaub, who belonged to the sect of warlike Sikhs, is situated at one side of the Hazuri Bágh, and close to the entrance of the fort. This building is raised on a double platform; the exterior is of white stucco, painted with graceful designs in bright colours; it has sloping eaves all round, and several small projecting balconies. There is one large dome in the centre, and numerous small kiosks and cupolas surrounding this. In the interior a corridor runs all round an open gallery, forming a second storey; the space in the centre is supported on marble pillars, and open up to the roof; in the midst is a small marble canopy, inlaid with the finest work in semi-precious stones. This may be about 14 feet in height. Above this there is a clear space to the ceiling, which is coved, and painted in bright colours, red and gold being the prevailing ones, and small pieces of looking-glass let in. The ceilings in the corridor are decorated in the same manner, only that, in some parts, red and green foil has been introduced beneath the pieces of glass, which has a pretty effect. In small recesses in the walls of the corridor there are statues of Ram Chund, or Rama (one of the incarnations of Vishnu), his wife Sita, and Lakhsman, his brother; also of Vishnu and his son, and of Kali, the goddess of cruelty.

In one of the smaller buildings near Ranjit Singh's tomb was a large statue of Kali, and small figures of other Hindú gods, and in another the tombs of Ranjit's son and grandson; and there we found an old Sikh engaged in reading the Granth, their sacred book. The presence of all these idols shows how much the Sikh religion must have changed since it was first founded, and how much of the debased form of Hindúism has crept in amongst this sect, of whose original form of worship I purpose giving an account later on.

Wazir Ali Khan's mosque was built A.D. 1634, by Hakím Ali-ud-dín, a Patán of Chiniot, who rose to the position of wazir in the reign of Shah Jehan. It is situated in a small open space, just within one of the gates of the native city of Lahore, and is approached by a short flight of steps leading to a square entrance gateway, domed within, though this is scarcely visible from the outside. There are small domed cupolas at each corner of the entrance gateway, and at each corner of the courtyard of the mosque is an octagonal minar. The interior of this quadrangle has small chambers all round it, all of which appeared to be inhabited. There are two small gateways on the north and south sides of the mosque, which, as is always the case in India, occupies the whole of the western side. The four minars, and the walls of the courtyard, are ornamented with medallions of the *kashi* work, and the exterior of the mosque is decorated in the same manner. The central doorway is entirely covered with this work: the designs have a decided Indo-Mohammedan character. Near the top of the minars are represented cypresses, of a very blue colour, and on other portions of the building there are vases of flowers, and Arabic writing, all in the same material. The interior exhibits a totally distinct type of work, and the designs are of a Persian character, both in colouring and form; so that one could well imagine that they had been copied from some Persian carpet. This work also differs entirely from the *kashi*, in that it has not been made of small pieces, which were afterwards cemented together; but the whole surface would appear to have had the designs painted upon it like fresco, and a sort of porcelain glaze put on afterwards. It seemed to us a great pity that these arts should now be lost, as, were the artists of our day able to execute such work, both the inside of our houses and their exterior walls might be adorned with the most exquisite designs, as, in all probability, a glaze of this kind would resist even our northern climate.

CHAPTER V.

PREPARING FOR CAMP LIFE IN KASHMIR, SRINAGAR—BOATS USED IN NAVIGATING THE RIVER JELUM—THE RACES WHICH PEOPLE KASHMIR—LIDDAR VALLEY—SNOWSTORM IN MAY—LOVELY VEGETATION—ANCIENT TEMPLES AT MARTUND AND AVANTIPORE—GULMURG—OUR LOG HUTS—RETURN TO SRINAGAR—DAL LAKE, ITS FLOATING ISLANDS—GARDENS AND PALACES ON ITS SHORES.

OUR chief business in Lahore was to engage servants and to buy tents and other camp furniture for our projected visit to Kashmir. Bedsteads, chairs, and tables are all made either to take to pieces or to fold up for the convenience of transport. At that time, the railroad being open only as far as Wazirabad, we had to take a carriage from thence to Rawal Pindi, 110 miles. This is a very pretty little station, within view of the Himalayas. It is very important that travellers intending to go into Kashmir should remember that it is advisable to engage as few servants as possible belonging to Southern or Central India; they should be chosen from the Punjaub in preference, as men from lower down country are quite unfit for the necessary roughing it in that colder climate.

We left Rawal Pindi about 7th April 1876, and as it was an unusually late season it was not possible to drive up to Murree (38 miles), nor could our baggage be sent up in carts, as is generally done. We had to ride the greater part of the way, and hire coolies to carry our tents, &c., which is the usual mode of conveyance all through Kashmir, where there are no roads for wheeled carriages. We arrived at Murree thoroughly drenched, having been caught in a storm of rain and hail. After remaining there one day, on 10th April we began our onward way. There are twelve marches between Murree and Srinagar, the capital of Kashmir, varying in length from 10 to 16 miles. The first two, each about 10 miles, being downhill, can easily be accomplished in one day, thereby reaching Kohala. On the next march, and soon after leaving the bungalow, the river Jelum is crossed by a suspension-bridge, and there we first entered Kashmirian territory. The next six marches took us through fine scenery, the valley contracting a good deal in parts, our paths sometimes running along the bank of the river, and sometimes many hundred feet above it.

Between Chata-Kalas and Rara, the river Nainsúk (a tributary of the Jelum) joins it. We were detained there some hours, being unable to cross this stream, for a mountain thunderstorm had caused such a rush of water as to render it impossible to gain the other side. Towards the afternoon, however, it was resolved to attempt it; and sending for a band of men from the village accustomed to such work, a rope was taken across by an expert swimmer, and made fast on the opposite side, the object of this rope being that a man might hold on to it and thus save himself from losing his footing, owing to the violence of the current. Even with this assistance the ordinary coolies utterly refused to carry our baggage over, but as soon as it was at all feasible these same villagers carried it, each man being supported by another, who held the rope with his other hand. When it came to our turn, it was rather nervous work; we were each carried across separately in a piece of carpeting fixed in a frame in shape somewhat like a boat, and having long poles at each end, which rested on the shoulders of the bearers. Four men carried this machine, two at either end; other four clung on to and assisted these. Our horses were forced into the water, and thus we all reached the other side in safety. On our seventh march from Murree, shortly before reaching Uri, we saw on our left hand a rope-bridge such as are seen in many parts of the Himalayas, and are in general use amongst the natives, though our road never led us where we had occasion to cross one. One, or sometimes two, ropes form the pathway; on either side there is a rope (held in position by forked sticks placed at intervals) which the passenger holds to steady himself, though once we saw a man pass over with a small burden, when this, of course, could not be done, as he had only one hand at liberty.

On the following march, near the village of Banniyar, and about three miles from Naoshera, there is one of the best preserved temples in the valley. Its dimensions are not large, being only 145 feet by 120, taking the measurement of the whole area, which is surrounded on all sides by a pillared colonnade. Between each pillar is a trefoiled arch, with a detached architrave, behind which is a niche, which, I suppose, may at some period have contained a statue. The space between this colonnade and the central temple has, in former times, as is the case of most, if not all, old temples in Kashmir, at least been capable of being flooded with water. The course of ages in this instance had brought down sufficient mud and silt to bury the temple itself in a great degree, but it was excavated a few years ago by the order of the Maharajah, and is now in an almost perfect state. The roof of the central building is of shingles, but it is doubtful whether this was always the case. The whole of this and the following march our road led us through a highly wooded district, the chief feature in which were the enormous deodaras. One, roughly measured by us, was seventeen feet in girth at six feet from the ground, and from thence grew up to a great height, gradually diminishing in size, and straight as the mast of a ship.

From the moment we got into Kashmir territory, after crossing the bridge at Kohala, the whole country at that season appeared one vast orchard, as it abounds in wild pomegranate, apricot, apple, and pear trees, which were then all in full blossom. Between Naoshera and Baramula the view is certainly most striking, as the course of the Jelum can thence be traced for a considerable distance; and the Woolar Lake is also visible. The last two marches being usually made in boats on the Jelum, at Baramula we embarked on board a so-called *doongah*. These boats are flat-bottomed, and about fifty feet long by eight feet wide in the centre, tapering to a point at each end. They form all the year through the permanent abode of the boatmen and his family, who occupy about one-third of the length of the boat: their cooking is carried on in two receptacles made of baked clay. The fire is placed in these, and huge jars of metal and pottery rest upon them—the former containing the family meal of rice, whilst the vegetables of the season are prepared in the latter. Mattings, formed of a kind of reed which grows plentifully on the lakes in Kashmir, separate the boat-people from the traveller, who has also a thick awning overhead formed of layers of the same, the space allotted to him being about twenty feet in length by eight in width. The front part of the boat must be kept clear for the boat-people to punt when occasion requires, though the more usual mode of progression is by towing the boat from the bank, the whole family joining in this except the mother, who, armed with a small paddle resembling in form the ace of spades, acts as the steerer. The planks of these boats are all made of the deodara; but as saws can hardly be said to exist, or to be used in Kashmir, they are formed by cutting away with an adze the whole of the exterior of the tree, till a plank of the required size is left in the centre.

Our party had by this time been enlarged—a young friend, Mr H., having joined us—so that when we left Baramula our flotilla consisted of five boats: my husband and I in one, J. and his young friend in another; a third was used as a cooking boat for the whole party; and the two remaining ones held our united baggage and the rest of our servants—the *saïs's* (or grooms) marching the ponies up by land. At stated hours the cooking boat is brought alongside that of the master, and the two are temporarily joined, the dinner, or whatever meal is required, passed over the side, the boats going on all the time, though perhaps their progress is slightly retarded.

The term "valley" is rather a misnomer as regards Kashmir, taken as a whole. The Jelum flows from south-east to north-west, through a plain, which tradition says was once a lake, and which must have been about eighty miles long by fifteen in width; but the greater part of the so-called valley consists of mountains, of raised terraces, and of glens, descending from the Himalayan ranges which surround it.

The seasons are divided into summer and winter, and are of nearly equal duration. Many of the mountains are clothed with rich forests, and at their base is a fine alluvial soil, which is very productive. The whole of the land is now the absolute property of the ruler, though this was not the case before it came into the hands of the Sikhs, as under former sovereigns grants of land had been made to many persons for various periods, but Ranjit Singh made a general resumption, thus reducing thousands to penury.

Under the present system, when the grain has been trodden out, a division takes place between the farmer and the Government: formerly this was an equal one, but the Government had advanced in its demands till it now requires seven-eighths of the produce of the land near the city, and three-fourths of the more remote crops. The *straw* belongs to the cultivator, and he contrives to bribe the watchman or overseer to let him steal his own produce. He is allowed to keep cattle on the mountains during the summer, may cut wood, and bring it into the city for sale, and may also sell wild-greens, butter, and milk. It would appear from this alone that the farmer is not too well off; but the case is aggravated by the method employed in disposing of the governmental share. This is sent into the market, a high price put upon it, no one is permitted to offer his produce at a lower rate, or sometimes even to dispose of it at all, until all the public corn has been sold.

The early chronology of Kashmir is much involved in obscurity. The first religion is supposed to have been the Naga or Snake worship. Hinduism, Buddhism, and, again, Naga worship, are said to have successively prevailed in the valley. According to Ferishta, the Persian historian, the line of Mussulman kings began A.D. 1326. General Cunningham gives 1334 as the date. Their rule lasted till 1558, when Akbar annexed it to the Moghul empire. After the death of Aurungzebe a state of anarchy prevailed in Kashmir for about a hundred years, when it was acquired by the Sikhs, who retained possession of the country till after the first Sikh war, when, in 1846, the British Government made it over to the present dynasty, who are of Rajput race, and were at that time rajahs of Jamu.

The native city of Srinagar is built on both sides of the river Jelum, and extends about four miles, or nearly so, following the windings of the river, though the right bank appears to be the most populous. There are seven wooden bridges connecting the two sides of the city: these bridges are formed of huge trunks of firs, or deodaras, laid in rows one above the other, each row being at right angles to the preceding one; the piers thus formed gradually widening as they increase in height, and approaching one another, till, when they are sufficiently close, they are connected by beams thrown across from pier to pier, and the roadway is formed. This same principle has been carried out in regard to all the smaller bridges in the interior of the country, and also in Ladakh—though where the streams are small no piers are necessary, and the beams are laid from either bank, each projecting beyond the former one, till they finally meet in the centre. Near the banks of the river are innumerable Hindú temples, the exterior of which dazzles the eye with their bright metal roofs. Though accustomed as we are to our grand Gothic cathedrals, and viewed by the side of Mohammedan mosques, the smallness of their size is very disappointing, yet the religion of the Hindús is not one of united public worship like that of the Christian or the Moslem.

The Maharajah's palace is on the left bank of the river—one of the largest of the Hindú temples almost joins it. Still higher up on the same side, and above the limits of the city proper, is a *baradurrie*—a large summer palace in which dinners or entertainments to Europeans are given. On one occasion when the Lieutenant-Governor of the Punjaub went up for the summer, it was given over to him as his residence. The Maharajah is himself a Hindú, as are also most of the principal officials who come up with him each summer from Jamu, his other capital.

The resident population consists of the Pundits—also Hindús, who are an educated class, inasmuch as they can read and write, and become bankers, merchants, &c. These are said to be descendants of the ancient inhabitants of Kashmir. Their Mussulman conquerors probably came from Afghanistan; and these last, though forming an immense majority of the population, are now in their turn oppressed by the Hindús. The Pundits are much fairer in complexion than the Mohammedans; have, many or most of them, a decided Jewish type of features; and some of their women belonging to the higher classes, who keep much in the house, are almost as fair as Europeans, though their skins are of a dead white; and they rarely have the red tinge underneath, though I have seen it occasionally. The dress of the Pundits is a long woollen robe, in form like a dressing-gown, made with very wide sleeves, and confined at the waist with a broad sash of cotton cloth. On the head they wear a turban folded in a peculiar manner. Their women wear a dress of the same form as that of the men, only the material is of a lighter texture, and is dyed a dark-red colour. A large white handkerchief is bound tightly round the head, so that not a particle of the hair is seen; over this again they throw a long piece of white calico, scarfwise, which envelops the figure down to the knees. Some of the Punditanas possess beautiful jewellery of a style which they alone wear.

The tailors, jewellers, workers in *papier-maché*, shawl-weavers and embroiderers, and also the servant class, are all Mohammedans. The boat-people, I believe, are likewise of this faith, though they seem to form quite a distinct class, and have a totally different type of features. The boat-people, both men and women, never appeared to wear anything but a long white calico dress buttoned close round the throat, and sometimes, though not always, a sash of the same material round the waist. The boatmen also arrange their turbans in a different manner to either the Pundits or the other Mussulmans. The boatmen's wives have usually a scarf of white calico thrown over the head.

Arrived in the European part of Srinagar, we stopped at the house of the officer on special duty, to whom we had been particularly recommended, and he caused one of the bungalows set apart for visitors to be opened for us. Those allotted to married strangers and their families are situated in the *munshi bagh*, or garden. The view from thence is one which must ever remain with pleasure upon the memory. Our bungalow was not more than fifty paces from the smoothly-flowing river Jelum, being only separated from it by a wide pathway and a sloping bank. On the opposite side of the river were richly-cultivated fields, which then were green, but later on took a golden hue; and in the extreme distance were to be seen the snowy heights of the Pir Panjal, which is the highest pass into Kashmir; and on the right hand, looking down the river, was a nearer and lower range of hills, on which on clear days a part of the mountain resort called Gulmurg can be distinguished. Hearing that cholera had broken out in the native city, and threatened to be serious, after two or three days' rest we left Srinagar, and moved on, with our servants, tents, and baggage, to the Liddar valley, going by water as far as Islamabad, whence two marches took us to Palgaum, about sixty miles from the capital.

In the Liddar valley we first saw how the Kashmirians supply their want of sugar, as the sugar-cane does not grow in their country. They use honey as a substitute, and have a rather singular method of obtaining it. A round hole is made in one wall of the house (their dwellings are for the most part, if not entirely, of wood), and in this hole they insert a tube of baked clay, lined with a plastering of clay mortar, which is worked up with the husk of rice, or with thistle-down. This tube is about 14 inches in diameter and 22 inches in length. Outside the house the orifice is closed by a platter of red pottery-ware, which has a small hole in the centre for the bees to enter. A dish of similar ware closes the tube within the house, and is also kept in its place by a plastering of clay mortar. When the comb is fit to be taken, the master of the house removes the plate within with some ceremony, and lays some burning grass near the entrance of the hive, which causes the bees to come out and stupefies them for a time only; after which they again return to the same place, though our Kashmiri servant, from whom I got much of this information, told me that an unskilful hand will often kill the bees outright. We remained altogether about five weeks in that valley—the gentlemen going away occasionally for a few days' shooting, taking only the small tents with them.

On 15th May we were overtaken by a snowstorm—such a thing at that season never having occurred before in the recollection of the *lumbadar*, or head-man, of the village, who was an old man. In the space of two hours the snow lay four inches deep on the roof of our tent. Had this happened in the night, or, as it was, had much more snow fallen before we could get efficient assistance to remove it, our tent might have collapsed and the consequences been serious. We were first aroused to our danger by the bending of the bamboo poles, and the strange appearance of the interior canvass on one side. As much as possible was at once removed; long poles to aid in knocking it off sent for from the village, together with several men, who were appointed to watch by turns all night for fear of another storm coming on, which, happily, was not the case. Before we left the Liddar valley I made two excursions with my husband, one being to Tannin—one march up the valley leading to Ambernath, where there are some caves which are much resorted to as a place of pilgrimage; our other expedition was to Aro, up the other branch of the fork which the Liddar valley makes at this point. The scenery on both these marches was very striking, and thoroughly repaid us for the fatigue and scrambling which was necessary,—for in neither case was it possible to ride the whole way. Whilst we were staying at Aro, where we remained two nights, we came upon some lovely wild-flowers: amongst others the wild peony, with large, white, single flowers, covered considerable patches of land; and we also saw one or two bulbous plants quite new to us.

One night a good number of *bara-singh* (a species of red deer), with immense horns, came down to our tents and much disturbed the equanimity of little Jip—a dog belonging to one of our servants who had attached himself to us; and had my husband brought his rifle with him, it being bright moonlight, no doubt he might have bagged one or more, so close did they seem to be, judging from the sounds we heard.

We left Palgaum finally the first days of June, and at that season found the whole road down to Islamabad, but more especially the last march from Eishmakán, one garden of wild-flowers. The sweet jasmine of our gardens was growing as a large bush in wild profusion; also a climbing rose, with large cream-coloured flowers, grew in a most luxuriant manner. Besides these, we saw what I believed to be two varieties of acacia, a dwarf and a tree species: both had magenta-coloured blossoms. There were also four or more other varieties of the wild rose, and numerous smaller flowering-plants carpeted the ground.

On this march we made a slight *détour* in order to visit the temple at Martund, the largest in Kashmir, whose position alone would render it worthy of a visit. Fergusson, in his volume on 'Indian Architecture,' states that the enclosure of this building was built by Lalitaditya, who reigned A.D. 725 to 751; that all authorities are agreed with him on this point; and adds it as his opinion that the same ruler also erected the temple itself, though there are no inscriptions which can enable its date to be fixed with certainty. General Cunningham, however, ascribes the building of this temple to Ranaditya, who reigned A.D. 578 to 594. The temple itself is situated about 500 feet above the plain, on a plateau of some miles in extent, directly behind which rises a mountain of considerable height. The view from the temple forms a perfect panorama on three sides. On one side can be seen Islamabad and the plain beyond leading to Vernag; and from this plateau can also be seen the mountains dividing the Liddar and the Sind valleys, a considerable portion of the course of the Jelum, and the mountains beyond it. The proportions of this temple, though infinitely smaller, are said to resemble more nearly than any other known building the temple at Jerusalem. It has evidently been much adorned with sculptures, though, from the friable nature of the stone, the subjects of these are for the most part hardly discernible. According to Fergusson, the building measures 60 feet in length by 38 feet in width; but this is supplemented by two wings which, singularly enough, are detached from the main building—a space of 18 inches or 2 feet existing between—and it is difficult to see the use of these side erections, which no one hitherto appears to have attempted to explain. Like the temple at Banniyar, already described, this also stands in the centre of a courtyard, and is surrounded by a colonnade. From the present state of the ruins one might quite fancy that this temple had been destroyed by an earthquake. Earthquakes are not uncommon in Kashmir. One was felt at Srinagar whilst we were in the Liddar valley, where we seem to have been beyond its influence.

Arrived at Islamabad we again took a boat, and on our return journey to Srinagar we stopped at Avantipore, where we saw the ruins of two temples which were excavated a few years ago at the suggestion of Bishop Cotton. One of these appears to have possessed a much greater richness of detail than the temple at Martund, for we noticed many stones which had evidently been sculptured on both sides, showing that the building had been richly adorned without as well as within.

On again reaching Srinagar, we found that the rains were shortly expected. These are there nothing compared to what is experienced in India; but they arrive about the same period, and usually last with more or less violence for six weeks or longer. We were told that Srinagar is not considered healthy during that time, and therefore we went up to Gulmurg (signifying "flower-meadow"), about thirty miles distant. It certainly deserves this name, for the quantity and variety of wild-flowers in the neighbourhood is quite extraordinary. Gulmurg lies at a height of more than 7000 feet above the sea (Srinagar is 2000 feet lower), and consists of a cup or hollow in the mountains of an irregular form. Surrounding this basin are several hills on which visitors build temporary huts or pitch their tents. In this hollow a small native bazaar rises every year, occupied by Parsees and other dealers, who bring up supplies and stores of provisions for the English visitors. A portion of the lending library is brought up, and the building where the books are kept forms a point of assembly where all congregate in the afternoons to read the papers, &c., or play at badminton on the meadow below. A small wooden church has been erected, and the chaplain at Srinagar for the time being goes up to Gulmurg for a few weeks each year. We fixed ourselves on the hill known as the Resident's, from the circumstance that the officer on special duty has a bungalow there—the only one in the place which is looked after and kept in permanent repair. J. discovered the remains of two rooms near this spot, and also a building of one room only, for himself. To the ruined edifice he added a dining-room and dressing-room, also a small verandah. To build these, put the rest into habitable repair, and mend our nephew's own habitation, cost somewhat less than £4. These houses, or rather huts, properly speaking, are built of rough planks, fashioned without a saw, like the boats before described. The coolies are allowed, under certain restrictions, to cut down trees for this purpose; into the interstices of these planks is put moss, &c. The roof is made in the same manner, and the whole dwelling is plastered outside with wet mud, which requires renewing to a certain extent every few days, especially the roof, after a hard storm of rain. With matting on the floors, these abodes are anything but uncomfortable; and we remained at least a month in ours, after which we returned to Srinagar, where the Yarkund Envoy, Yakoob Khan, had arrived with his suite. He was attended by an English officer, and passed through Kashmir on his way to visit the Viceroy at Simla, and to take part in the proclamation at Delhi, *en route* for England.

Yakoob Khan was a fine-looking intelligent man, of perhaps forty-five years of age; his face bore the impress of thought to a much greater extent than is usually seen in the countenances of natives of Eastern countries. He speaking nothing but Persian, we could only converse with him through an English interpreter. He was anxious to know if we intended visiting Yarkund, and said he would give us every facility in his power for doing so, &c., &c. From this conversation, I think, began to date our desire to go part of the way thither at least, and finally led to our going to Ladakh.

The envoy, during his stay in Srinagar, gave an entertainment at the Naseeb Bagh, an old garden dating from the time of the Emperor Jehangir, and situated on the Dal, or city lake. On going thither on the appointed day we found awnings and tents prepared, the ground beneath these covered with the richest Persian carpets, and a feast provided which, alas! none of us Europeans could partake of, as far as the meats were concerned, for want of knives and forks. There were kids and lambs roasted whole, and no doubt stuffed with pistachio nuts in the orthodox manner, had we only possessed the means of ascertaining it.

There is a river flowing out of the Dal which connects it with the Jelum; but this communication is capable of being completely shut off by means of large flood-gates, which are closed when the lake sinks below a certain level. The lake is fed by streams flowing into it from the mountain on its eastern side; and possibly it may also have springs in its midst, for a very considerable body of water usually flows out of it. The Shalimar and the Nishat gardens, on its eastern shore, are of large extent; they both contain pavilions and fountains still in working order. These gardens were also laid out by Jehangir, who, together with his wife Nur-Mehal, used constantly to visit Kashmir.

The lake now brings in a considerable revenue to the state, chiefly derived from the Singhara, a species of sweet nut growing in the water, which, when first boiled, and then roasted, is not unlike the Spanish chestnut in flavour, and forms an important item in the food of the people, who also eat the stems of another water-plant, the Nymphæa lotus, when boiled till tender. The floating gardens which have been formed on this lake are also very curious. A long kind of rush, which grows in great abundance, is cut off just below the surface of the water. On these stalks, when laid flat and pressed somewhat closer together, reeds and sedges are put, and mud piled, which sinks into the mass of matted roots; long stakes are then driven into the ground beneath to keep the whole in place. Floating gardens are thus made which vary in size: some (possibly by being afterwards added to) are of considerable extent. On these islands are grown sweet and water melons, cucumbers, vegetable marrows, and gourds, in great quantities. One inconvenience attends them, which is, that a man's neighbour will occasionally remove the stakes and transport the whole island bodily, in the course of a night, to a distant spot, rendering it impossible for him to swear to his own property.

CHAPTER VI.

STARTING FOR LADAKH—SONAMURG—ASCENT OF THE ZOJI-LA PASS—DRAS—NATIVE POLO PLAYING—NAMYIKA AND FOT-LA PASSES—LAMA YURU—CHINESE ACCOUNT OF THE ORIGIN OF THE THIBETANS—THEIR RELIGION—EXCLUSION OF EUROPEANS FROM CHINESE THIBET—VISIT TO LAMA SERAI, OR MONASTERY AT LAMA YURU—DESCRIPTION OF A RELIGIOUS SERVICE HEARD THERE—NATURE OF COUNTRY BETWEEN LAMA YURU AND LEH.

About the 4th or 5th of September we left Srinagar for Ladakh, starting in the evening, going in a boat as far as Ganderbal, at the entrance of the Sind valley, and the next morning riding on to Kangan. In this valley there are some fine walnut-trees, and also very large planes: these last are one of the trees most commonly seen in Kashmir, and yet they are not indigenous, for we were told they do not ripen their seed, but are always multiplied by cuttings; in fact, I believe they are known to have been introduced by the Moghuls. From Kangan it is three marches to Sonamurg, or the "Golden Meadow," which lies at a height of 9000 feet above the sea. Several valleys converge at this spot. Some native huts are situated in a hollow or cup, which may have anciently been the bed of a lake; and here is also a small wooden church, and four or five wooden houses, in the style of those at Gulmurg. A large glacier, at the upper end of a narrow valley, faced the bungalow in which we were. Pouring rain detained us there one day, but the following one we were able to march on to Baltal, before reaching which cultivation almost ceases. The scenery is, however, very grand, and the mountains on either side of the valley are clothed with dense pine forests: the lower slopes are used as grazing grounds, to which the sheep are taken in great numbers during the summer. At Baltal the Sind valley ends. There being no accommodation but a large log-hut used by natives, we pitched our tents almost at the foot of the Zoji-la Pass (11,500 feet), which leads into the Dras valley. Two streams here unite to form the Sind river: one comes down a lovely wooded ravine to the south; but we went northwards, and parallel with the stream, which rises beyond the top of the pass. The ascent is very steep and trying; during the winter and early spring it is only practicable by following up the gorge of the river, which at those periods is filled with snow to the depth of fifty feet. The view in ascending this pass becomes very striking after a certain distance. Behind is the richly wooded Sind valley; and in front, the sterile though grand mountains of Ladakh. After the steepest part of the ascent has been overcome, there is a difficult and steep descent, and a snow-bridge has to be crossed; after which a gradual ascent leads to the water-shed—whence an easy descent brought us down to Mataiyan, where we halted for the night, and the next day reached Dras. There the valley becomes wide and undulating, with good pasturage. There is a small fort, and the people began to have the Tartar type of features; though they said they were not Buddhists, but Hindús or Mohammedans.

At Dras we first saw the native game of polo played, which is said to have had its origin in Thibet. Music is with them an indispensable accompaniment when they are playing: the instruments were drums, and a rude kind of clarionet. On the next march to Tashgam we still saw grass, but beyond that the vegetation becomes very scanty. During the whole of this march we followed the Dras river till it joins the Kargil river, which is again followed till Kargil itself is reached. This place is the headquarters of a district, and, like Dras, has a fort, garrisoned by about twenty soldiers. At Shergol, the next stopping place, we saw the first Budhist monastery, and there also we first saw the men with pig-tails in the Chinese fashion. Just where the two races meet can be contrasted the great difference between the Kashmiri proper and the Thibetan, or Bôt. The former is invariably melancholy looking, as if he were living under a harsh and oppressive rule, and rarely or ever laughs or smiles; whereas the Bôt, though now living under the same government, is always merry and gay, and spends his spare time in laughing and joking with his associates.

Religion and race may both have something to do, perhaps, with this difference of temperament, but it must be remembered that the Mohammedans of Kashmir have been much longer under foreign rule, having been terribly ill-used by the Sikhs. Ladakh was only conquered by the father of the present ruler of Kashmir, and had up to that time been independent, and governed by its own rajahs. We must also take into account that the present Government treats the Bôts much more leniently than its Mussulman subjects: perhaps the country being thinly populated, and much of the land sterile and mountainous, it is impossible to make any heavy demands upon them.

I will illustrate the manner in which the people are ground down in Kashmir by the heads of villages or others invested with a little authority, and relate here an anecdote told us by a friend who was in that country a year or two before our visit. He wished to give new *puggrees* (or turbans) of a particular colour to the boat-people who were regularly in his employ, in order that he might recognise them at a distance. But these men all prayed him not to insist upon this, but if he was satisfied with them, give them a little money instead, as after he had left, the officials seeing them with any good new clothes would say, "Oh, the sahib has been very good to them, and no doubt has given them lots of presents," insist on obtaining from them all they could of their hard-earned summer wages on the strength of this, and thus squeeze them more than they would otherwise have done.

On the next march, about three miles beyond Shergol, we saw a colossal image of Buddha, in *alto-rilievo*, about twenty feet high, carved on a huge isolated rock; and shortly afterwards began to ascend the Namyika Pass (12,000 feet). The ascent is about five miles long, and a very gradual one. At Karbu there are the remains of a large fort, on an inaccessible-looking rock. The following day we had to cross the Fot-la Pass (about 14,500 feet). Lama Yuru, our next stopping-place, was about 2000 feet lower, and is just visible from the top of the pass. When we reached the summit, I observed a Bôt, who accompanied us, on reaching this point, look towards that place, place his hands together in the attitude of supplication, and apparently repeat a prayer.

At Lama Yuru the scenery is of the most rugged description; and, as a rule, the soil is very barren. Much of the land around it is a mass of lacustrine deposit, which sometimes rises to 15,000 feet above the sea level, which would seem to show that at one time a large inland sea had existed there, or probably large detached sheets of water, with the higher peaks projecting out of them.

We there first saw some of the walls called "Mānés," which are formed of stones placed one upon the other without any mortar, and are usually about four feet high, and four feet wide. Some of these walls are as much as a quarter of a mile in length, and are made, we were informed, with the following object: When a Buddhist undertakes a journey, or makes a vow, he chooses a flat stone, takes it to a monastery, and gets a lama (or monk) to engrave some rude characters upon it, which are said to be usually, "Om mani padme Om," which has been translated to mean, "All hail to the jewel in the flower of the lotus!" though some give other interpretations to these words. When his stone is thus prepared, the individual places it on the top of one of these walls, which on their upper surface are almost covered with such engraved stones. Thibetans, when passing these walls, always keep them on their right hand, and frequently go out of their direct road in order to do this.

Chinese historians say that the Thibetans are descendants of the aborigines of China, and are therefore one and the same race as those who still people the mountainous districts of Kweichow and Kwangse; and add, that some of these aborigines wandered westward and southward, and eventually settled in large numbers in Thibet, leading a nomadic life, and living on the produce of their flocks and herds. History does not say when they first had a supreme ruler; but it is stated that, about A.D. 627-650, Lung-tsan, King of Thibet, married a Chinese princess of the blood-royal. The queen, accustomed to the luxuries of the Chinese Court, did not relish the simplicity of her new home, and was especially disgusted with the custom of painting the face red, which prevailed there. The king built her a palace, forbade the use of the disfiguring red paint, and also introduced Chinese silks instead of the woollen materials which, up to that period, had been worn by all classes. The queen converted her lord to Buddhism, and induced him to send to India for copies of the Buddhist writings for the instruction of himself and his subjects. His envoys brought back an alphabet, framed on the Devanagari, which was adopted as the national written character, instead of the Chinese form. The king's nephew and successor also prayed to have a Chinese wife sent him; and from that time Buddhism of a certain kind took a firm hold in Thibet, though its people did not enter into the subtle beliefs and ritualistic practices of Sakya Muni. Thus a species of Buddhism sprang up, which was engrafted upon their original wild magic worship.

Towards the middle of the fifteenth century a sect of reformers arose amongst them, under a leader called Tsungk'aba: these adopted a yellow cap, to distinguish themselves from the older sect, who wear a red head-dress. On the death of Tsungk'aba, in 1478, two of his chief disciples agreed to divide the power, it having been told them by their master that they should be born again, generation after generation, Tsungk'aba promising that his spirit should be always with them. These two men took respectively the titles of *Dalai Lama* and the *Panshen Lama*. The first Dalai Lama reigned as king of Thibet, and occupied himself with political affairs; and the Panshen Lama would appear to have concerned himself only with spiritual matters.

The exclusion of Europeans from Chinese Thibet dates from the early part of the present century. In 1792 the cupidity of the Gorkha Rajah of Nepaul was aroused by the stories which were related to him by a refugee Thibetan monk respecting the great treasures contained in the Panshen Lama's palace at Tashilumbo. He at once sent an army into the field, and marched to Thibet, at the head of 18,000 men. The palace at Tashilumbo fell a prey to the invaders; but the then Panshen Lama (an infant) was carried to Lhassa for safety, and an appeal for help sent to the Chinese Government. That country, always ready to tighten its hold upon Thibet, sent an army, and, after some hard fighting, the Gorkhas were driven back into Nepaul, and gladly accepted humiliating terms of peace in order to save their own capital. After the conclusion of this campaign, the Dalai Lama wrote to Lord Cornwallis, the then Governor and Commander-in-Chief in India, to tell him of the defeat of the Gorkhas, and warn him against giving them any support should they attempt aggressive measures in future. The Chinese Government at that time had taken up the idea that the British Government had aided and abetted the Gorkhas in their invasion; and the authorities at Pekin, therefore, decided to stop all intercommunication with India, and for this purpose closed all the Himalayan passes leading thither; and this order is still in force.

The Dalai Lama is assisted by four ministers, nominated by and under the control of two Chinese officials called Ambas, who thus are, in reality, the real rulers in Chinese Thibet. In the 'Journal of the Royal Asiatic

Society,' vol. iv., part 1, there is a description of the ceremonies which took place in 1841, on the election of a Dalai Lama. On that occasion the candidates for this office were four in number. They are commonly, if not invariably, infants under the age of two years, at whose birth miraculous signs have appeared. These four children were all taken to the Sangha monastery, near Lhassa, and on a fixed day the Chinese Ambas, the Chancellor, and the superior orders of clergy, all went thither to put these infants to the proof. The image of Buddha, and various other articles which had belonged to the late Dalai Lama, were placed before them, together with exact duplicates of them. All the children at once picked out the ones which had been the property of the late Dalai Lama, thus proving their pretensions to miraculous powers. The name of each child was then written on a slip of paper, and placed in a golden urn before the effigy of the Emperor Kien-lung, who finally subdued Thibet in 1746, and still posthumously receives homage as sovereign of the country. The senior Amba then inserted his hand into the urn, drew out one of the slips of paper, opened it, and read out the name of the successful candidate. The new Dalai Lama was afterwards enthroned by virtue of an imperial mandate. Money and other gifts, to the value of more than £3000, were sent to him from China. The chief Amba read out the imperial mandate, to which the newly-made Dalai Lama listened on his knees, and made three genuflections and nine prostrations in the direction of the imperial abode. The father of the fortunate infant, who was a scavenger, was raised to the rank of a noble.

When at Lama Yuru we visited its monastery, which, like all such buildings, is situated at some height above the village. This one, we were told, was the third in importance and size in all Ladakh. It consisted of various buildings on different levels or platforms, some containing grain, &c.; one had within it three very highly decorated *dungtens*, or tombs of a peculiar form. We were told that those particular ones contained the ashes and relics of defunct lamas of high degree. These tomb-like buildings are called both *chodtens* or *dungtens*, the former being dedicated simply as an offering to the deity, and the latter word signifying bone or relic receptacle. Within this monastery was also a *chaitya*, or place of worship, about 30 feet square, supported on wooden pillars. Along the wall facing the entrance there were three or four tiers of shelves, on the lowest of which was a seated figure of Buddha; on either side of him were smaller statues, representing, as they told us, his prime minister, physician, &c.; and the upper shelves were crowded with old and discarded statues of the same personages, arranged in the same order. There were small lamps burning in front of the favourite Buddha; and offerings of grain, rice, and flowers had also been deposited there. Against both the lateral walls were wooden shelves, on which were laid an enormous number of manuscripts in the Thibetan language.

We were fortunate enough to arrive there at the hour of one of their services, which I believe take place at 9 A.M. and 3 P.M. It was conducted in the following manner by six or eight lamas, who are all seated on the ground. Three or four of these recite together some prayers out of a book in a sing-song sort of chant, inclining their bodies backwards and forwards all the time; as many more monks, perhaps, place themselves at a short distance from these, with singular-looking musical instruments before them, comprising four brass tubes, widening out in their whole length something like a clarionet (two of these instruments were at least six feet in length, the other two each about a yard long); a fifth man struck at intervals a sort of gong, which was suspended from a pole placed on a stand. When the reading party were exhausted, the musicians set up the most unearthly din. Their praying wheels are not the least curious part of their worship: every man on entering or leaving a monastery gives the wheel a twirl. It is usually placed in a niche near the entrance doorway, but woe be to him who turns it the wrong way! These wheels are cylinders of wood or copper, having round them a roll of paper or parchment on which a prayer is inscribed; each time this is turned round is considered equivalent to repeating a prayer. Most of them are turned by hand, but in some places the larger ones, we were told, are turned by water. There are also small prayer wheels which can be carried in the hand, and used at home or on a journey: one of these last is in my possession.

Women, as well as men, can be lamas: all are such from their infancy,—the eldest, or even more sons (if no son, their daughter or daughters), being dedicated to the monastic life. They always wear a distinctive dress. Those we saw wore a long loose robe of a dark red colour, confined by a sash at the waist, shaved their heads, and had a yellow cap of a peculiar form. The number of lamas is consequently considerable, but, of course, only a certain number can reside in a monastery at one time, and the rest live with their families till they are wanted, employing themselves in the cultivation of the ground, and in other ways.

Lama Yuru is four marches distant from Leh, the capital. Before reaching the valley of the Indus, our road led us for some miles through a very narrow and rocky ravine with high precipices on either side. At the termination of this gorge the Indus valley comes in sight, and that river is crossed near the fort at Kulsi. It is not very wide at this point, but is very rapid and apparently deep, as a large body of water rushes by. There are orchards of pear, apple, and apricot trees near Kulsi, and a good deal of cultivation exists for a couple of miles beyond that place. Several villages are passed along this part of the route; these lie for the most part at a high level above the river, being placed on spots where the land can be irrigated by side streams coming down from the great snowy Kailas range, which divides the Indus and the Shayok valleys. Each such spot of fertility reminded us of an oasis in the Sahara which we had visited some years previously, though with this difference—both countries being rainless—that in the African desert cultivation, only possible, of course, by means of irrigation, is *there* limited by the amount of water, whilst in Thibet it is restricted by the quantity of flat land available for the purpose.

At each of the next stopping-places there is an oasis of cultivation. Near Snimo, about twenty miles from Leh, we passed some extraordinary mud-pillars, some of which must have been more than fifty feet high, each having a large stone on the top. These mud-pillars look as if the least push would topple them over. The origin of them is supposed to be, that the whole valley having been originally filled up with clay, these large stones happening to be on the surface, the clay beneath them was thus protected from the rain, which in course of ages washed away all the surrounding parts, so that the pillars remained. These singular columns would appear to indicate that at some very remote period the climate of Ladakh was totally different to what it is at present. Beyond Snimo the valley becomes from six to eight miles in width, and there are villages and fields near the river ; but between the cultivated ground and the foot of the hills is a waste of sand, gravel, and large boulders.

CHAPTER VII.

LEH, THE DRESS OF THE INHABITANTS—FESTIVAL OF THE DASERA—REVIEW OF TROOPS—NATIVE DANCES—LAMA RELIGIOUS DANCES—VISIT TO THE RANEES—HOW TEA IS MADE IN THIBET—FUNERAL RITES—BUDDHA AND HIS EARLY HISTORY—RETURN TO SRINAGAR—DÉTOUR TO THE TEMPLES AT WANGAT IN THE SIND VALLEY—TEMPLE AT PANDRETHAN, NEAR SRINAGAR—LEAVE KASHMIR BY BANIHAL PASS—SIALKOTE—PROCLAMATION CEREMONIES AT DELHI.

ABOUT 25th September we reached Leh. The road on the last march keeps close to the river, till when within four miles of it Leh is seen on the left hand, situated on a plain of some extent between two ranges of hills, and backed up by the snowy peaks of the Kardung pass, which is 18,000 feet above the sea, and begins to rise almost immediately behind the city. On the furthermost of the two lateral lower ranges which bound the city of Leh on either side is placed the *lama serai* (or monastery), and below that again is seen the old palace belonging to the rajah: this building is large, and has an imposing appearance from a distance. Its owner, together with other small rajahs of the upper valley of the Indus, was deprived of his sovereign rights by Goolab Singh, the father of the present ruler of Kashmir. They all still bear the title of rajah, and a considerable amount of respect is shown them by the people. The present owner of the palace at Leh was a boy of twelve, who possesses a certain quantity of land at Stok, a village on the other side of the valley about ten miles distant. He spends the greater part of the year there with his mother and another of his father's widows. We rode through the bazaar at Leh—this is walled round, and can be closed at either extremity by large gates—and going on about half a mile further, we came upon an enclosed open space overlooking the town and the plain beyond. Inside these walls there was ample ground for pitching tents; and there was also a small building containing four distinct sets of rooms, each giving sufficient accommodation for a married couple.

It was a daily amusement to go down to the bazaar and see the natives of Yarkund, Turkestán, and Iskardo, as well as those of the country itself, all in their peculiar and distinctive costumes. The men of Ladakh wear the *chogá*, a kind of dressing-gown with wide sleeves, confined round the waist by a wide sash; their robe is woven from white sheep's wool. Some wear a cap of brown wool, made somewhat in the form of a pudding-basin; others have as their head-gear a long bag made of black sheep's wool,—part of it covers the head, the rest hangs down behind, and is moved from side to side at the pleasure of the wearer when the sun incommodes him.

All the men wear the pig-tail, which with some attains a respectable size, though in most cases this is formed of only a small wisp of hair tightly plaited. The women wear the same shaped dress as the men, but theirs is invariably made of cloth woven from the wool of the black sheep. Over their shoulders, both in summer and winter, the women hang a sheepskin, with the wool inside, and tied together on the chest by a string. Those who are better off dress precisely in the same manner, only in their case the outside of the sheepskin is covered with pieces of red and green cloth arranged in a symmetrical pattern. The women plait their hair in seven or more small tails, with which is mixed false hair of black wool to lengthen the plaits. All the tails of hair are united some way below the waist, and there tied together, a large tassel of black wool forming a finish at the bottom. An ornament called a *parak,* made of leather, or sometimes covered with silk, and in shape somewhat resembling a cobra, is fastened to the parting of the hair in the centre of the forehead, and gradually increases in width till it reaches down to the waist behind. On this head-dress are sown numbers of large rough turquoises and quaint cornelian brooches, with characters engraved upon them. In the case of rich ladies, like the rajah's mother, these brooches are of gold, set with fine pearls and well-cut turquoises. Amongst the men, also, the more wealthy wear a brooch of this kind on the pig-tail at the nape of the neck; the poorer ones entirely dispense with this ornament. In Thibet no woman is supposed to marry until she is provided with a *parak,* it being considered absolutely indispensable to a lady's dower. One thing struck me very much in regard to the people of Ladak, and I should much like to know if other travellers have observed the same —viz., that the men seem to have invariably a Tartar-Chinese cast of features, and that I only saw one woman (a lama) of a similar type; the women generally all having long oval faces, straight and longish noses, and large, dark, straight, almond-shaped eyes.

In Leh, lying as it does at a height of 11,500 feet above the sea, the cold is very severe during the winter months, therefore the women all protect their ears with small flaps of fur, the furry side being placed next the skin, and kept in position by being tied round the head beneath the plaits of hair. In the case of the ranees, these flaps were of the finest sable, and their value about £5 sterling, I was told. The Hindú festival of the Dasera happened to fall whilst we were at Leh, and in consequence we were able to witness some purely national scenes and sports, which only take place at such times.

The Dasera is supposed to relate to the autumnal equinox. On the last day of the feast, the image of Durga (the wife of Shiva) is thrown into the water, in memory of her victory over the buffalo-headed demon Mahashasur, after having been worshipped for nine days, and the Hindús decorated their houses with flowers. We did not see any part of the religious observances, but in the afternoon Mr Johnson, the Maharajah's representative in Ladakh, sent to invite us to go down with him to an open space, and there witness a review of the troops. Some of the army were styled *irregulars*, and were certainly very much so. The so-called *regulars* had very little in common with each other except their caps, which were all of one pattern. There was also a small battery of artillery, consisting of six or eight guns, and the gunners showed more precision in firing than one could have expected from seeing them. The officer who acted as commander-in-chief was resplendent with gold-lace and a coat of a spinach-green colour. After certain evolutions had been performed, and so many rounds fired, all the troops passed in single file before the place where Mr Johnson and ourselves were seated. The little rajah headed the procession; each man in his turn offered us, in the hollow of his two hands, a sum of money in the current coin. This is called offering the "Nuzzur," and, we were told, ought to amount to as much as the daily income or pay of each man. *We* all had simply to touch each man's offering, and then remit it; but had the Maharajah himself been there, it must have been laid down in a heap before him, and he would have appropriated the money.

This ceremony over, we all adjourned to the bazaar, where from the balcony of a house we could look down upon the natives playing the game of polo. It was played somewhat differently to our English mode, and we could not rightly understand it: the most curious part was to see the man who began a game take the ball in his left hand and the stick in his right, then, arrived at the middle of the course, and the horse galloping at its utmost speed, the player would throw the ball up in the air, and hit it as it descended. After this came *nautching,* or native dancing, which there was executed by men and women together. When we had thrown down small coins for a general scramble, we moved on to a large house standing by itself in an enclosed court-yard, and from an upper room we witnessed what was to us the most singular part of the whole entertainment —viz., three or four different lama religious dances, which were executed by them before us. The dresses were varied in all of them, and we wished much to have ascertained their respective meanings, but were unable to obtain any explanation. The lamas were all dressed up in the most magnificent Chinese stuffs, embroidered with silks of various colours: each wore a sort of *papier-maché* mask, with grotesque features of a gigantic size. Some of these masks were ornamented on the top with fruits or flowers modelled four times the natural size. I have called these *masks*, but they were not so, properly speaking, as they covered the whole head of the actor. In one of these dances two men were dressed up to represent a Chinese mandarin and his wife; and in another, the two last figures which came on the scene had masks representing very ferocious-looking dogs. The whole dance consisted of a slow undulating movement performed in a large circle. Then came sword-dances, and mock fights between two combatants, which ended the day's performance.

The day after the Dasera, Mrs Johnson wrote to ask us to go down to her house to see the three ranees, who had come to visit her. These ladies were two of them widows of the Rajah of Stok, the younger one being the mother of the younger rajah already alluded to, and the third was the wife of a rajah of another district. All three were dressed in the national costume, as was also the widow of the former treasurer, which office is hereditary; and the holder of it being a lad about the age of the little rajah, a deputy acts for him, but the boy went daily to the office to learn the business. The rajah's wife was by far the best-looking woman we saw in Thibet, and, indeed, would have been thought pretty in any country. All three ranees sat down near us on cushions placed on the ground; the little rajah was also seated on one at his mother's feet. These ladies laughed and joked with their male and female attendants in a manner not usual with royal personages; but, at the same time, a considerable amount of state was kept up, and much respect shown to them—as, for instance, when any of their female attendants had to pass near them, they rolled their petticoats tightly round them, lest these should by accident touch the ranee's dress. Also, when the little treasurer's mother, who was standing behind them, was called upon to exhibit her jewels to us, she showed much hesitation in coming forward, which arose from the circumstance that it was not etiquette for her to pass in front of the young rajah. His mother, however, seeing her difficulty, cut the gordian knot, by making her son rise, on which she shoved him outside a window which opened down to the ground on to a small enclosed court; and the little fellow appeared again, a few minutes later, through another door with his hands full of sweeties, which he had bagged in passing through the kitchen!

The Thibetans are all passionately fond of tea, which comes to them from China, in the form called *brick* tea, and their method of preparing it is so singular that the process merits a description. It is as follows: A tea-cupful of tea is put into three pints of water, a large spoonful of carbonate of soda is strewn over it, and the whole is boiled. A milling-churn is then taken, such as is used for making chocolate in Spain and in the south of France; a pound of fresh butter and some salt are placed in this, a part of the boiling contents poured upon these, and milled like chocolate; some cream or milk is then added to what is left in the saucepan, the milled tea is poured on this and boiled again, once more put into the churn, and so on till all is properly milled. It is then strained through a cloth, and when well made resembles chocolate in colour. This quantity would suffice for five or six persons. An Englishman who had often tried it on his march to Yarkund, told me that it was far from being unpalatable, and that he found it most refreshing and nourishing after a long and cold march.

The Abbé Huc, in his work written some years ago, states that the Thibetans use dogs in their funeral rites. He speaks of the great number of gaunt and famishing dogs he saw wandering about, and adds that four different modes of disposing of their dead are practised by them: 1stly, burning; 2dly, immersion in rivers or lakes; 3dly, exposure on the top of a mountain; 4thly, they cut the corpse into small pieces, giving these to be eaten by dogs. The ownerless wandering dogs devour the poorer classes, whilst the rich are eaten by the more distinguished animals, which are kept in all the *lama serais* for that purpose. Ancient authors say that burial inside dogs was esteemed by Scythians and others. We ourselves saw some most fierce-looking dogs in the monastery at Lama Yuru, and the lamas with much difficulty prevented them from attacking us. They were a very large and powerful breed. We were informed that their masters can very rarely trust them, as they seldom become attached to man, which would seem to bear out in some degree the Abbé Huc's statement. In cases where a body is burned, after cremation water is poured on the ashes, out of which a figure or medallion is made, which is first worshipped and then thrown into a sacred river, and a *chodten*, or *dungten*, erected on the spot where the body was burned.

Buddhism, in its commencement, partook much more of a social than of a religious character. Its founder, Sakya Muni, the last and only historical Buddha, was the son of Suddhodana, Rajah of Kapila, and his wife Maya. Kapila was a petty principality near the modern Gorakpore. Sakya Muni first began by undermining the Brahminical system of caste; and renouncing the splendours of his royal position, he travelled about as a beggar. He did not shrink from contact with any one, and, unlike the Brahmins, did not require his followers to undergo severe penances, or excommunicate those who had sinned, but simply required a public confession of sin and a promise of future amendment. Buddha (or the Enlightened, as he afterwards called himself) was by birth of the Kshatriya or warrior caste. He derived the name of Sakya from his family, and that of Gautama from his clan. The rapid rise of Buddhism excited much opposition from the followers of Confucius and Lao-tse. The latter declared that Sakya Muni, or rather Sakya Buddha, was but an incarnation of their own master, who had died soon after the date of Buddha's birth. This was resented by the Buddhists, who, in consequence, put back the date of their founder's birth to 687 B.C., and afterwards fixed still earlier periods as the date of that event.

It was not till 65 A.D. that Buddhism was officially recognised in China as a third state religion, side by side with the doctrines of Confucius and Lao-tse. After taking leave of his father (his mother had died shortly after his birth), Sakya Muni first went to Vaisâli and put himself under a famous Brahmin who had 300 disciples. Having heard all that this man could teach him, Sakya Muni went away disappointed; he had not found the true way of salvation. He then tried another Brahmin teacher, but with no better success—left him, taking five of his disciples with him. Together with these, he retired into solitude, where they all remained six years. At the end of that time he was still dissatisfied, and believed he had not yet found the right way. On this the five disciples left him. After some time had elapsed, he felt he had attained true wisdom, gave himself the name of Buddha, and thus became the founder of a religion which, after the lapse of 2400 years, is still professed by a very large part of the population of Asia. Buddha then proceeded to Benares, where his first converts are said to have been the five disciples who before deserted him.

The Buddhists are bound by their rule not to eat after mid-day, except when sick or travelling. At one time the Buddhist religion was persecuted in China. In A.D. 423, in the reign of Shaou-ti, the second emperor of the Sung dynasty, it was made a capital crime to make idols of earth or of brass, or to worship foreign divinities. In A.D. 451 there was a relaxation of this severe rule: one Buddhist temple was allowed in each city, and forty or fifty of its inhabitants were allowed to become priests; but in A.D. 458, after the discovery of a conspiracy, headed by a Buddhist priest, stringent rules were again enforced, one of which was, that no nuns were to be permitted to enter the royal palace or to converse with the emperor's wives.

Having started for Ladakh so late in the season, we were unable to remain at Leh as long as we could have wished; so, after little more than ten days' stay, we started on our return journey, and met with no adventures worth recording, till, on reaching Sonamurg again, after a double march of twenty-eight miles, which also included the crossing the Zoji-la Pass, we found ourselves at 8 P.M. at Sonamurg without provisions, nor were any to be obtained. Our beds, too, had not turned up, so at about 11 P.M. we were just resigning ourselves to lying on the floor, wrapped up in the folds of a tent, when we heard cries below us: this was our baggage arriving. We had then something to lie upon, though it was out of the question to have food prepared at that hour.

On the way down to Srinagar we stopped a couple of nights at Kangan, in order to visit the old temples at Wangat, about twelve miles off, up a valley on the right bank of the Sind river. We rode there and back in the day, which did not allow us as much time as we could have wished to spend on the examination of the ruins. They are situated about three miles beyond the village of Wangat, which lies on the right bank of the river Kanknai, a tributary of the Sind. The temples consist of two groups of buildings of various sizes, all more or less in a ruined condition. In the first group are six temples enclosed by a wall with a gateway. There do not appear to have been colonnaded courts as in the former examples I have cited, nor do the temples seem to have been symmetrically arranged. One of the largest of this group is 32 feet by 30 in outside measurement; the smaller ones are 10 or 12 feet square. The date of the erection of these temples has never yet been fixed with any certainty, though they appear to be of a later period than the other principal temples in Kashmir. On returning to Srinagar we also visited a small temple at Pandrethan, an hour's walk up the river: it can be approached in an hour and a half by boat, when a few minutes' walk takes the traveller to the spot. This temple is supposed to have belonged to the *Nagas*, or snake-worshippers, and now stands, as it has always done, in the middle of a tank; but owing probably to the decay of a causeway or bridge, it can now only be approached by swimming, or in a boat. The roof of this building is of stone, and in an almost perfect state, the apex of its double pyramidal roof being only wanting.

We did not finally leave Srinagar till the middle of November. My husband and J. employed this interval in going to the Lolab valley, and also to Nagmurg, a mountain situated beyond and overlooking the Woolar lake. As the weather was by this time becoming too cold for tent life, I did not accompany them on this expedition, but remained in Srinagar during their absence. Nearly all the visitors having left the country, I could at times almost realise what would be the feelings of the oft-quoted New Zealander, though till the last day or so of our stay there were still one or two European stragglers left in the place. Intending to leave Kashmir by the Bannihal Pass, we all embarked, on 15th November, for Islamabad, and marched on from thence to Vernag, where we remained a few days that the gentlemen might have some bear shooting. At Vernag, and also in other parts of the Kashmir valley, we found mistletoe, identical with our English species, growing on the walnut-trees, the fruit of which is an important article in the food of the people, who also express oil from the nuts. At Vernag there is a rest-house, which we found very cold at that season, as it is built more in the style of a summer-house, having open staircases and corridors. Close to the bungalow there is a tank about 18 feet deep, whence rises a very large spring of clear bluish-looking water: this tank was literally swarming with fish, which are so tame as almost to eat out of the hand. This spring is said to be one of the sources of the river Jelum; the fish are considered sacred, the natives consequently will not eat them. On my asking if they were good eating, a Hindú pundit replied no, they were poisonous, though, as far as the eye could see, they were identical with some we had constantly eaten out of that river. The day we left Vernag we crossed the Bannihal Pass (9000 feet). It is ordinarily an easy pass to go over, but at that time it was difficult, for, owing to the lateness of the season, snow had fallen, then melted, and again become frozen, which rendered it almost impossible for our horses to keep their footing up the steepest parts of the ascent,—so much so, that the one I rode that day, being the stoutest animal of the three, was the only one that could manage at all with a rider on its back, my husband and J. being forced to get off and walk. The summit of the pass is carpeted with short green sward, and there is a small lake near the top. After this seven more marches brought us to Jamu, the winter capital of the Maharajah, and the place where he mostly resides. We had a special permission to take this route, which without this is not open to European travellers, and therefore is not kept in such good repair, as the others: coolies, and provisions also, are not abundant.

Jamu is a town of considerable size overlooking the river Toui, a tributary of the Chenab: this city is situated on the first range of low hills which rise from the plains of the Punjaub. It is about 25 miles from Sialkote, and 14 from the English frontier. After remaining a couple of days at Jamu, and seeing its bazaars and the Maharajah's palace, we rode down to Sialkote, making one halt by the way. This place is situated nearer to the Himalayas than most other European stations; from one part of it we obtained a fine view of the snowy ranges of Kashmir. It is much liked, too, for the reason that its climate is very superior to that of most places in India. At a village about six miles from Sialkote are made various articles of steel, inlaid with gold. The pattern intended to be worked out is first engraved by hand on the steel with a fine-pointed tool. The gold being beaten out to a very thin wire, is laid into the design so engraved, and the surface scraped level. The article is rubbed and polished with a smooth stone, and is afterwards subjected to a moderate heat, till the steel acquires a blue colour. The same kind of work is also made at Goojerat, in the Punjaub; but that manufactured near Sialkote is much more highly finished. Such things as armour, complete suits of chain-mail, inkstands, pen-trays, candlesticks, brooches, and ear-rings, &c., are made in this style. Sialkote is distant barely 30 miles from the railway at Wazirabad.

On once more reaching English territory, we found the principal subject in the newspapers and in every one's thoughts was the assemblage about to be held at Delhi, and that a very large proportion of the native princes were intending to be present at the proclamation of her Majesty the Queen as Empress of India. This ceremony was practically a return to the usage of ancient times, when the rulers of Hindostan asserted their supremacy in a peculiar manner, and held similar gatherings which the feudatory rajahs were expected to attend. A horse played an important part in this ceremonial, of which there are very few recorded instances.

A horse was sent round to all the rajahs of India by the prince who claimed universal sovereignty, as a challenge to any one who disputed his right, and afterwards sacrificed. This sacrifice was consequently equivalent to claiming sovereignty over the whole of India. I have a fine gold coin in my possession, belonging to the Gupta series, which has on one side a very spirited horse standing near a fire-altar; and on the other, a female figure holding a *chauri*, or fan, to keep the flies from the animal. This sacrifice was performed by Rama, the hero of the Ramayana, or earliest epic poem in Sanscrit; and the Pandoor brothers also demanded the right of performing it. The unwillingness to allow this latter claim led to the great war which formed the subject of the Mahabarata, the other great Hindu poem. These two poems occupy to this day much the same position in India as did the 'Iliad' and the 'Odyssey' in ancient Greece.

We were detained in Lahore nearly a fortnight, waiting for our heavy luggage from Sialkote, which, in the end, did not arrive in time for us to reach Delhi to see the Viceroy's entrance as we had intended, so we spent Christmas-day at Lahore, and went on the day after. All the newspapers at that time were full of accounts and representations of the great spectacle, so it is useless here to enlarge upon it, except in so far as personal impressions are concerned respecting the general *coup-d'œil.*

Our destination in Delhi was the Punjaub civil camp, where a tent had been promised us. J. left us at this time to join his father, who, with his regiment, was encamped about six miles from us. Our camp was placed just outside the Kashmir gate, and consisted of upwards of 30 tents, a very large mess-tent being at the upper end. The mess-tent was of an enormous size; it had been lent for the purpose by some rajah. From 120 to 150 persons used to sit down to dinner in it; and as nearly every one had his own servant, and besides these there were attendants belonging to the camp, some idea may be formed of its size.

On *the* great day—1st January 1877—every one flocked to the vast domed daïs which had been erected about three miles from the city of Delhi. A large turfed oval space surrounded this, and on either side of the daïs semicircular stagings had been put up, fitted with rows of raised seats arranged in blocks, each block being duly numbered with a letter. One of these semicircles was appropriated to the native princes and their suites, and the other was set apart for the European visitors, where we took our places in virtue of the tickets with which we had been provided. During the ceremony we were too far off to get more than a general view of the whole pageant, but the sight was a most striking one, from the gay assortment of colours, the flashing of the jewels worn by the Eastern princes, and the dazzling effect of the emblazoned and richly embroidered banners which floated behind the chair of each. As soon as the Proclamation had been read, we all descended to the open space below, and there saw all these splendours more closely. The little Nizam of Hydrabad in the Dekhan, the young Gaekwar of Baroda, and other notabilities, were pointed out to us.

The same day, as soon as it was dusk, we went out to see the fireworks and illuminations. The principal bazaar, called the Chandni Chowk, was one running blaze of little oil-lamps; the fireworks were set off from a staging placed in front of the Jumma Musjid, or large mosque. We were fortunate enough to find seats in a small balcony high up in the façade of this building, and though we had seen finer displays of the same kind in Europe, these were very good; and it was amusing to watch the purely childlike enjoyment of the whole scene by the lower class of natives, who crowded every available spot below us.

On 3d January the whole business was concluded by a grand march past of all the troops. First and foremost came the elephants and mounted attendants of all the native princes, the elephants having trappings of cloth-of-gold reaching down to the ground on either side; upon their backs were placed *howdahs* of gold or of silver; and each chief's retinue made obeisance as they passed in front of the Viceroy, the most splendid train being that of the Gaekwar of Baroda, whose silver guns were drawn by milk-white oxen with magnificent trappings. The dresses of all the mounted guards of the different princes would be a perfect study—the Maharajah of Duttia's people, for instance, wore helmets and suits of armour made of chain-mail. Some of the elephants had been trained to make obeisance, which they performed when arrived opposite to the Viceroy, by facing round, putting up their trunks, and making a peculiar noise. Some of the horses too, performed likewise, stopping in one spot, raising the two fore-legs, and dancing up and down for a minute or so, like a child's rocking-horse. When these had all gone by, came the turn of the European troops, who went past—horse-artillery, artillery, and infantry regiments, as well as both the native cavalry and infantry in the Queen's service—at slow march, quick march, gallop, or run.

All things must come to an end—this was the finale. After this all the multitude who had been brought together began to disperse north, south, east, and west, we ourselves amongst the number, our destination being Benares, where we stayed nearly ten days, and, of course, saw its temples, &c.; but being myself very unwell at the time with an attack of influenza, which complaint was very prevalent at Delhi, I saw everything almost as in a dream. As we spent some time there a few months later, when I could carefully go over the ground again, I shall reserve my impressions of it till after our second visit.

CHAPTER VIII.

BELGAUM—SKETCH OF THE HISTORY OF THE DEKHAN, AND RISE OF THE MAHRATTA EMPIRE—SEVAJI, HIS BOLD INCURSIONS—COUNTRY ROUND BELGAUM—ITS CLIMATE—OLD JAINA TEMPLES IN FORT—'IDGAH AT KURAR—OLD FORT AT SATTARA—BUDDHIST CAVE TEMPLES AT CARLEE.

FROM Benares we went to Bombay, and then by steamer down the coast to Vingorla, whence a two days' journey in a small carriage brought us to Belgaum, which is almost the most south-westerly point of the Dekhan.

In the reign of Mahommed Toghlak, the empire of Delhi extended from the Himalayas of Assam on the east to the Indus on the west; towards the south it may be said to have comprehended the whole peninsula, with the exception of a long narrow tract along the western coast and the extreme south. Owing to the misgovernment of this sovereign, two of the rajahs of the Dekhan revolted, and the territories of Telingana and Carnata again came under Hindú rule. The former of these provinces comprised what is now known as the Coromandel coast, and the latter included what is now styled the Carnatic, and also the district for some distance inland.

The Mussulman frontier was still further altered by these princes bringing also other parts into dependence upon them, thus forming several states, which were soon powerful enough to contend with their Mohammedan neighbours. This re-conquest took place about A.D.

1344, and was succeeded in 1347 by the grand rebellion in the Dekhan, whereby the power of Delhi was driven beyond the Nerbudda. Some time elapsed before a further dismemberment took place; Guzerat, Malwa, and Jounpore freed themselves during the minority of Mahmoud (the last king of the Toghlak dynasty).

In 1398, on Tamerlane's invasion, the remaining provinces threw off the yoke, and nothing remained to Delhi but a few miles of country round the capital. In 1347 A'lá ud-din Hasan Shah, a Brahmin's servant at Mahommed Toghlak's court, had headed a successful revolt against that ruler, and founded the kingdom of the Dekhan, which throne was occupied by his descendants for several generations during a space of 178 years. This is known as the Bahmani dynasty, and had for its allies the rajahs of Bijyanagar and Warangol. Their struggle with the Mohammedans was a long one, though these last were the conquerors in the end. The Hindús, immediately before their fall, had gained territory in Orissa, and also extended their conquests as far as Masulipatam on the east, and to Goa on the west.

The curious part of these early wars seems to be, that men of both faiths entered freely into each other's service: the King of Malwa's army, during his invasion of the Bahmani territories, is said to have consisted of Afghans and Rajputs; whilst the Hindú Rajah of Bijyanagar had Mohammedans serving under his standard, and built a mosque especially for them. His state long maintained its position amongst the powers of the Dekhan.

The Bahmani possessions were split up to a certain extent about the year 1437, when Yúsuf Adil retired to his government of Bijapur, subsequently took the title of king, and became the founder of the dynasty of Adil Shah. Yúsuf Adil was a son of the Ottoman sultan. On the accession of his brother Mahomet II. to the throne of Constantinople, he alone escaped being put to death with the remainder of his brothers, his mother secretly conveying him to Persia whilst yet an infant. At the age of sixteen he was obliged to fly from thence on account of some suspicion of his birth,—was then induced to go to the Bahmani court, and there sold as a slave.

In 1565 the Mohammedans formed a league against Ram Rajah; a great battle was fought on the Kishna, near Talicot; after a fierce conflict the Hindús were defeated, and the monarchy of Bijyanagar was at an end, though, owing to the jealous spirit which prevailed amongst the victors, their territories were not much extended, and a great deal fell into the hands of certain petty princes. The Mohammedans had still not recovered a great deal of what had been possessed by them in the time of Mahommed Toghlak, but this was all that they re-acquired up to the time of Aurungzebe.

That part of the Dekhan in which Belgaum is situated is inhabited by a Mahratta people, who occupy a large tract of country reaching from the southern watershed of the Nerbudda on the north to a little below Belgaum on the south, its western boundary being the Indian Ocean, and its eastern limit extending inland about 300 miles from the coast,—its extreme length from north to south being about 350 miles. Its great feature is the line of Ghâts, which vary in height from 3000 to 5000 feet, and run along its western side at a distance of thirty or forty miles from the sea. Native legends say that the sea once washed the foot of these Ghâts, and that the Concan was rescued by a miracle of one of their gods.

The Maḥrattas are hardly mentioned by Mussulman writers till the beginning of the seventeenth century. They differ essentially from the Rajputs in character as well as in appearance, being small sturdy men, well made, though not handsome. They are wanting in the dignity of manner and the pride which the Rajputs possess, and think any means justifiable by which they can accomplish their ends; whereas a Rajput warrior, as long as he does nothing to dishonour his race, is almost indifferent to the result of his arms.

Sevaji, the founder of the Mahratta empire, could lay claim to Rajput blood on his mother's side. His paternal grandfather, named Maloji, was an officer in the service of Malik Amber, a relation of the Rajah of Orissa. On one occasion Maloji and his little son Shahji, a child of five years old, attended a great Hindú festival which was held under the roof of Lukji Jadu Rao, who had attained to the command of 10,000 men under the same prince. During the festivities, Jadu took the little Shahji on his knee, together with his own little girl, who was only three years of age, and laughingly said they made such a fine couple that they ought to be man and wife. On this Maloji jumped up, and called the assembled company to witness that the daughter of Jadu was affianced to his son. Jadu was naturally indignant at the mean advantage which had been taken of what he had said in a mirthful spirit. As time progressed, Maloji's fortunes prospered, and he became the commander of 5000 horse, and the possessor of a large estate, of which Poona was the chief place. Still maintaining his claim to the hand of Jadu's daughter for his son, this was acceded to, as in his then state of prosperity their relative positions were no longer so unequal. Sevaji was the second son of this union.

The Mahrattas being as a rule illiterate, their affairs were generally managed by Brahmins. Sevaji, like the rest, employed himself in horsemanship and military exercises. His chief companions were the soldiers of his father's horse regiments, or the inhabitants of the neighbouring Ghâts: these last seem to have been for the most part plunderers, who went about in gangs. It was these people whom Sevaji afterwards employed in going after higher game, such as taking possession of some of the remote and ill-garrisoned hill-forts belonging to Bijapur, by means of surprise or stratagem. His father in vain remonstrated with him; and grown more bold with success, we find him seizing two forts belonging to Shahji, and about this time also bribing its Mohammedan governor to surrender to him Singhar, a very strong fort about twelve miles from Poona. All this was done without bloodshed or disturbance. The possession of these points of vantage enabled Sevaji to intercept and plunder a convoy of royal treasure in the Concan on its way to Bijapur; after which he took five other hill-forts. One of his leaders surprised and took Callian, and occupied the whole province. The Court of Bijapur, firmly believing that these encroachments had been made at his father's instigation, seized an opportunity of taking Shahji prisoner, and threatened to wall him up in his dungeon if Sevaji did not give in his submission within a given period. He, of course, was greatly alarmed at this threat, but still held out, and endeavoured to gain Shah Jehan over to his cause.

The emperor listened to him favourably; and it was

probably owing to his intercession that Shahji was released from captivity, though he was detained four years longer at Bijapur. Sevaji remained tolerably quiet during this interval, but after that he again began to form ambitious plans, took possession of some of the hill country to the south of Poona, procuring the assassination of its rajah, and then profiting by the consequent disorders to seize his territory. He went on much in the same manner till the year 1655, when, on Prince Aurungzebe's being sent down to the Dekhan, Sevaji made as though he wished to hold what he had acquired under imperial authority, but he soon threw off the mask, thinking that troublous times were in store for Aurungzebe, and for the first time invaded Moghul territories; but the prince made rapid conquests; and when he was going against Bijapur, Sevaji tried to obtain from him forgiveness for this act of disaffection.

Aurungzebe, on being recalled to Delhi in 1658, pardoned him, on condition of his furnishing a body of horse to the Imperial armies; but Sevaji contented himself with promises alone, and renewed his attacks upon Bijapur. A large force was sent against him by the regent of that state, the king having died, and his successor being a minor. Sevaji sent humble letters of submission to Afzul Khan, the commander of this force, by a Brahmin in his employ, who persuaded the khan that Sevaji was really in a state of great alarm; and the general allowed himself to be drawn on through intricate valleys to the fort of Partabghar, where Sevaji was then residing, in order to grant him a personal interview, and thereby assure him of forgiveness.

Afzul Khan started with a small escort only, and during the latter part of the way had only a single attendant with him. He was dressed in a thin muslin robe, and carried a straight sword, more fitted for show than use. Sevaji descended from the fort to meet him, being to all appearance unarmed; but beneath his white dress he wore a suit of chain-armour, and had a concealed dagger. Besides this protection, he had also sharp steel hooks fastened on to his fingers, which could not be seen when the hand was closed; these are known by the name of tiger's claws. Sevaji came along humbly crouching to the place of meeting, and at the moment of their embrace he stuck these claws into the unsuspecting general, and before he had time to recover from his amazement despatched him with his dagger. Sevaji had previously disposed his troops so as to surround Afzul's army on all sides, and the Mussulmans were driven back with great slaughter. Those who were made prisoners were all well treated; many who were Mahrattas entered Sevaji's service.

Another army was then sent from Bijapur, and he was besieged in the almost inaccessible fort of Panala; but at the end of four months he contrived to escape under the cover of night. The king then took the field in person, at the head of an immemsely strong force, and in 1661, at the end of one year, Sevaji found himself stripped of nearly all he had acquired; but the king's attention being at that moment called off elsewhere during the two years following, Sevaji was able to recover his former possessions, and even make additions to them. At the expiration of this time peace was made by his father's mediation: Sevaji, by the agreement then concluded, was to retain a district comprising a part of the Concan, and also some of the land above the Ghâts.

He kept a standing army of 7000 horse and 50,000 foot, on a territory about 400 miles in length by 100 in width at the widest point. Sevaji was still animated with a restless spirit, and in a very short time came to an open rupture with the Moghuls, though it does not appear what led to this. His horsemen began to ravage the country almost to Aurungabad; but Shaista Khan, the maternal uncle of Aurungzebe, whom he had made Viceroy of the Dekhan, marched against him, drove his forces out of the field, and took up a position at Poona, where he considered himself secure. Singhar, whither Sevaji had retreated, was only twelve miles off. This latter, knowing all that was passing, and how secure the Mohammedans considered themselves, left his fort one evening after dark, and posting small bodies of infantry along the road to support him, he went on to Poona, accompanied by only 25 followers, entered it by joining a marriage procession, and proceeded direct to the house of Shaista Khan, who had barely time to escape from his bed-chamber, two of his fingers being cut off as he was letting himself down from an upper storey to the court below. His son and most of his followers were cut to pieces. Sevaji then retreated to Singhar as rapidly as he had come. His next exploit was to plunder the rich town of Surat during the space of six days, and to carry off large booty. Soon after this he heard of the death of his father, Shahji, who, though very old, was killed by a fall when out hunting. Sevaji then once more went to war with Bijapur. Establishing a fleet, he took several Moghul ships, and sacked Barcelór, a wealthy port, situated in the province of Canara, which belonged to Bijapur, and also plundered the adjoining districts; nor did he leave the country above the Ghâts in peace.

What enraged Aurungzebe the most was his capturing some vessels which were conveying pilgrims to Mecca, and also his plunder of Surat—which city has a kind of sanctity, from being the place where these devotees embark.

About the year 1665, soon after his father's death, Sevaji assumed the title of rajah, and began to coin money, one of the principal marks of the assertion of independent sovereignty. Rajah Jei Sing, with whom Dilir Khan was associated on equal terms, was therefore sent against him. Jei Sing undertook the siege of Singhar, and the other chief that of Purandar. Both places held out for a time; but Sevaji, apparently despairing of making a successful resistance, negotiated for peace, and made the humblest professions of future obedience. By the arrangement then concluded, Sevaji was only to retain twelve out of the thirty-two forts he then possessed, and these he was to hold in fief under the Moghul emperor. A high military command was given him, and he joined the imperial forces in an invasion of Bijapur. He seems to have acquitted himself to the emperor's satisfaction in this campaign, and after it was over was invited to go to Delhi. Sevaji might have become a warm adherent of Aurungzebe's had he been well treated at this time; but the Moghul emperor, either from religious intolerance or jealousy, put a number of small slights upon him. After his arrival at Delhi, he found himself on one occasion placed with officers of the third rank, and no notice taken of him; his haughty spirit was unable to brook such treatment, he changed colour, and fell down in a swoon. On coming to himself again, he said they had better take his life since he had been deprived of his honour, and then retired without waiting to take leave or receive the usual gifts. From this moment he was virtually a prisoner, and guards were posted round his dwelling; but feigning sickness, he gained over some of the Hindú physicians who attended him, and also sent presents of sweetmeats to be distributed amongst fakirs and other holy men, both of the Hindú and Mohammedan faiths. In this manner his guards became accustomed to seeing hampers and baskets pass in and out. At length, when all his measures were arranged with those outside, one evening he concealed himself in one hamper, his little son was placed in another, and they were thus carried out through the midst of his guards. Sevaji mounted a horse, which had been placed at a certain lonely spot for this purpose, and taking his boy up behind him, rode to Muttra, where he put on the disguise of a Hindú mendicant. Leaving his child in trusty hands at Muttra, he made his way back to the Dekhan by unfrequented paths, and reached the fort at Raighar nine months after leaving Delhi.

This was about the most prosperous period of Aurungzebe's reign, the only exception being the ill success of his army in the Dekhan. Jei Sing was consequently removed from his command, and died on his way back to Delhi. The new leader of the Moghul armies was more favourable to Sevaji, and was even suspected of having received bribes from him. Anyhow, in 1667, he obtained peace for him on very easy terms, and the acknowledgment of his title of rajah. Sevaji then once more turns his attention towards Bijapur, and forces its ruler and the king of Golconda to pay him an annual tribute.

A long period of tranquillity then ensued, which Sevaji employed in properly organising his government and army, placing both these departments upon a system which was perhaps even more strict and regular than that of the Moghuls. Aurungzebe was the first to break the compact which had been made between them, and gave orders for an open attempt to seize Sevaji's person. This last retaliated by endeavouing to seize the fort of Singhar, near Poona, where, knowing its importance, the Moghuls kept a strong force of Rajputs under a tried officer; yet its capture was accomplished by 1000 men, who, led by Sevaji's great friend Tanaji Malusri, contrived to scale the rock at night, and escalade the walls before they were discovered. They were met by an obstinate resistance; their leader and several of their number were killed, but they at length overpowered the garrison. Sevaji again plundered Surat about this time, also ravaged Kandeish, and for the first time levied what is known as the *Chout*, afterwards so celebrated in Mahratta history. This was a permanent tax, amounting to about one-fourth of the revenue of a district, and if regularly paid exempted it from plunder.

In A.D. 1672 Sevaji for the first time defeated the Moghuls in open action in the field; after this the vanquished party seems to have concentrated its forces at Aurungabad. The King of Bijapur dying shortly after this, and that province falling into disorder, Sevaji once more turned his forces in that direction, and in the course of the two following years made himself master of the whole of the southern Concan, except certain parts held by the English and Portuguese, and also a tract above the Ghâts. Though Sevaji had long enjoyed the privileges of sovereignty, he now thought it necessary to be crowned: this ceremony was accordingly performed at Raighar in the same manner as a Moghul coronation, including his being weighed against gold, and distributing rich presents to all. Not long after this, the Moghuls made an incursion into his territory, but had reason to repent of this, for Sevaji sent detachments into the Imperial possessions, and for the first time crossed the Nerbudda, penetrating as far as Guzerat. His next plan was to try and recover his father's *jagir* (or landed estate) in Mysore and in the present Madras Presidency, which had fallen into his younger brother's hands. He was successful in this undertaking; but in the end the two brothers came to a compromise, by which Sevaji was to receive half the revenues. About the year 1679 Sevaji's son, Sambaji, went over to the Moghuls, who received him with open arms, hoping to make use of him against his father. Aurungzebe did not endorse his general's views respecting this youth (who seems to have been given up to pleasure, and to have possessed none of his father's traits except his courage), and ordered Sambaji to be sent a prisoner to his camp, but Dilir Khan connived at his escape.

Sevaji's eventful career was at length cut short by an illness which carried him off in 1680 at the age of fifty-two. His early career was almost that of a bandit chief, or of one of the German robber barons of the olden time, who were in the habit of descending from their mountain fastnesses to plunder and take toll of travellers and merchants; but as Sevaji's opportunities were greater than theirs, so he aimed higher, till by degrees he and his followers did not even hesitate to attack the imperial forces, though their earlier style of warfare had much of the guerilla element in it, and was conducted chiefly by surprises and stratagems.

After this unavoidable historical digression, we must return to the description of the journey from Vingorla to Belgaum. The first day's drive brought us to the top of the Ghâts, and we had some very pretty views; but on the second day the scenery was very uninteresting and the country bare. I believe this was more especially the case that particular year, owing to the drought of the previous one, though the whole of that district can at no time have a very green appearance, for, except just in the station of Belgaum itself, there are few if any trees, and the deep red colour of the soil of the whole surrounding country gives it an arid look. Belgaum has been cited as being quite one of the choicest stations in India; but I think its climate rather a treacherous one, for in the month of February it was intensely hot after 8 A.M., and each day regularly at 4 P.M. a cold wind sprung up which came from the sea, so that within half an hour the extremes of heat and cold were felt. Up to the latter hour the thinnest clothing was desirable, and all in a moment a winter dress was required. The friends whom we went to visit lived inside the fort, which is surrounded with high walls, and contains several houses with well-kept gardens.

Within the fort at Belgaum there are three old Jaina temples. Mr Burgess, the archæological surveyor for the Bombay district, gives A.D. 1200 as their probable date, and says that in the Museum at Bombay there is an inscription which is said to have been brought from a temple at Belgaum (the ancient name of this place was Venigrâma). This writing is in the Hala Kânadâ language, and is to the effect that a rajah, called Sena, after first enumerating his own virtues and those of his sons and his daughters-in-law, goes on to state that he caused a temple to be erected, in which were installed Sir Santinâtha Deva. . . . And that for the expenses of the said temple he gave, A.D. 1205, the village of Ambarvami, &c. One of the three temples I have spoken of is inside the commissariat compound; another is just outside this; the third has been so much added to that its original outward form is no longer distinguishable, though the pillars in the interior do not seem to have been disturbed. Other temples, however, must have existed at one time in that neighbourhood, for one often sees old Jaina pillars used as gate-posts, and fragments of sculpture scattered about. The shrine of the temple outside the commissariat is wanting: it was probably destroyed in order that the road might be carried that way. There now remains a porch which goes the whole width of the building: a screen separates this from a hall which is supported on sixteen pillars and the same number of pilasters. The four central columns stand on a platform about three inches high. It was customary for the worshippers to pass round this in order to perform their devotions, it not being considered reverential to approach the god direct. A latticed screen of pierced stone-work originally divided the side aisles from the centre part of the temple, but of this only a small portion now remains. A narrow ledge runs all round the interior of the building: this has been made a little wider at one part, as if to admit of an image being placed upon it. Above this, and at a height of about five feet six inches from the ground, there is a stone shelf about eighteen inches wide, and rather more than six feet long.

The only representations of living objects within this

building are cobras on the capitals of the pillars, and dancing satyrs on the door of the shrine, which is now blocked up; but over the entrance to the hall, or ante-temple, which I have just been describing, numerous figures are carved. Those represented on the screen are almost all dancing, or have musical instruments in their hands. The shafts of the pillars are formed of a single stone. Some of the slabs used in the walls are of a very large size. Mr Burgess is of opinion that the temple inside the commissariat compound has also been originally Jaina-work, but adds that it is often very difficult to determine this point, for sometimes these buildings have been appropriated by other sects, and their distinctive images destroyed. The one I am now speaking of has four distinct chambers: an open hall surmounted by a carved dome, an inner temple, a small ante-chamber, and also a shrine. The image is no longer there, but in the shrine there is the throne for the idol, on the back of which is carved the cushion, such as is usually placed behind Jaina images; and above this there are sculptured numerous circular or wheel-shaped flowers. The ante-chamber has a carved roof, and the domed hall possesses, I think, almost the most beautiful carved pendentive roof which I have yet seen in India. It is slightly damaged at the point, and hangs from a circle nearly eight feet in diameter. There is also a mosque within the fort, which we were informed has been closed by order of the Government ever since the Mutiny, for at that time, under pretence of holding religious services in it, the Mussulmans made it a place for secret meetings.

Whilst we were at Belgaum we went one evening to see some native theatricals. The actors were all Brahmins, except one, who was a Parsí, and the women's parts were taken by young boys. The piece was founded on an incident which occurred in the time of the old kings of Delhi. Each act began with prayers, which were recited in the Sanscrit language; but the dialogue of the play was in Hindostani. Not the least curious part of the entertainment was a dance in which the whole of the performers joined. A pole was set up on the stage, to the top of which were attached many long streamers, alternate red and white. Each man took hold of one of these, and, by describing certain figures, the dancers caused them to entwine and form different patterns. After this the dance was slightly varied by their taking also a small club in each hand, with which, whilst rapidly threading their way in and out, they struck their neighbours' sticks, and thus beat time with most astonishing regularity.

Leaving Belgaum towards the end of March, we drove to Poona, a four or five days' journey, stopping one day at Kholapore, the capital of the native state of that name. Its rajah was still a minor. The revenues seemed to be judiciously employed in erecting schools and other buildings. One of the improvements was that of bringing water from a considerable distance for the supply of the city. The new waterworks were to be opened a few days after we passed through. In every street of the town there were to be several drinking-fountains, and larger ones at intervals for the use of animals, and for washing purposes.

At Kurar, another halting-place, there is the finest 'Idgah I know in India. This building is composed of a long high wall, very solidly built and having several buttresses, which forms one side of a large square, which on the other three sides is enclosed by a low parapet.

The 'Idgah is used by the Mohammedans for special services on three principal occasions in the course of the year. These are the Bakri 'Id, or Id'-i-Kurban, when they commemorate Abraham's sacrifice of Ishmael, as they have it; the Mulad-i-Nabi, or 'Id Mulad, which is kept by the Shiah Mussulmans only; and the 'Id-ul-Fitr, which terminates the fast of the Ramazan, and varies its date each year. In 1877 it fell early in November. On that day all Mohammedans are required to bathe, to put on new clothes, and give food to the poor. All then proceed to the 'Idgah (every place which has a Mohammedan population seems to possess an 'Idgah of some kind), repeating, "God is great," "There is no God but God." The moollah then ascends the *nimbar*, or pulpit, and, after repeating a short prayer, reads the Kutbah, or Friday sermon. He then descends to the lowest step, recounts the virtues of the ruler, and prays for him. General prayer being ended, all rise and shout, "Din" (Faith), and fire off muskets; after which they return to their homes, and in every house feasting and merriment go on.

We made one day's halt also at Sattara in order to see its fort, which occupies an immensely strong and commanding position, being placed on an isolated table-land of basalt, whose perpendicular cliffs rise 500 feet above the plain. Even with the present missiles of war, it could hardly be reached from any of the heights around it. From the top we could also see many other old disused Mahratta forts on various distant summits. We then drove on to Poona, an important station on the top of the Ghâts, the summer capital of the Bombay presidency, and the favourite resort of Europeans from Bombay during the rainy season.

CHAPTER IX.

A HINDÚ WOMEN'S FESTIVAL AT SAUGOR—FAMINE IMMIGRANTS—FOOD OF PEOPLE IN THAT DISTRICT—GHAZIPORE—OPIUM FACTORY—TOBACCO CULTIVATION AND MANUFACTURE—AFGHAN POPULATION AT LUMANEAH —BUDDHIST REMAINS AT SYDPORE—LÂT AT BITHRI.

On 1st May 1877 my husband sailed for Europe, family affairs obliging him to return to England for a few months. I went up country again to stay with some relations, and spent the period of his absence partly in Jubbulpore, but mainly at Saugor. All who know life in an Indian station will understand the sort of stagnation which comes over every one during the hot season, and also the difficulty there is in writing, even should there be anything to write about. Saugor boasts of no architectural buildings or remains, and during the summer the natives even seem more than commonly apathetic.

Early in September I witnessed a native festival, which is purely Hindú, and, as I was informed, is observed only in the Central Provinces. It is called the *Jowaree*, and is conducted entirely by women and children. There is a lake at Saugor, near the native city. This piece of water is some miles in circumference, and we witnessed the gay scene from a large boat. It was a very pretty and animated sight to see the crowds of women, in their new and bright-coloured *sarees* (a large piece of muslin enveloping nearly the whole person), come flocking to the lake from every direction—the poorer ones themselves carrying, the richer having carried after them, trays covered with pots made of leaves fastened together with the thorns of some tree, and filled with earth, in which were growing young plants of wheat, or of *jowaree*, the leaves of these being of a pale yellow colour from having been raised inside their dwellings. Arrived at the lake, the burdens were deposited on the ground. Numbers of women formed themselves into circles, and, joining hands, walked round and round these plants, singing all the while. After a time all the pots of grain were taken down the steps of the Ghât to the water's edge, where the women washed the grain till it was free from the earth in which it had grown, and distributed the plants amongst their friends. This festival takes place just before the sowing of the wheat crops. Crowds of men were present, but as lookers-on only.

Although Saugor itself was not in a famine district, yet during the early autumn the prices of grain were seriously affected by the distress which prevailed in Gwalior, Bhopul, and other parts of Central India. At first a few families came, who did not look very ill-fed or very badly off—some even had brought a few half-starved looking cattle with them; but in a very few days the number of these emigrants increased so enormously that certain sanitary regulations were enforced respecting them, and special camping-grounds set apart for them.

It was at that time resolved by those in authority that their numbers should be counted; and I heard from a reliable source that 160,000 passed through Saugor in less than a fortnight; and when questioned, their reply was, that they came where they could get water. Scarcely any of these people cared to remain there to work; the general idea amongst them seemed to be, that if they could only reach the railway, all would be well with them. Whether owing to want of food or, as many believed, from damaged grain sold to them by the merchants, a sort of famine-cholera broke out in several of their camps, which afterwards turned to true cholera in the case of some of the soldiers of the native infantry; and though it was of the form which medical men call *sporadic*, and the cases were isolated ones, yet for precaution's sake the European soldiers were for a time forbidden to frequent the native bazaars; and in order that they might not think this restriction unjust, no one who was not actually obliged to do so went near the native lines or bazaars for more than three weeks, so that our morning rides were considerably curtailed. These regulations, and the lateness of the season, probably contributed to make the visitation a mild one.

In the district near and round Saugor, where I had opportunities of making inquiries, I was told that the natives seem to subsist almost entirely on grain food for the greater part of the year, with little or no admixture of vegetables, and none of meat; and it was the opinion of some who had means of observation, that this system could only be pursued (consistently with the maintenance of health) by constantly changing the species of grain. Almost every month in the year a different kind is eaten—maize and wheat, which are the most heating, the natives use during the cold weather only. Indian famines would seem not to be a purely unmixed evil, for, owing to the fact of the Hindús being forbidden to eat beef, the number of oxen is greater than the land can possibly support, so that in years of scarcity the weaker animals die off, which would otherwise contrive to drag on a miserable existence.

I remained at Saugor till 15th November, and, travelling *viâ* Damoh, where I stayed a day and a half with a friend, reached Jubbulpore on the evening of the 18th. This journey was rather a wearisome one, as it had to be made partly in a bullock-tonga and partly in a palanquin over roads which were not of the best. My husband rejoined me on the 20th, and after resting a day or two, we proceeded to Allahabad, where we were most hospitably received by a friend; and then we went on to Ghazipore to stay with other friends, travelling partly by railway and partly by *dák gharrie.* This conveyance could only take us to the banks of the river, there being no bridge over the Ganges at that point: we were therefore conveyed across in a boat with paddles, worked by men on the principle of the tread-mill—our course being a very roundabout one, owing to a large sandbank which has there formed in the river within recent times, and is said to be increasing yearly in size.

The house in which we stayed was built in former days for the English Resident, and now belongs to the Rajah of Benares. It is raised upon a high terrace overlooking the river, and at no great distance from it, and consists of two buildings connected by a vaulted stone passage, and divided by a small garden. One would appear to have been built as a dwelling-house; the other, the larger one, contained the reception-rooms. If report be true, the fashion of living in a double house was suited to Anglo-Indians of former times, who are said to have very frequently adopted the domestic arrangements of the natives of India.

Ghazipore and Patna are the two places where the British Government has agents to receive the opium produce. Opium is only allowed to be cultivated under certain restrictions. Every cultivator must possess a Government licence; at the proper time of year each man brings in his produce, which is carefully weighed and tested by the officials, and paid for according to its percentage of solid matter, which ought to be 70 per cent. The opium, when found to be pure, is made up into balls about the size of cannon-balls; these are covered with layers of the dried leaves of the poppy flowers instead of paper, and are stored up each in a small earthen saucer on wooden stagings, in buildings holding, each of them, upwards of 9000 of these balls. When dry enough, they are packed up and sent to Calcutta, whence their destination is China—that prepared for the Indian market being treated rather differently, and made up into square bricks.

If a cultivator's opium is found to be adulterated (and I was told that about a dozen different substances are employed for this purpose) it is confiscated, after being subjected to various tests in a laboratory attached to the premises. The confiscated opium afterwards goes through a process, by means of which morphine and narcotine are extracted from it. Opium is also produced in the native states of Malwa in Central India; this pays a customs duty to the Government. The total net revenue derived from opium is about six millions sterling annually.

At Ghazipore there is a monument, designed and executed by Flaxman, to the late Marquis Cornwallis, Governor-General and Commander-in-Chief in India, who died in that place on his march from Calcutta in the early part of the present century. A tobacco manufactory was at that time just being started by an English company, under the management of an ex-Confederate officer from Virginia, assisted by two Englishmen. They had leased about 1700 acres of land from the Government, which was formerly a stud farm, and on this the firm was growing tobacco: some of the land they have underlet to cultivators for the same purpose.

The whole process of its manufacture was shown to us. The leaf is hung up till it has become dry to a certain extent; it is afterwards dipped in a mixture of boiling sugar and other ingredients, hung up to drain, then given over to women's hands, in order that the mid-rib of each leaf may be removed; after which men are employed to make up the leaves into small bundles, the dipped leaves being placed in the centre and dry ones wrapped round them. The bundles are then transferred to the pressing-room, and after passing through three machines they come out as flat, dark-looking, oblong cakes, about eight inches long by four wide. This establishment probably has in it the germs of what may in time become a very important industry in that district. It was the opinion of the manager that they would be able to produce a larger quantity of tobacco per acre than in America, and equally good in quality. Labour, too, is much less expensive: in India the women employed each receive about three halfpence, the men threepence daily. Enterprise of this kind has hitherto been much retarded by want of capital and means of communication.

Whilst at Ghazipore an accidental circumstance led me to a research into the history of that district, and I found that at two different periods—viz., about the year A.D.

1685, and again about A.D. 1750, certain Afghans had taken possession of lands there, and that their descendants still exist. Mirza Sultan, a prince of the royal family, and the tenth in descent from Timur, or Tamerlane, was the Viceroy of Ghazipore in A.D. 1615. After him succeeded two other rulers; under the second of these, and during the reign of Aurungzebe, four brothers (Neanee Patáns) were soldiers in the viceroy's army. On one occasion the viceroy's wife was making a tour with him in the provinces, when, in the hurry of a sudden march, she and her palanquin were left behind in a forest. These brothers, finding her thus, took up her palanquin and conveyed her with the greatest courtesy to the viceroy's camp, in return for which service permission was given them to settle down in the Ghazipore district. One of the brothers, named Ghous, built the village of Ghouspore; his descendants in the fifth generation are still living there, and though in great poverty, are still the nominal owners of the village, which is so heavily mortgaged that they cannot redeem it.

Again, about the year 1750, the Rohilla Afghans, having wounded and defeated the Viceroy of Oudh, sent a force to occupy Ghazipore, Fuzl-Ali being the then ruler of that province. This same Fuzl-Ali seems to have been a fair specimen of the Indian ruler of the old school: having seen men put to death by every means except that of drowning, he caused a boat to be filled full of people, and then scuttled in the Ganges before his eyes. The history of these Afghans who settled at Zumāneah illustrates how the Mohammedans have gradually encroached upon the Hindús. The present colony at that place was formed by a regiment of these Rohilla Afghans; their descendants are, even at the present day, quite unlike any of the Mohammedans of the district, whom they are said to despise, and never to intermarry with. Some Pushtoo words still linger amongst them, and are used at their marriages and other important ceremonies. Some of them have acquired land, but for the most part the men become soldiers or travelling merchants.

On 17th December we started for Benares with the friends with whom we had been staying at Ghazipore: it was a four days' march with tents and camp equipage. The first march brought us to Nungunj, where there was nothing of interest; but the following day we reached Sydpore, where there are some interesting remains, which good authorities consider to be Buddhist. They owe their preservation to the circumstance that a Mohammedan fakir named Sheikh Summan made one of them his dwelling, and was buried there after his death. In the same enclosure there is now also a mosque. Of the two Buddhist buildings, which may have been *chaityas*, or places of worship, the larger one is 26 feet in length by 23 in width: it is open on all sides, and supported on pillars, of which four placed in the centre support a roof covering the tomb. The shafts of the pillars are all square; the bracket capitals are cruciform, each limb being nearly two feet in length, and bearing the usual Buddhist bell ornamentation. The roof generally is composed of long stone slabs; the centre part of it, however, which rests upon the four pillars, has a primitive Buddhist ceiling, consisting of four triangular stones placed upon the architraves. A square slab of stone, which is ornamented with a lotus blossom, rests upon these, and forms the centre of the whole. Each of the four triangular stones has also this flower carved in relief upon it. The smaller building is in the same style.

From Sydpore we made an excursion to Bithri, about four miles distant from it. Shortly before reaching that place we crossed a small river, and there saw the remains of an old bridge of Mussulman workmanship, and made of carefully-hewn stones, which would seem to have been taken from the ruins of the ancient city. With a small outlay this bridge might again be made passable for wheeled vehicles. After passing over the river we saw, on either hand, irregular mounds, which looked as though they concealed the ruins of a street of houses; and a little further on was a so-called *'Idgah*, which is a building used by the Mohammedans in their worship on certain occasions during the year.

About half a mile beyond the 'Idgah stands what is styled a *lât*, or stone pillar. The inscription on this *lât* has been deciphered, and it has thus been ascertained that it was erected and inscribed by the orders of Chandra Gupta II., who is supposed to have lived between the third and fifth centuries A.D., but the dates of the kings of India at that period are very uncertain. The inscription is on the base of the pillar, which is square; the shaft is round, and rather more than 15 feet in height. The stone has been smoothed in order to engrave the inscription, but part of the base below this still bears the mark of the chisel. The capital of this pillar is 3 feet 2 inches in height, and reeded like the capitals of the Asoka pillars, or what Fergusson calls a Persian capital. A portion of it is broken off on the western side, thus exposing a narrow socket, which would appear to have held a metal spike. Near this pillar there are several mounds, consisting of brick-work ruins, some of which, the head of the village said, had been already excavated.

The kings of the Gupta dynasty would most of them appear to have been Hindús; but the greatest of all, Chandra Gupta II., and his son Kumara Gupta, were Buddhists; and Sitaditya, the great king of Oojene, or Ujain, who overthrew this dynasty, was a Buddhist also. Our road led us again through Sydpore, and at a distance of about two miles beyond it, on the Benares road, and overlooking the Ganges, we came upon some fine old trees, underneath one of which was a stone platform about four feet high, where were placed two figures, one said to represent the Boar incarnation of Vishnu, and the other Krishna with his milk-maids. Both are old, and in good preservation. Around the base of another tree were also numerous ancient fragments of sculpture. Amongst these were two small stone elephants, one of which had the *mahout,* or elephant-driver, sculptured upon it, as if he were lying flat upon the animal: another fragment, we conjectured, may have formed the capital of a column. On it was the complete figure of a man, doubled up, as it were, the legs being bent back, so that the back of the heel touched the back of the elbow. After resting that night at Chumbulpore, one more march took us to Benares.

CHAPTER X.

BENARES—HIONEN THSANG, THE CHINESE PILGRIM, VISITED SARNATH—STUPA THERE—REMAINS OF SUPPOSED BUDDHIST BUILDINGS NEAR THE BAKARIYA KUND AT BENARES.

BENARES is situated on the banks of the Ganges, and is considered by the majority of Hindús *the* sacred city of all India. The date of its foundation is unknown, but it is regarded by them as being coeval with the birth of their religion. The Hindú longs to visit it as much as the Mussulman does to go to Mecca, or the Christian to see Jerusalem. All that is known of its origin is, that Sakya Muni, the only historical Buddha, who, as I have before stated, was the founder of the Buddhist religion, proceeded to the Vihara, or monastery of Sarnath (which is about four miles distant from the modern Benares), in the sixth century B.C. Sarnath at that period was a celebrated city. It was famous amongst the Buddhists, not so much for its religious buildings, as because there Sakya Muni first turned the "Wheel of the Law" (or preached). According to an article by Mr Edward Thomas, the celebrated archæologist, which appeared in the 'Athenæum' of 2d November 1878, the Jains have a fixed date for the Nirvana, or absorption of Mahavira their great saint, in which both their sects, the Svetambaras and the Digambaras, agree, and arrive at the year 526 B.C. as the time of the death of Mahavira. But Buddha's date varies immensely, according to different authorities, and it is not improbable that the Chinese are correct, when they state that this period was ante-dated from time to time in order to give Buddha priority over Confucius and others. General Cunningham seems latterly to have come to the conclusion that Jainism was the more ancient of the two faiths: he adopts Colebrooke's view, and now reasserts that the Nirvana of Buddha must be placed at 478 B.C., a result which he arrived at in 1854 by original figure-calculations. In a passage from the Bhagvati, translated by Professor Weber, it is related "that the holy Gautama [Buddha] in whom faith, doubt, and curiosity arose and increased, rose up, and having arisen he went to the place where the sacred Cramana Mahavira was." The doctrines of Buddhism, by the energy of its missionaries, became spread over a large section of the globe. It has many traditions in common with Jainism, which some good authorities now believe to be the parent creed, and possibly owes these to the meeting of the founder of the one faith with the representative of the other. Buddhism has now become extinct in India proper, though Jainism still survives.

Two Chinese pilgrims, Fa Hian and Hionen Thsang, the former of whom visited India about the middle of the fifth, and the latter in the seventh, century A.D., have both of them left us accounts of the state of Sarnath during the later days of Buddhism. Hionen Thsang was born in a provincial town in China. His father had retired from public employ, and devoted himself to the education of his four children. The afterwards celebrated pilgrim was sent to school at a

Buddhist monastery, and became a monk at the age of thirteen, but still continued his education, and travelled about with his elder brother, in order to follow the lectures of distinguished professors. At the age of twenty he become a priest—and even then his great book-knowledge had already rendered him famous. After this he travelled about for six years longer seeking information; and when at length he found he could obtain no more in his own country, he resolved on going to India, and applied to the emperor for permission to leave his country. This was refused to him, and to several other priests also who had wished to accompany him.

At length he set off secretly. People were despatched to capture him; but the governor of the province before whom he was taken, and who had had strict orders not to allow any one to cross the frontier, was so much struck with his resolution and determination, that he permitted him to proceed on his way. He started quite alone, without a friend or a guide; but the next morning a man joined him, who acted as his guide as far as the confines of a desert, and there left him. He had still to pass five watch-towers; no road was to be seen except that indicated by the hoof-marks of horses and the skeletons of men and animals. On his arrival at the first watch-tower, the officer in command, who was a zealous Buddhist, allowed him to proceed, and gave him letters to the officers in charge of the four other towers. He had then to cross another desert; and his skin of water having burst, he stopped and began to retrace his steps, when he thus communed with himself: "I took an oath," he said, "never to make a step backwards till I had reached India: it is better that I should die when proceeding to the West than return to the East and live." He then marched on for four days and five nights without water; but, comforted by his prayers, continued his road, and reached a small lake, in the country of the Oigour Tartars, who received him only too well; for one of the Tartar khans, who was a Buddhist, insisted on his remaining with him to instruct his people. Hionen Thsang's remonstrances were for some time of no avail: he would not give in; and at last he said, "The khan, in spite of his great authority, has no power over my mind and my will," and refused all nourishment, persevering in this course for three days, at the expiration of which the khan yielded, and allowed him to depart, making him promise, however, to visit him on his return to China.

Thus this adventurous pilgrim once more set forth on his journey. On reaching the mountains he had to traverse glaciers, and encounter heavy snowstorms and violent tornadoes of wind, so that fourteen of his companions perished during the seven days that were required to fight their way over those Alpine passes.

Hionen Thsang says that he found a high state of civilisation then existing in the part of Asia which borders on the western frontier of China. Agriculture had made great progress; and he enumerates many of our English fruits amongst its productions. The inhabitants wore silk and woollen stuffs, and the chief cities supported musicians. Buddhism was at that time the principal religion of that district; but he found traces of the Bactrian fire-worship. Entering India by way of Cábul, he passed through Peshawur, and relates that, at no great distance from the modern city, he visited a mountain cavern, within which both he and Fa Hian assert that they saw the miraculous shadow of Buddha.

In the case of Hionen Thsang, the shadow did not appear to him till after many prayers and much time spent in devotion at that spot. According to his own account, as many as one hundred prayers and confessions of sinfulness did he make before the vision was vouchsafed to him. To-Yung (a Chinese historian) relates that, on a mountain not far from this cave, Buddha with his own hands made a pagoda 115 feet high; and he adds: "They say that when this tower sinks down and enters the earth, then the law of Buddha will perish."

After visiting Kashmir, the Chinese pilgrim reached Magadha, or the holy land of the Buddhists, and remained there five years, studying Sanscrit and Buddhist literature. He then traversed Hindostán, hoping to reach Ceylon, the chief seat of Buddhism; but baffled in this, he visited Benares and some of the principal cities of Northern India, and returned to Magadha again, spending some years there. At length he was obliged to return to China; and going through the Punjaub, Kabulistán and Bactria—passing also through Turkestán, Kashgar, Yarkund, and Koten—he made his way to his own country after an absence of sixteen years. By this time his fame had spread far and wide; and the poor pilgrim, who had been obliged to leave his home by stealth, on his return was received with public honours by the emperor himself, and made a triumphal entry, all the streets being covered with carpets, banners displayed, and flowers scattered around. The emperor received him in the Phœnix Palace, gave him many costly gifts, and wished him to accept a high post under Government; but Hionen Thsang declined this, saying he would dedicate the rest of his life to the law of Buddha. The emperor then requested him to write an account of his travels, and assigned him a monastery in which to prosecute his literary labours. He spent the rest of his life in translating Sanscrit manuscripts; and when he felt his death approaching, he divided all his property amongst the poor, and invited all his friends to go and see him, and take, as he expressed it, "a cheerful leave of the impure body of Hionen Thsang;" adding, "I desire that whatever rewards I have merited by good works may fall upon other people. May I be born again with them in the heaven of the blessed, be admitted to the family of Mi-le, and serve the Buddha of the future, who is full of kindness and affection. When I descend again upon earth, to pass through other forms of existence, I desire, at every new birth, to fulfil my duties towards Buddha, and to arrive at last at the highest and most perfect intelligence." He died about A.D. 664.

For these details of Hionen Thsang's life we are indebted to a French Orientalist, M. Stanislas Jullien, who by twenty years of hard labour prepared himself for the task of translating this book from the Chinese. It was necessary that he should first master the Sanscrit, Pali, Thibetan, Mongolian, and Chinese languages. In 1838 he succeeded in procuring an entire copy of Hionen Thsang's travels; and nearly twenty years later his work was completed. M. Stanislas Jullien is, I believe, acknowledged to be the only man in Europe capable of doing it.

According to Hionen Thsang's account, in his time Sarnath, and the country round it, contained a mixed population of Hindús and Buddhists. The people were partly Aryans and partly aborigines: Aryans, because he mentions the Brahmins; and aborigines, because it is known that some centuries later these last were numerous, and masters of the country. The ruins of Sarnath are in an enclosure which had an area of about half a mile, and was called the deer park, and also the park of the *rishis* (saints or devotees), because a *rishi*, or holy man, dwelt a short distance to the east of it. Concerning this deer park the following curious legend is related :—

The Rajah of Sarnath, who was very fond of sport, had slaughtered so many deer, that the king of the deer remonstrated with him, and offered to furnish him with one deer daily throughout the year if he would abstain from killing them. The rajah consented. At last it came to the turn of a hind to be sacrificed : she objected, saying that this would involve the sacrifice of more than one life ; on which the king of the deer, who was really Bôdhisatwa, the future Buddha Sakya, offered himself instead. The rajah would not allow this, and gave up the park for ever to the deer.

In Hionen Thsang's time many towers were existing at Sarnath, but only two now exist. One of them is a mound of solid brick-work, 74 feet in height ; the date of this is uncertain. On this mound is an octagonal building, which was erected to commemorate the visit of Humaion, son of the famous Emperor Baber. This mound has been excavated, but no relic-chamber was found in it.

The other building is a Buddhist *stupa*, or *tope*, called Damek, about a quarter of a mile distant from the first-mentioned tower. General Cunningham fixes its date in the sixth century, but Fergusson inclines to the opinion that this stupa was of a much later date, and thinks, with Captain Wilford, that it was probably erected by the sons of Mohi Pala, but injured, and the work interrupted by the Mohammedans in 1017, before its completion. Damek is a solid round tower, 93 feet in diameter at the base, and 110 feet in height. The whole is built entirely of large hewn stones, clamped together with iron, the upper five courses excepted, where only brick-work is now visible : this part may have been faced with stone, or perhaps plastered. The lower part of this monument has eight projecting faces; in each of these, at a height of about 20 feet from the ground, is a semicircular-headed niche, and in each of these niches is a pedestal nearly a foot in height, where a statue has evidently been placed. General Cunningham, in an account of this stupa, printed in the 'Journal of the Asiatic Society of Bengal,' says "that none of these statues have hitherto been discovered, but that there can be little doubt that all the eight statues represented Buddha the Preacher in the usual attitude, with his hands raised before his breast, and the thumb and forefinger of the right hand placed on the little finger of the left hand, for the purpose of enforcing his argument."

On our second visit to Sarnath, in December 1877, I was fortunate enough to discover a mutilated statue of Buddha in sandstone. The base of this statue measured two feet eight inches in width; it was headless, and would, when perfect, have been a little more than three feet in height. The god is seated cross-legged, with the soles of the feet uppermost. In the centre of the sole of each foot is sculptured a lotus flower, and a large flower of the same kind is carved in the centre of the small pedestal at the base. The arms are wanting; but carved in the centre of the breast is a thumb, and the way in which this is attached to the body of the statue would give the hands the exact position of Buddha the Preacher as described by General Cunningham. On the throat is a necklace of pretty design, which first attracted my attention to it, and in seeking to make a drawing of this I saw the thumb. The whole of the statue, except the shoulders and a portion of the necklace, were fast embedded in soil mixed with large stones, and had evidently lain undisturbed for a considerable time. The statue was in a recumbent position, about three feet below the surface; and there it had probably been ever since it was thrown down and mutilated by the fanatic Moslems. Some years ago General Cunningham opened a tunnel right through the stupa close to the spot where I discovered the statue, and the rains which have since fallen have no doubt washed away the earth and stones which then hid it. The small size of this statue renders it possible that it was not one of those which filled the niches, for they are five feet and a half in width, and the same in height; though, on the other hand, the place in which it was found (almost immediately beneath one of these niches) makes one imagine that may have been its position.

A triple band of ornament still exists on parts of this stupa. One of these bands is composed of various geometrical figures, the main lines of which are deeply cut; above and below this is a band composed of lotus flowers. Over the upper part of one of these bands is carved a garland, with small bosses at intervals; and above this, again, some smaller ornamentation. On the lower side the decoration is much more rich and varied. Near the centre of the now existing ornamental portion is a human figure seated on a lotus flower, and holding a branch of lotus in each hand. On either side of this figure is a lotus scroll, very graceful in design, formed of lotus flowers and buds. Below, and on each side of the seated figure, are two full-blown lotus flowers, shown in a side view; each of these supports a Brahmini goose. Above the goose, on the right-hand of the figure, is sculptured a frog. Below this lower ornamental border are three plain projecting bands, with carving between each. Near the top of the stupa, on its north-west face, is a stone pierced with a round hole, which was apparently meant to hold a flag-staff. Flags and streamers are at this day very commonly placed outside Buddhist religious buildings in Ladakh. All around this tope, in places where the outer stone casing had fallen away, we found a great many so-called "mason's marks" in the row of masonry next behind.

William Oldham, Esq., in his historical and statistical memoir of the Ghazipore district, gives drawings of certain of the Gupta coins. Singularly enough, some of the same symbols may be distinguished on them as we found at Damek amongst the mason's marks. This would seem to open out a wide field for investigation, unless the resemblance be purely accidental, which can hardly be the case, as they occur in several instances.

Not far from the great stupa, and to the west of it, are the ruins of an old Buddhist *vihara*, or chapel monastery, and also other extensive remains. There are also other Buddhist buildings in the neighbourhood of Benares—viz., those at the Bakariya Kund (or tank) at the north-west corner of the city. On its western bank is a massive breast-work of hewn stones; and a flight of steps in the centre leads down to the tank. In this wall are some richly carved stones, many of which have evidently been taken from older buildings; and I also discovered a few mason's marks where the facing had fallen away. Ascending this terrace, and passing other ruins (some of which have been partitioned off with mud walls, and used as zenanas by the Mohammedans, so that their original form is hardly discernible), a small mosque is seen, which appears to have been originally a small Buddhist temple. Near this is what formerly may have been a monastery: the foundations are extensive, though four columns only now remain. Beyond this again is a platform faced with stone: it is 130 feet long by 90 in width, and about 5 feet high. It sustains what is now used as a Mohammedan burial-ground.

The most remarkable and interesting ruins are the remains of a Buddhist temple on which the Mohammedans have placed a dome, and erected a tomb beneath this. It is impossible to say what the exterior form of this building was originally, for it has evident marks of having been continued in every direction. It now consists of a square building which has been supported by double pillars: these pillars, which are square, are in groups of four at each corner, and are surmounted with the Buddhist bell ornament. To this central building were attached four porches, one of which is wanting—at least, it seemed so to us when on the spot, though, on afterwards looking at Mr Sherring's work, entitled 'The Sacred City of the Hindús,' I saw he was of opinion that there was no porch on the western side, but simply a sort of projecting buttress, on which the chief idol stood.

There are also some interesting ancient remains near what is called the Raj Ghât, leading to the bridge of boats over the Ganges. Just before beginning the descent, a bad road on the left hand leads to the fort, before reaching which, at a short distance on the right, is a building which is said to have been converted into a mosque about eighty years ago, and was used as such till 1857, and regarded by the Mohammedans as peculiarly sacred; but during the Mutiny it was turned into barracks. At present it consists of two cloisters,—the larger one 84 feet in length, the smaller 66 feet. They are of uniform breadth, but differ considerably in height, the pillars in the larger cloister being at least a foot higher than in the other. As the pillars now stand, they form three colonnades, which extend the whole length of the two buildings. One row of pillars is built into the back wall, and there are three detached rows of columns in front of these. Some of the pillars are covered with very deeply-cut carving, and represent the lotus in a scroll form, and a Brahmini goose is sculptured at the base of each; others have a kind of geometrical pattern upon them; and some pillars, again, have no ornamentation whatever. These pillars have a genuine Buddhist character, are interesting in an archæological point of view, and some, in addition, are of great beauty. The ceiling, as is common in most Hindú temples, is divided into squares, and richly decorated in some parts.

CHAPTER XI.

MODERN BENARES—PARTICULARS OF A CONVERSATION WITH A LEARNED HINDÚ PUNDIT—POOJA, OR CERTAIN FORMS OF HINDÚ WORSHIP AS PRACTISED AT BENARES — DESCRIPTIONS OF VARIOUS TEMPLES IN THAT CITY — CURIOUS STATEMENTS TAKEN DOWN FROM THE MOUTH OF A HIGH-CASTE BRAHMIN.

THE modern city of Benares is situated on the left bank of the Ganges. At distances along the river are ghâts, or flights of steps leading down to it. Some of these, as well as some of the temples, are in a ruined state, standing quite in the water, or being very much out of the perpendicular, owing to the banks of the Ganges having given way. The city is believed to contain about 1400 Hindú temples, and of Mohammedan mosques a considerable number. On the other side of the river is the suburb of Ramnagur, in which is the palace of the Maharajah. A pilgrimage to Ramnagur is performed during the cold weather, the Hindús having the idea that should they chance to die there they will become donkeys in the future state, but that by making this pilgrimage such danger will be averted. The Maharajah, whenever he feels ill, causes himself to be conveyed across to Benares. The origin of this idea is said to be as follows: There are two great sects amongst the Hindús—the worshippers of Shiva and those of Vishnu, these being the two principal gods of the Hindú pantheon. The Vishnuvite Brahmins, jealous of the influence of their Shivite rivals, wished to establish another sacred city on the opposite bank of the river, but were foiled in this by their adversaries persuading the people that all who should die there would inevitably, in their next transmigration, take the asinine form.

It will not be inopportune in this place to give some account of the respective differences in belief and worship between the followers of Shiva and of Vishnu. Whilst we were at Benares, my husband had a conversation with a learned pundit, which I will insert in the colloquial form as it occurred. This pundit, when asked whether he were a Vishnuvite or a follower of Shiva said, "I am a worshipper of Vishnu; only bad men worship Shiva and Brahma. Vishnu is the only god, the great god, the almighty, the all-powerful, the all-wise." C. said, "Who then is Shiva?" "He is the spirit of darkness, or of destruction, and all evil," the pundit replied. C. again asked, "Do you believe in the incarnations of Vishnu, —that he was Krishna, for instance?" The pundit answered, "Yes; Vishnu appeared on earth in the form of Krishna." "How then was it that all the children of this almighty god were killed by one of his enemies? that he was defeated in battle, and at length himself was killed? are these and the stories of Krishna's immoralities allegorical?" The pundit replied, "No, they are not; they are strictly true: they happened exactly as they have been related. Krishna did no harm; no person was hurt by his immoralities." He added that the Brahmin worshippers of Shiva drink wine, and eat meat, and that there are great numbers of such in Bengal. Two or three days later I was present when a Mahratta

Brahmin from Poona, one of the Chitpawn caste, came to see us. According to his account, the *Chitpawn* form one of the three great divisions or castes amongst the Brahmins. Pershám, some say—a warrior god, one of the incarnations of Vishnu—made these divisions. The word Chitpawn signifies dead bodies. The second division are the *Kuradhay*, who are bound by their religion to kill some man, therefore our friend the Chitpawn said he would not dine with one of the Kuradhay without considerable hesitation. The third division are called *Dashust*, or the people living on the ghâts. There are many subdivisions of these.

The visit of this Brahmin, Eknath Kanáré by name, was most opportune, as he being a Shivite we were able to hear his views on religion, and compare them with those of the Vishnuvite pundit. Eknath Kanáré told us that all over the Dekhan there are Vishnuvites and Shivites; the former place Vishnu, and the latter Shiva, in the middle, or place of honour, when their principal gods are represented; that these are five in number—viz., Shiva, Vishnu, Gunputi (otherwise Ganesha, the elephant-headed god), Surajkanth, and Sonamuki (or gold stone). Even Shivites, he added, somewhat inconsistently, acknowledge Vishnu to be the head; Brahma is not a god, is not worshipped by any one; he was simply made by Vishnu that he might create the world. Shiva is their Saviour, but Vishnu the Creator and supreme god of all. At Gya, near Patna, they believe that they see the imprint of one of Vishnu's feet, and have a tradition that the other is to be seen at Mecca. According to this Brahmin, certain Brahmins have been to Mecca, and some still occasionally go thither, and offer balls of rice, as at Gya. He also said that at Mecca a bell sometimes rings of itself, and if a Hindú be there at that moment, and he answers the summons, saying, "I am here," the Mohammedans then allow him to go within the holy place. He added that formerly it was strictly prohibited to all Hindús to go beyond the Indus, but that this rule is relaxed, and they may do so if, on their return, they worship the *agni*, or fire, say certain prayers to it, give charity, and make a feast to the Brahmins. Eknath Kanâré, who is in the receipt of £20 a-month, told us that were he to go it would cost him £100 on his return to be readmitted into his caste. He also added that, after Benares, Poona was formerly the most learned city in India, and that Shivites worship the sun daily, and the serpent once a year only, on a day which falls within our months of July and August.

When we were at Benares in January 1877, just after the Delhi assemblage, a great number of the native princes were there, desirous before returning home to perform certain rites required by their religion from all Hindús, in order that they may wash away their own sins and also purify the souls of their ancestors. I will here describe this ceremony, which is called doing "Pooja," as I took it down from the mouth of an intelligent Brahmin who is *babu* (or clerk) to a friend of ours.

The pilgrims are required first to bathe in the Manikarnika Kund (or tank) near the ghât of that name, taking with them flowers and uncooked rice. After dipping themselves several times in this tank (the water in which is anything but clean looking or inviting either to sight or smell), they must make presents to the *pandas*, who are certain privileged hereditary Brahmins. Whilst the pilgrim is in the water, the pandas repeat some Sanscrit verses; the former meanwhile takes up some water in the hollow of his two hands, and, inclining his body, pours a libation to the four quarters of the compass : this they believe cleanses away their own sins and those of their forefathers who have died before them, and also those of their friends and relations who have no sons of their own, all of whom they mention by name. This part of the ceremony is called "Turpan," and can only be performed by males: the women also do pooja, but omit this. The pilgrim then goes to the temple of Bisheshamath (one of the numerous names of Shiva), which signifies "Lord of the World," and is better known under the name of the "Golden Temple." Arrived there, offerings of flowers, rice, and also money are made, the pandas repeating more Sanscrit verses; and from thence the temple of Anya-purna must be visited. This is one of the many names by which Shiva's wife is known, and there similar rites must be observed. In his different aspects, Shiva is called Mahádéo, Bishéswar, Kedáreswar, Sangaméswar, &c.; and Durga in the same manner has the names of Sati, Parvati, Parbuti, Kali, Gauri, &c. The pilgrim must next feast, at least, twelve unmarried Brahmin girls, and worship at the feet of one of these, with the same worship as he gives to his gods, and present her with good clothes and ornaments. Such girls are considered equal in rank to Durga, and are called "Bhagvati," or mistresses of the world. He must then give food to at least twelve Brahmins, after which these all receive presents according to the means of the pilgrim, and then feed twelve married women of the Brahmin caste, who need not necessarily receive any presents. Then comes the turn of twelve pundits, who are each presented with a basket of sweetmeats and a gift of money.

I was told that when the Maharajah of Kashmir was at Benares at the time of the Prince of Wales's visit, he gave sixteen rupees to each Brahmin, and twenty-five to each pundit; these last also each received a shawl. The pundits are the learned class amongst the Brahmins. The Maharajah is said to have disbursed altogether at that time the sum of 100,000 rupees, or about £10,000 of our money. The most learned men in all India are to be found at Benares: some of them hold what may be called degrees, conferred on them by their societies.

The bodies of all Hindus who die at Benares are burned at the Manikarnika Ghât. Thousands of people go thither from all parts of India simply to die in the sacred city. Any one having very old parents is bound, if within a reasonable distance, to send them to it; and any Hindú dying at Benares is believed to have his sins entirely washed away, and to become incorporated with Shiva. With apparent inconsistency, the only exception to the rule of burning the bodies seems to be in the case of the Gossains, who are members of a kind of Hindú religious fraternity, and of those who die by an accident or from the bite of a serpent; in the two latter instances they give us a reason that such do not die by the hand of God. Children dying under the age of two years are also buried.

The pilgrim's duty does not end here; for he must also make the circuit of the Panch Kosi road, which is so called because at no part of its course is it more than five *kos* (or ten miles) from Benares. This road comprises a circuit of fifty miles, and this area is esteemed very sacred. Hundreds of shrines are scattered along this road; the pilgrim is bound to worship at as many of these as possible. All the land within this space is called Benares. The Hindús believe that whoever dies within this enclosure is sure of happiness after death—and this applies, they say, to Europeans and Mohammedans, even to Pariahs and outcasts. After completing this circuit, the pilgrim must then visit the temple of Sakhi-Bináyaka, or the witness-bearing Bináyaka, in order that the fact of his pilgrimage may be verified. Were they to neglect this, the whole would have been performed in vain.

I will now begin to describe some of the Hindu temples at Benares, premising that I will speak about none which I have not myself visited; and the same rule must be considered to apply to any other monuments, unless the contrary is especially stated. The temple called Durga-Kund, or tank of Durga, is not far from the Manikarnika Ghât, but it is at least three miles from Sikraul, as the English quarter at Benares is named. It is best known as the "Monkey Temple," from the great number of those animals which it maintains. When we were there we gave some money to one of the attendants to buy grain, and on strewing it about, the monkeys, old and young, large and small, came down to the feast in great numbers from the temple and its surrounding colonnades. A certain old mamma monkey had a baby with her who was afraid to undertake the final downward leap with her, the little animal staying on the top of the colonnade and crying like a child. Mamma could not endure this for long, so, in spite of her evident fear of losing a part of her share of the food, she turned round, stood upon her hind-legs, held out her arms, and the little creature jumped into them.

The Durga Kund temple is built on the same plan as

all Hindú temples, but has no minute carving or sculpture upon it, therefore I shall go on to describe that of Bishesharnath, commonly known as the Golden Temple, from the plates of gilt copper which cover the central dome, and one of the pyramid-like roofs on either side of this, beneath one of which is the shrine of the god. These roofs are covered with small pinnacles placed one above the other, the whole terminating at the summit with a single tall and graceful pinnacle. The entrance doors are very handsome, being made of gilt brass or copper, and consisting of small squares, each of which contains a figure of some god in *basso-rilievo:* a richly wrought arabesque border surrounds the whole. After passing through these doors a large court is seen, round which is a platform with a sloping roof supported on pillars, with partitions at intervals, which form recesses. The whole building is of sandstone, coloured a bright red.

Once when we were there we saw more than one painted devotee seated on this platform, apparently absorbed in meditation, having a few flowers, or perhaps a few leaves of a book, on a mat before him. In his right hand was a kind of a sock or bag of a peculiar form, made of bright bits of cloth sewn together in a particular arrangement of the colours. This bag is sometimes embroidered with figures of Krishna, the Brahmini bull, the sun, &c. In it he holds his rosary, and, muttering certain prayers, counts his beads. The dome and the two pyramidal-like structures already alluded to are on a platform, about four feet in height, in the centre of this court. All these buildings are richly carved on their exterior, being covered with minute work representing sprays of flowers, conventionally treated, the lotus blossom being often repeated. Beneath the dome, and in all the recesses round this temple, are numerous Mahádéos, or emblems of Shiva.

The temple of Anya-Purna has also been mentioned as one of those which every pilgrim is bound to visit. Anya-Purna may be called the goddess of plenty, as she is supposed to feed all the poor. Tradition says that when Benares was first peopled, Anya-Purna was fearing that the task of supplying their wants would be beyond her power. The goddess Gunga, or Ganges, came to her assistance, and said that if Anya-Purna would give a handful of pulse to every applicant, she would contribute a *lota* (a brass vessel) of water. From this has now arisen the custom that all who can afford it daily put aside a quantity of pulse or rice, which they moisten over night, and in the morning give away in handfuls to the poor. Only one handful is given to each person; but a whole family, after collecting a supply from a number of donors, by the middle of the day can obtain a goodly quantity, which they first dry, and then either cook for food or sell in the bazaar. Milk is also given to them—the produce of the sacred cows kept in the precincts of the temple.

This building is worthy of notice, being built of a very white kind of stone, and covered with paintings of flowers in bright colours, amongst which the lotus has a prominent place. On entering the doorway the usual square court is seen, with the temple in the centre, but differing slightly from other buildings of the same nature, inasmuch as all round the courtyard there is a covered colonnade slightly raised above it, wherein cows, calves, and even bulls are kept, which are all so tame as to be not a little intrusive. A number of gay peacocks also strut about this enclosure. The centre building, or temple proper, is supported on twelve columns, and is open on all sides but one, where it is joined to a small covered building containing the shrine of the goddess. The flooring is of black and white marble, arranged in geometrical patterns. Under the central dome is a bell, sounded by a clapper: this is almost constantly going, for all, when they have performed their devotions, sound it in their turn on quitting this temple, which is said to have been erected about 150 years ago.

About a mile beyond it, and overlooking the Ganges, is the so-called Nepaulese temple, erected to Shiva by a Maharajah of Nepaul about a century ago. Singularly enough, there is a considerable resemblance, both in form and construction, between this temple and the Mohammedan mosques in Kashmir. It is a large square building, elevated on a platform about four feet high. At the principal entrance are steps by which the temple is reached. On either side of these there is a lion carved in stone, but on the right hand, between the steps and the lion, there is a stone head of Shiva in *alto-rilievo*. The hair is arranged in a double row of curls, standing out like the sun's rays; below the ears, and round the neck, most lifelike-looking snakes are coiled. From the platform rises the temple—a building about 24 feet square and the same in height. Sloping eaves, about 6 feet wide and roofed with small tiles, project all round—the eaves being supported by wooden brackets richly carved. Above this rises another square building of smaller dimensions, which likewise is furnished with similar sloping eaves. Along the edge of each of these eaves hangs a row of small bells, placed at short distances from each other, which must tinkle when there is any wind stirring. Above this again is a sort of pagoda. Smaller ones of the same kind occupy each of the four corners. From an iron rod at the summit is suspended a large bell. A trident—one of the emblems of Shiva—is also attached to the centre pagoda, and stands out nearly at right angles to it: the trident, as well as the pagodas, are all gilt. There are four doors to this temple, each with a window on either side of it. The doors, as well as the shutters of the window, are all of wood, and richly carved. The principal entrance has a figure of Shiva in duplicate upon it; the other three doors have Shiva and Parbuti, side by side, represented upon them. Over each door is a segment of a pointed arch, which is surmounted by the well-known "*chattur*," or umbrella-like ornament. The most prominent figure in this piece of carving is that of Garuda, the King of the Vultures, one of the heroes of the Ramayana. The window-shutters have small bells carved all over them.

Adjoining this temple is a building with some handsome carving upon it, erected by the same Maharajah. Such places are called Baradurries; and in the one I am speaking of any Hindú pilgrim of good caste receives board and lodging gratis. Foundations of this character abound in Benares, and render it a very paradise of beggars.

The temple of Baironath is built on the same plan as all the others, and is of sandstone, painted a bright red. The temple itself is supported on fluted pillars. The small inner shrine contains a statue of this god, covered with plates of silver. In the colonnade there are statues of Hanuman, or the monkey god; of Kali, and also of Rama and his brother Lakhsman, who are seated one on each shoulder of another statue of Hanuman. Baironath is looked upon by the Hindús as a spiritual *kotwal* (or police magistrate) of Benares and its suburbs. He is bound to keep the city free from evil spirits and evil persons, and to expel them should he find any such. This being his office, it was deemed only right to arm him with a truncheon, which in this case is no sham weapon, but a very real one of stone, and is called the "Dand-pan." The Hindús believe it to be divine.

Singularly enough, this weapon is not placed close to the magistrate's hand—which would perhaps appear to be its natural and proper place—but we had to thread at least a quarter of a mile of intricate and narrow streets after leaving the temple before we came to it. The Dand-pan is inside a small building, and consists of a pillar of black stone about 4 feet 6 inches in height, tapering slightly upwards. There appeared to be some ornamentation at the top, but the pillar was so covered with wreaths of flowers which we dared not remove, that we were unable to examine it very narrowly. The Dand-pan is specially worshipped every Sunday and Tuesday, on which days a priest sits near it, and, with a rod made of peacocks' feathers, taps each comer; he is thus supposed to punish them for any evil they may have done. The word for this pillar was originally Danda-pani, which we were told signifies in Sanscrit, "Stick in hand." Its meaning seems to have become almost forgotten, and the pillar itself is now worshipped as a real deity, which shows one of the changes Hindúism has undergone even within a few centuries.

There are certain wells, too, which the Hindús consider sacred. One of these, the Kál-kúp, or "well of fate," is in the same building as the Dand-pan. The well is so situated, with regard to a square hole in the outer wall of the building, that at mid-day the sun's rays strike upon the water in the well below. People go there at that hour to search into the future, and woe be to him who cannot then see his own shadow in the water, for within six months he is certain to die!

There is another famous well called the Gyan Bápi, or "well of knowledge," in a large open square near the Golden Temple: the Hindús say that this well is the residence of their god Shiva. They throw offerings of flowers into the water, and the mass of decaying vegetable matter which is there accumulated makes the smell it emits anything but agreeable. An orthodox Hindú believes that whoever in ancient times drank of this water was blessed with knowledge; but that now, owing to want of faith, this gift is withheld. They have a tradition that once upon a time no water fell in Benares during a space of twelve years, and that there was great distress in consequence. When they were reduced to great straits, in order to relieve them, one of their *rishis* —who was a mythical being, not divine, but certainly not mortal—grasped the trident of Shiva, and dug at that spot, when a plentiful supply of water sprang up.

A large oblong building, supported on forty-eight columns, and open on all sides, covers this well; and to the east of this, on a separate platform, with a canopy over them, are placed statues of two deities in *alto-rilievo.* Four very steep steps lead up to the platform; and whilst we were there we saw a very decrepit old womam perform this portion of her pooja. As she ascended these steps she touched each one with her forehead; and when arrived at the top, she placed marigold flowers on the foreheads of these images, strewed some also on the ground, and wound up by well shampooing both these gods!

One side of the open square, where the Gyan Bapi is situated, is occupied with a mosque of considerable size, which is modern, and has nothing curious about it. But the back wall of this mosque has evidently at some time formed a portion of a large old Hindú temple, which is said to be the ancient temple of Shiva, and must have been on a much grander scale than any of the temples of the present day.

Besides those I have enumerated, there are also four temples in Benares dedicated to Sitala, the goddess of small-pox, whom they consider a sevenfold deity, and, therefore, in her temple is a *bas-relief* representing seven female figures. Another building is sacred to the *Naugrah*, or nine planets—viz., the Sun, Moon, Mars, Mercury, Jupiter, Venus, Saturn, Raha, and Ketu. The first seven give their names to the days of the week. We could only peep through a grating at these images, as this last temple remains closed all the day, and is only opened in the very early morning, when a priest comes and worships the idols, and makes the necessary offerings.

Although the city of Benares may now be regarded as sacred to Shiva, yet it would appear that it was not always so, as divine honours were at one time, they say, paid to a rajah called Divodas. Brahma had made this man Rajah of Benares, and given him jurisdiction over gods and men; and all other gods were banished from the city. These, headed by Shiva, of course tried to unseat him, but were unable to do so, until they could get Divodas to commit some sin, when his divine power and authority would be at an end. They were unsuccessful until Ganés, or Ganesha, the elephant-headed god, the eldest offspring of Shiva and Parbuti, came to the rescue, and in the character of a great *guru*, or teacher, went to Divodas. The rajah was so much struck with his learning and conversation that he asked to sit under him and be his disciple. Ganesha refused, but asked only that the rajah would follow out whatever instructions should be sent him in a dream. These came, and were simply that he must quit Benares. Feeling bound by his promise, the rajah abdicated his throne, retired from the place, and was conveyed by Shiva himself to the Káilas mountain. The other gods then entered Benares, and Shiva became their supreme ruler and head of the city.

A short account of Ganesha will not, I think, be out of place here, as statues of him figure in all the temples and in nearly every street of the city. The following is from a statement made to me by an educated Brahmin, and given, as far as possible, in his own words :—

"As time went on, and a veil of ignorance had covered the true Hindú philosophy, a belief in the Trinity, much resembling the Trinity of the Christians, was introduced into Hindú society. It was believed that the deity manifested himself in three distinct forms: Brahma, Vishnu, and Mabeshwara, or Shiva; these representing the Creator, the Preserver, and the Destroyer. Men ascribed to each of these a physical nature akin to the human, and considered them members of society.

Popular mythology further asserts that before the creation of man "Bhagvati," like Eve, was created out of the body of Mabeshwara, and was married to him. The first-fruit of their marriage was Ganesha, who is said to have had the head of an elephant. Mythology also adds that Ganesha was, at his birth, a charming little babe with a human head, and that a very unhappy circumstance made his appearance so monstrous. His birth caused great joy amongst the gods, and they all went to see the child except Shaui, or Saturn, the god of evil, dreaded by gods as well as by men. Bhagvati seems to have taken Shaui's absence as a pointed insult to herself. The other gods then summoned him by means of a mysterious mental process, and he immediately made his appearance. No sooner, however, had his first glance fallen upon Ganesha, than the babe's head vanished. It is said that Shaui's first look always causes irreparable evils, whilst his second glance gives what one may hardly expect.

The gods were horror-struck to see this change in the child, but bethought themselves to try if any living creature could be found at that moment in the whole ethereal region who was fast asleep with his head towards the north. They found Airavata, the famous elephant of Indra; and his head being in the desired posture, was chopped off, and brought to the scene of the accident. At the second glance of Shaui, the unwieldy head of the elephant was fastened on to the babe's slender body. All this was done in the twinkling of an eye, so that Bhagvati had only to bewail the metamorphosis. This, however, distressed her so very much, that the gods, to console her, assured her that her son would be held in the highest honour, and that his worship would precede the worship of the rest of the gods. Ganesha accordingly receives the first offering in pooja of all kinds; and his name is, as a rule, first uttered whenever the Hindú scriptures are read."

CHAPTER XII.

COMMISSIONER'S DURBAR AT BENARES—MARCH TO JOUNPORE—INTERESTING MOSQUES AT THAT PLACE.

On 1st January 1878 we were still at Benares, being detained by rainy weather, which prevented the tents from being struck. We thus witnessed a *durbar*, as it is called, which was held by special command by the Commissioner as an anniversary of the Proclamation at Delhi the previous year, this official acting as a representative of the Empress of India. The ceremonies were much the same as those used on such occasions by the Prince of Wales or the Viceroy. The Commissioner was seated on a chair of state at the upper end of a long room. On either side of this room, down to the entrance door, were also seated a double or triple row of native princes and gentlemen, those of the highest rank having places nearest to the seat of honour.

On a small table in front of the Commissioner were placed certain medals, the same as those distributed at Delhi, which were to be given away on this occasion. In the chief seats I noticed four native gentlemen, evidently very different in type and appearance from all the rest, and most unmistakably Mussulmans. On inquiry I found that these had the title of Shahzadas, which I believe means princes, and were lineal descendants of

Timur, or Tamerlane. They continue to receive pensions from the English Government, as belonging to the dynasty of the Moghul emperors of Delhi, their ancestor on that throne being Bahadur Shah, a son of Aurungzebe.

Bahadur Shah, who began to reign A.D. 1707, may be said to be the last emperor who ruled in Delhi while it existed in all its splendour and magnificence, for after him each ruler became more effete, and more incapable of governing, till the final death-blow was given to their nominal sovereignty in 1857. One of the sons of Bahadur Shah—possibly during the contest which ensued amongst them directly after their father's death in 1712—came to Benares, and these Shah-Zadas are his descendants. They have the privilege of demanding a private interview with Royalty or with the Viceroy, and exercised this when the Prince of Wales was in India in 1875-76.

The rest of the ceremony consisted in giving the medals to those for whom they were intended. One of the minor rajahs, and some old men who had done good service during the Mutiny or otherwise, each received one. After this came an act of homage (the giving of the Nuzzur) by every native prince or chief personage; *attar* and *pan* were then handed round, and all took their leave.

From Benares we went, with tents and camp equipage, to Jounpore, thirty miles distant. At Baragawn, our last halting-place, about a quarter of a mile from our camp, and facing a tank, there was a very curious Hindú temple, consisting of two chambers, each about six feet square—the roof of the inner one being of stone, and its construction the same as that of the roofs of the

Buddhist temples at Sydpore and Benares, which I have already described. A huge peepul-tree (*Ficus religiosa*) grows against one side of this building; its roots have completely embraced the whole of the inner temple. There is an entrance to each chamber; the door-posts of the one facing the tank have stone pillars about six feet high, which are octagonal at the base, then become sixteen sided, and are round at the upper part. The second chamber has likewise two stone pillars: on each of these is carved a female figure, about two feet six inches high, having a bird on its head. The lintel has also figures carved upon it. In the centre of the inner chamber is placed a huge stone head, sunk about a foot below the ground, with a low stone balustrade all round it. This head is rounded at the top, and is now worshipped as an emblem of Shiva. The inner chamber has two brick recesses, and its entrance door is at right angles to that of the first chamber. We thought this a most curious and interesting little building, and it must be of considerable antiquity.

The fort at Jounpore, as it at present exists, has nothing worthy of notice but its commanding situation and the fine view of the surrounding country to be obtained from it. It was rendered entirely defenceless shortly after the Mutiny of 1857: it was so strongly and well built that our engineers had considerable trouble in blowing up the walls. This fort was originally built by Firoze Shah, the third ruler of Delhi of the Toghlak dynasty, who began to reign A.D. 1351. Firoze Shah demolished several temples for the purpose of making this fort, and was proceeding to destroy the Atala Devi temple, but such an outcry was raised against this that he was forced to desist. He entered into a written agreement that neither he nor his successors would touch it, part of the contract being that the Hindús were not to restore what had been destroyed.

There were three more sovereigns of the Toghlak line who succeeded him; and after this came a period of thirty-six years, when there was no real kingdom of India. Kasir Khan, a governor of the Punjaub, and three of his descendants, governed the country in the name of Tamerlane, without taking the royal title; and this formed the so-called government of the Seiads, the last of whom, Ala-ud-din, made over Delhi and his pretensions to Beholi Khan Lodi, who assumed the title of king. Beholi's ancestors had been in commerce, and his grandfather was governor of Moultán under Firoze Shah.

About the year A.D. 1400, the *soubahdar*, or governor of the province of Jounpore, assumed an independent sovereignty. He founded a dynasty called the Sharki Patán. Under this rule Jounpore remained independent for nearly three quarters of a century, but was reconquered in 1478 by Beholi Lodi, the then sovereign of Delhi, though it still retained a kind of independence till the time of the great Akbar, when it was finally united with the Moghul empire. General Cunningham, in his report for the years 1871-72 of the Archæological Survey of India, says "that the style of building adopted by the Mohammedan kings of Jounpore was formed by a fusion of the styles of the Ghori Patáns and the Khilgi Patáns of Delhi, and that the mosques of the Sharki kings of Jounpore fill an important gap in the history of the Patán architecture of Northern India." He considers these the latest examples in which the lofty front, towering high above the main dome, forms the principal point of the building.

Near the Jumma Musjid, or great mosque, they still show the tombs of some of its rulers. A very old Mohammedan, living in a little house close by, told us that he himself was a direct descendant of these kings, pointed out his father's tomb in this enclosure, and said that they only and their descendants had the privilege of being buried there. We had heard beforehand that the mosques at Jóunpore were well worth a visit, but we were little prepared for such striking, interesting, and, at the same time, such puzzling buildings, inasmuch as in part they would appear to bear a decided Hindú character.

The Atala Musjid is by far the most highly decorated, and consists of a large square court with two-storied cloisters on three sides, the mosque proper forming the fourth and western side. These cloisters may well have been formerly part of a Buddhist *vihara*, or temple monastery, and seem at first sight almost as perfect as when they were built, though, when all has been summed up that has been said on both sides of the question, it would appear that most antiquarians are of opinion that none of these buildings, as they now stand, are Buddhist erections. From the circumstance that the Buddhists did not use the arch, there was no risk in removing any part of a building, even a single pillar. Consequently the builders of the mosques could have demolished any side or part of the cloisters, and joined new work on to the old.

The lower storey of the cloisters contains a series of small cells, such as are known to have been used by the monks and students in Buddhist institutions. Fergusson, who is a great authority on such matters, in his 'History of Indian and Eastern Architecture,' gives us his opinion that in this instance such was not their original use, one of his reasons being that the cells all open outwardly. General Cunningham, in his volume of the 'Archæological Survey of India' for the year 1874, differs from him, however, and says distinctly that the Atala Musjid is known to have been originally a Hindú temple converted to Mohammedan use by Ibrahim Shah Sharki, between the years 1403 and 1440 A.D.; and the opinion of Mr Beglar, one of his assistants, seems to be that the alteration was the work partly of Hindú and partly of Mohammedan masons—but his reasons are too numerous to detail here. On a close examination of the interior of some of these cells, for the purpose of finding some of the so-called "mason's marks," we found one of the emblems of Shiva five times, and another three times, repeated within one of them: these marks would hardly have been made by a Mohammedan. The upper storey of these cloisters is open on both sides, and supported on six rows of pillars, the outer rows being formed of double pillars. Over the north and south entrances to the cloisters the Mohammedans have erected small domes, but there is no dome over the eastern one.

The mosque proper, occupying the whole of the western side of the court, has a large dome in the centre, and a smaller one on either side of this. Judging from what General Cunningham states of the architecture of Jounpore, the mosques there would appear to belong to what is called the Ghori Patán, joined to the later, or Khilgi Patán style. Their great peculiarity seems to be the absence of minarets; and also, that in front of the domes of the mosque proper towers a propylon, or pyramid-like gateway, high above them, as if the architects of those days thought that the domes they had then only begun to use were not sufficiently perfect in their external form; or that, perhaps, the public eye was hardly accustomed to seeing them. In the Atala Musjid the centre propylon, which hides the large dome, is 86 feet high, and has a square doorway of the Ghori Patán style; whilst the smaller doorways on either side of this, in front of the smaller domes, have the horse-shoe arch, ornamented with the trefoil, which marks them as being Khilgi Patán work.

The mosques at Jounpore are further remarkable and interesting as possessing the first domes ever placed in India on buildings of that nature. In the Jumma Musjid the cloisters exist likewise in part, though much more alteration and adaptation has there been carried out. Like the cloisters of the Atala Musjid, these also have their cells opening exteriorly, and are two-storied; but the ground in the interior of the courtyard has been filled up as far as the top of the lower storey, so that, when inside it, only the upper storey is seen, which is open and supported on pillars, as in the former instance. Should the conjecture be correct that these cloisters were of Buddhist or Hindú construction, may there not, in the case of the Jumma Musjid, have been a tope, or tumulus, in the centre of the cloisters, and it have been, in consequence, less inconvenient to fill up the space than to remove the obstruction? In this building the entrance gate facing the mosque is in ruins, and bears all the marks of having been destroyed by violence.

On inquiry, one of the moolahs told us that they had a tradition that this gate was blown up by the orders of Beholi Lodi, who, when he conquered Jounpore, wished to destroy the whole mosque as an evidence of his victory, but the moolahs telling him that this would be against the Koran, the emperor said, that in order to show he had defeated them, he would at least blow up the gate, which was accordingly done. By this act, however, Beholi Lodi has rendered posterity one service, and thereby clearly shown how that the Mohammedans did destroy older buildings and afterwards use their stones; for there, where the construction of the walls of this gateway is exposed to view, they are plainly seen to have been made up interiorly of large stones, many having fine carving upon them—these stones having been placed there loosely, anyhow, without mortar, and cased on both sides with carefully-hewn masonry. Some say that the Jumma Musjid was erected in order that a certain old saint might be saved the labour of walking a mile barefoot to his Friday prayers. Others have a tradition that, during a seven years' famine, the money which had been granted for distressed persons being given to those who were not in need of relief, a labour test was instituted, and the rule enforced that only those persons who worked in casting up the mound in the interior should receive relief.

There is still one more mosque at Jounpore, the so-called *Lall Darwaza*, which is the least perfect of all. The cloisters, as now seen, are one-storied, and have neither domes nor cells. The mosque itself has a dome, and a propylon in front of it; on either side of this is a row of open pillars, double the present height of the cloisters.

Hearing that there was a great deal of sickness at Lucknow, we gave up our intention of going thither, and returned to Benares *en route* for Allahabad, where we were engaged to spend a few days with a friend. On leaving Benares, when we came to the bridge of boats over the Ganges, we found it was covered with a mass of bullock-carts, which were three in a row in some places, and not knowing exactly how much time we had to spare before the departure of the train, we got out of our carriage and walked across. We had some difficulty in threading our way and avoiding the horns of the bullocks. When we at length reached the railway station, on the further side of the river, we were surprised to find it crammed, inside and outside, with sacks of grain. My husband inquired the cause of this great traffic from an Englishman who had charge of the unloading and transport, and learnt that, in consequence of the want of rain in the district, on the Benares side and in Oudh, grain was pouring in so rapidly as almost to produce a block.

Only a few months previously, this person said, the grain traffic had been all in the opposite direction, but at that moment 460 carts were employed daily, each furnished with three bullocks, to convey the food across the river, chiefly to supply the Jounpore and Fyzabad districts, in consequence of the apprehended scarcity there. This was to us a conclusive argument in favour of the extension of railways in India, where they would seem to be more necessary even than in Europe, owing to the enormous distances to be travelled over, and the periodical famines which seem to be either taking place or apprehended every year in some part of this vast country.

CHAPTER XIII.

ALLAHABAD—ITS FORT—MIRACULOUS TREE IN ANCIENT TEMPLE—LÂT OF ASOKA—SECOND VISIT TO AGRA—MY HUSBAND'S IMPRESSIONS OF TAJ—FUTTEHPORE SIKRI.

THE fort at Allahabad seems to contain the only very ancient remains that place now possesses. Shah Jehan gave this city its present name: it was founded by Akbar, A.D. 1572, on the site of an old city called Pragaya. Hionen Thsang, the Chinese pilgrim, visited Pragaya A.D. 687, and relates that he found there a Brahminical temple, to which whoever contributed one piece of money gained as much merit as he who gave a thousand elsewhere. Before the principal room of the temple there was, he says, a large tree with spreading branches, which was said to be the dwelling of a demon; and he found this tree surrounded with the bones of pilgrims who had sacrificed themselves there. The temple described by Hionen Thsang is believed to be the one now shown in the fort. The lapse of time, and the consequent accumulation of soil, has filled up the ground around it, so that the temple is now quite underground, and a flight of steps has to be descended in order to reach its level, when a long narrow passage leads to the temple itself, which is in the plain Hindú style, having square pillars with bracket capitals. The building is not perfectly square; we counted eleven pillars one way, and nine the other. Owing to the absence of daylight, and the very imperfect light given by our guide's little lamp, we could not get any general idea of it as a whole; but in one place we saw two of the forks of an old tree, which appeared to be of the Banian or sacred fig species: each limb was about a foot in diameter. The people all hold this old stump in much reverence, and say that it never dies. One special day in the year pilgrims come in crowds to visit it, and firmly believe that this, their holy tree, is undying; though the sergeant of the guard at the fort, on the eve of this festival, would probably best know the reason of its flourishing so vigorously on that particular day, as report says a new one is, or was till within a year or two, smuggled into the fort by the Brahmins in the dead of night. At any rate, when we saw it, the limbs did not look dead or sapless, which might be due to the dampness of the vault, but there were no twigs or leaves on them.

On the ground in front of this tree there was a small image of Shiva, with a silver face; in another place there was a statue of Brahm, commonly called the first person of the Hindú Trinity. To the right of the tree the priest in charge pointed out a small stone passage not more than two feet high, which he declared, and seemed to believe, led to Benares; though, on being questioned, he said he himself had never made the journey, nor did he know any one who had done so.

In the arsenal at the fort is the audience-hall of Akbar's palace. This appears to have been originally in the centre of a courtyard which had colonnades all round it, these having a two-storied room at each corner. In the upper storey of one of these corner buildings is an inscription on a pillar, the purport of which is to commemorate the coming of some rajah to visit Akbar; and on a stone outside one of the windows of this room is some writing, to the effect that a certain rajah (country and name not decipherable) came to bathe in the Ganges, and derived so much benefit from doing so that he returned again and built a temple. The audience-hall in the centre of the quadrangle has also been a large two-storied building, each storey being surrounded by external colonnades supported on pillars, the capitals of which are formed of elephants' heads carved in stone. In the arsenal is shown a small-coiled steel cannon, on which the name "Mahabir" has been read; also the word "Futteraj," a place some distance to the south of Allahabad. This gun was discovered during the time of the Mutiny.

The *lât* or stone pillar erected by Asoka, B.C. 250, for the purpose of inscribing upon it certain edicts regarding Buddhism, is also inside the fort. The original site of this pillar is not known: some think it was brought from a place now called Kossám on the Jumna, about thirty miles off. About A.D. 200 Samudra Gupta next used this *lât*, and his inscriptions partly obliterated those of Asoka. Samudra Gupta recorded on it his extensive sovereignty in India, extending from Nepaul to the Dekhan, and from Guzerát to Assam. This column was re-erected by the Moghul emperor Jehangir, to commemorate his accession to the throne. In 1838 it was placed where it now stands.

The old city of Pragaya would seem to have totally disappeared, and it is thought very probable that the various Buddhist remains may have been washed away by the river Jumna even before the final abandonment of the city, as its course is known to have been gradually changing.

After leaving Allahabad, we again went to Agra, wishing very much to see the Taj once more, and also to go to Futtehpore Sikri, which the limited period of our stay two years before had prevented our doing. On this our second visit my husband noted down his impressions of the Taj Mehal, as contrasted with other buildings in Europe, taking a view of it which I think has not hitherto been adopted, therefore I will quote it entire in his own words, as follows:—

"No photograph or plan ever gives an adequate idea of the Taj, partly on account of the flatness of its surfaces, which in the marble original are relieved by mosaics in cornelian and jasper, and also because no copy on a small scale can do justice to the refinement and softness of the outlines of its dome. Beyond this, however, there is a secret in its fascination which is not easily explained. It stands single and alone among the great monuments of the world, not only in its purpose and in its architecture—which last cannot be likened or compared, or even contrasted, with that of any other building—but also in its effect on the mind of the spectator, which is more akin to that produced by an exquisite and costly jewel than by a vast and splendid edifice. This effect is probably due to the fact that the Taj appeals to the fancy more than to the imagination, and also to something peculiarly evanescent in its beauty, or, as it may be called, its exceeding prettiness. Often while we gaze upon it, its beauty seems to fade away; and when we closely and coldly criticise it, especially if we are absent, we deem it faulty and imperfect; but on returning to inspect it deliberately and dispassionately, all coldness, all calm criticism vanishes, when we behold its pure white dome gleaming against the blue sky.

"It is not difficult to find imperfections both in the design and in the details of the Taj, but the spectator feels under a spell. However architecturally incorrect he may suppose it to be, he is conscious that it is exceedingly lovely—and this not because its beauty is of the highest order,—it possesses neither the refined simplicity, subtle elegance, and antique massiveness of a Hellenic temple, nor the picturesqueness and sublimity of a Gothic cathedral; it is rather distinguished by something essentially feminine, or, as some might say, effeminate; but its lace-like tracery, its sculptured vases and flowers, the soft and flowing lines of the mosaics, the swelling form of the dome,—all these things are not inappropriate in the mausoleum of a queen.

"The Taj would not impress men as it does did its group of buildings not culminate in a large and lofty dome, which rises to a height of 243 feet from a base 186 feet square; but its size is felt rather than seen. It pleases, charms, and attracts; if it awes, it is by its purity and stately grace, and a certain indefinable sadness, and not by its vastness. It seems to be not so much the product of high genius as of exquisite taste, feeling, and sensibility, and to owe its charm to sentiment more than to skill and science."

Futtehpore Sikri is about twenty-two miles from Agra, and in order to enjoy it thoroughly we decided to remain there a few days, and with this end obtained permission to occupy one of the reserved bungalows. Futtehpore Sikri is situated in a walled but not fortified enclosure about seven miles in circumference. It was built by the Moghul emperor Akbar, who took a fancy to the site, elevated as it is above the plain; but it was hardly finished before the court deserted it,—as some authors say, owing to the badness of the water. It is said that its selection as a royal residence was principally owing to the circumstances attending the birth of Akbar's son, Prince Selim, afterwards known as the Emperor Jehangir. His mother was Hindú—a Rajput (the Rajputs constitute the warrior caste); and Akbar married her, it would seem, in pursuance of his plan of making the Hindú and Moslem races amalgamate. By this lady he had twin children, who died in infancy.

On one occasion, when Akbar and his wife were returning to Agra by that road, they went to visit a holy man—a hermit—named Shaikh Suleem Chishtee, who lived at the top of this hill. The royal couple, it would seem, remained some little time at this spot, and paid more than one visit to the hermit, whose baby son, aged only six months, one day asked his father why he looked so sorrowful, and why he had sent the conqueror of the world away in despair? The holy man said he must grieve, because he knew that all the emperor's children would die in infancy, unless some one gave his own child to die instead. This very precocious infant then said that he would die rather than that his Majesty should want an heir, and instantly expired. The tomb of this wondrous baby, about large enough for a moderate-sized doll, is shown just behind the mosque. Akbar's son and successor was born the following year.

The walls encircling the whole area of Futtehpore Sikri, and all the buildings, with the exception of one tomb, are of red sandstone, and have the square Hindú pillars. On entering the enclosure, we first passed through a massive quadrangular outwork, and then through another court, before we reached what is now the Dák Bungalow, but is said to have been the emperor's record office. This, and all the other houses which were occupied by the emperor, his ladies, and his ministers, are entirely of stone, and as perfect as the day they were finished. Not a particle of wood seems ever to have been used in their construction: the apertures for light are in stone, perforated in geometric patterns, and the doorways seem to have been closed by heavy curtains, or *purdahs*, as they are called in India.

On the north side of the square, containing the record office, is another very large quadrangle where there are some interesting buildings—viz., the *Khwabgah* and the Turkish queen's house. In front of the Khwabgah is a large square reservoir for water, with four stone causeways leading to a platform in the centre of this tank. The Khwabgah itself is a large square building open on all sides and supported on many pillars; this is supposed to have been the place where the emperor and his more intimate male friends took their siesta. Over this is a square room, very massive and simple, believed to have been Akbar's bedroom; this has a wide sloping colonnade all round, roofed with huge slabs of stone, which are supported on pillars.

The Turkish queen's house is a one-roomed building, with exquisitely minute work within and without. It has colonnades all round; at right angles to it a similar colonnade comes from the other side of the courtyard; and between these are three wide steps leading to another court, where is the Dewan-i-Khas, or privy council chamber; also the Dewan-i-Am, or public hall of audience, and another building, which is supposed to have been Akbar's treasure-house.

The Dewan-i-Khas faces the Khwabgah, and though built in the same style as the rest, yet its construction is so singular as to merit description. As seen from without, it appears to be a two-storied building, but it is really open from pavement to roof, and a single pillar rises in the centre of the interior to the level of the first storey. This pillar has an immense capital, several times its diameter, and from this start four stone causeways, each ten feet in length, and resting on large brackets in each corner of the hall. A small staircase leads up to a narrow gallery running all round the building. One tradition is, that the emperor himself used to sit on the top of the centre pillar, while in each corner was perched one of his ministers, who there received his commands for the four quarters of the world. Others are of opinion that the ministers were thus placed in order that if any thing were stated for or against them by the people below, they being obliged to shout in order to make the emperor hear, all could be certain that their complaints or requests were properly brought before him. Again, another story relates that Akbar used to deliver his judgments from the summit of this pillar, and also listen to criminal cases, and on this account a minister had to sit in each corner at the end of these causeways to prevent any chance of the assassin's knife reaching the great emperor. This building is richly carved in the interior, though in a bold style. In what is supposed to have been the treasure-house there were secret coffers in recesses in the walls, closed by massive sliding slabs of stone; all these have, of course, been rifled long ago.

In front of the so-called treasury there is a tiny little

pavilion, which is said to have been occupied by a Hindú teacher who was tolerated by Akbar. Its architecture is, in some respects, of the Jaina character: each of the architraves is supported by two very curious struts, which issue from the mouth of a monster, and meet in the middle like the apex of a triangle.

The Dewan-i-Am, or large hall of audience, forms one side of this court; it consists of a small hall, with a deep verandah beyond, looking out into another vast courtyard 360 feet by 180, having colonnades all round, where the people could sit secure from sun or rain and witness the administration of justice, the emperor being seated in the verandah at a height of about 10 feet from the ground.

We will now return to the courtyard of the Dewan-i-Khas, and there note the *pucheesee*-board in the centre of the pavement, the use of which has been already described when speaking of the fort at Agra. Abutting on this courtyard, and to the south-east of the Dewan-i-Khas is the Panch Mehal, a five-storied little building, each storey being open and supported on pillars, and smaller than the one beneath it, so that at the very top there is a small kiosque only. This is said to have been the place where the female servants were stationed, as it overlooked the courts appropriated to the seraglio. The pillars on the ground-floor of the Panch Mehal are without ornamentation, but in the row above this they are curious, inasmuch as every one is carved, but, as far as we could see, no two were alike.

Due south of the Panch Mehal, and only a few yards distant from it, is the bungalow we occupied, which is known as the Mehal Sonari, and also as Beebee Mariam's, or the Christian lady's house, it being stated by some that a Portuguese lady, one of Akbar's wives, lived in it, though I believe there is no good authority for the statement that he ever had a Christian wife. In the verandah is an inscription which, when translated, runs thus :—

"If I say its window is of higher dignity than the sky, I should be saying what is proper.

"It is well for me to consider its threshold grander than the sun.

"It is an abode of riches, and an asylum of peace and safety;

"A place of refuge for the nine heavens, and a temple for the nine planets.

"The sky is to the floor of this place as morning is to . . . (defaced).

"The threshold of this palace is so high, that it serves as an axis for the sky."

In the recesses on the exterior of the Mehal Sonari are still some remains of fresco paintings. I made out some groups of flowers, also elephants, and in one place a camel led along by a man; on the animal's back was a species of *howdah*, in which was a seated figure, but whether of a man or a woman I could not determine.

On the ground-floor of this house there is one large and three smaller rooms; in the upper storey there are three small rooms only, and over the larger one is a small stone canopy supported on pillars, where, no doubt, the lady or ladies sat occasionally to enjoy the view. The walls of one of the three small rooms on the ground-floor have been originally painted in fresco; the remains of colour are clearly to be seen, but in other respects the architecture of this house is plain and unadorned, and forms a contrast to the enclosure containing the so-called palace of the empress, or to the house of Beerbul, both of which are quite close to it. Leaving the Mehal Sonari on the right hand, a doorway leads into a quadrangle about 170 feet by 150 : it is surrounded by a colonnade, which has domes at each corner, and two-storied buildings in the centre of each of its four sides. Facing the grand portal is a hall opening into the courtyard, and adorned with pillars of an early Hindú type. In this hall was the first and only fireplace I have ever seen in buildings of that date in India : there is a large hearthstone and a chimney in the back wall. Some say that this was the palace of Jodh Bai, Jehangir's mother; but others affirm that it was the residence of Akbar's chief wife, Roogeea Soultan Begum, the daughter of his uncle Hindal.

Beyond and to the west of this is Beerbul's (or rather his daughter's) house, a perfect gem in its way, from the extreme delicacy and minuteness of its finish, both within and without—though red sandstone is such a coarse material that it would hardly be thought capable of lending itself to such fine tracery. Each of the four rooms on the ground-floor of this house is about 15 feet square; they are ceiled with slabs of stone 16 feet in length and 1 foot in width. The two rooms in the upper storey, which are placed at right angles to each other, are of the same dimensions as the lower rooms, and crowned with domes.

Rajah Beerbul was one of Akbar's Hindú grandees, and a man of letters. Being, however, sent on a military expedition to the north-west frontier, he miserably mismanaged the affair, and perished, together with 8000 men and officers. His death is said to have been long mourned by his master Akbar. At the back of Beerbul's house there is stabling for 102 horses, there being 51 stalls, and each constructed to accommodate two animals. The mangers and rope-rings, both of stone, are still quite perfect. The doors, which were of the same material, have all disappeared except one.

On looking down from the raised platform near Beerbul's house, we saw a singular tower below us just outside the walls. It is round, and bristling all over with projections, which were intended to represent elephants' tusks. Akbar used to resort to this tower when he desired to have some easy sport; antelopes and other game were then driven towards him. To get near this tower we had to go down a steep causeway and pass through two gates, the furthermost of which is called the gate of the elephants, as on the outer side are the remains of two huge ones made out of large slabs of stone, so carved as to resemble those animals. This gate is the earliest specimen of the true arch with a distinct key-stone we have met with in India.

The mosque at Futtehpore Sikri is said to be an accurate copy of the one at Medina, and is also the grandest and the largest that Akbar ever built. The *durgah*, or sacred quadrangle, is of vast size, being 433 feet by 366. The principal entrance was originally at the east end facing the mosque; but the archway at the south side far exceeds it in size. This last is called the Buland Darwaza, or gate of victory. It is 130 feet high, and was built after the mosque was erected, to commemorate some conquest made by Akbar in the Dekhan: from its great height it has the effect of dwarfing the other buildings. Just outside and to the west of this gate there is a large well, into which men and boys leap, for a small reward, from a part of the mosque about 60 feet above the level of the water. Even if Hindús, whatever money they receive for performing this feat, they invarably give a fourth part of it to the shrine of Suleem Chishtee, being convinced that they would come to grief if they did not. This monument is entirely of white marble; on all four sides there are pierced lace-like designs carved out of solid slabs of that material. The tomb of the saint is within; it very much resembles a four-post bedstead. The supports and canopy are all incrusted with mother-of-pearl, so that it gives one the idea of a casket of jewels in an outer box of marble. On the pavement near the shrine are a number of tombs, said to be those of the women of Akbar's household; and beyond these, again, is a large building of red sandstone containing the tomb of Islam Khan, the saint's grandson.

At the time that Akbar built this mosque, he was thought to be trying to work out his system of so-called "Divine Monotheism," by attempting to throw off the rules laid down by Mohammed, and substitute a religion founded by putting together the systems of Zoroaster, the Brahmins, and of Christianity, only retaining some Mohammedan forms. The mosque proper is, as is usual in India, on the western side of the enclosure. It consists of seven halls, each communicating by an arched doorway with the one next adjoining. The central hall has a large dome. Its walls are ornamented with white marble, inlaid in geometric patterns. The spaces between these are filled up with flower designs in fresco painting. The whole of this chamber is decidedly Mohammedan in style, whilst the six lateral halls—three on each side of this—are essentially Hindú in character. Four have flat roofs, supported on pillars reaching from floor to ceiling, and the remaining two have small domes.

Since writing the above I have read a paper published by the Archæological Society of Agra, wherein certain good authorities seem to think it is very possible that the true structural arch may have been known to the Hindús long before the Mohammedan conquest, but that, like the ancient Greeks, for some reason or other they did not use it, or at least never employed it in their buildings when they were of a monumental character. Fergusson says "that even at the present day the Hindús refuse to use the arch, for, as they express it, 'an arch never sleeps,' meaning that by its thrust and pressure it is always tending to tear a building to pieces, and thus hastens the destruction of a monument which, if constructed on more simple principles, might last for ages."

CHAPTER XIV.

MUTTRA—ANCIENT BUDDHIST STATUES FOUND THERE—DISTRESS AMONGST THE NATIVE POPULATION—OLD AND MODERN TEMPLES AT BINDRABUN GOVERDHUN—TEMPLE OF HARI DEVA—DEEG—BHURTPORE.

WE left Agra finally on 13th February 1878, having had some letters of introduction given us by friends to enable us to make a round and visit some of the adjoining native states. Our first move was to Muttra (or, more properly, Mathurá). During our stay there we were much indebted to the kindness and courtesy of Seth Govind Dás, a wealthy Hindú banker, to whom we had three letters from different persons. He lent us a carriage and horses to convey us to Muttra, and one of his carriages was placed at our disposition during the whole of our stay, to enable us to see the place and the objects of interest in the neighbourhood.

The Seth and his family formerly belonged to the Jaina sect, but are now staunch Vishnuvites. This is a very singular circumstance, as I believe the hatred of these two sects to each other is very great—at any rate, it is peculiarly so on the part of the Vishnuvite Hindús, who have a saying that it would be better, on meeting a mad elephant in a narrow street, to stand still and be trampled to death rather than escape by crossing the threshold of a Jaina temple.

Some time ago the Seth returned his property for income-tax at over £20,000 a-year; besides this, he owns much land, and has house property both in Muttra and Agra. He himself chiefly resides at Bindrabun. He and his family belong to the reformed or Sampradáyas Vishnuvites, which sect was unknown at Bindrabun until he and his brother were enlisted in its ranks. It is the oldest and most respectable of the four modern communities of this faith, and is based on the teaching of one Ramanuja, who lived in the eleventh or twelfth century of the Christian era. Their distinctive caste mark is two white perpendicular streaks down the forehead, joined by a cross line at the root of the nose, and a streak of red between the white lines. In the case of the Shivites, these lines are three in number, and placed horizontally in the form of a bow. The special tenet of the Vishnuvites is faith in Krishna (at least it is so in the Muttra district). This can be expressed, they say, by the mere mention of his name, without prayer; if they only have belief in him they are saved, and may commit any sin, for are they not free?—is not Krishna their friend?

It is very strange to find the familiar dispute between faith and works existing amongst a heathen people. It will be unnecessary here to go into a more detailed account, but from a comprehensive statement of their belief which I met with, I was induced in my own mind to class the Vishnuvites as belonging to the Low Church, and the Shivites as representatives of the High Church in the Hindú religion. The chief dogma of these Sampradáyas, or reformed Vishnuvites, is the assertion that Vishnu, the one supreme god, though invisible as *cause*, is visible as *effect* in a secondary form in material creation. During nine months in the year there is a continual stream of pilgrims going to Muttra: some hold that place as far superior in sanctity to Benares, and say that one day spent there is more meritorious than a whole lifetime passed at Benares. This is, of course, the Vishnuvite view of the matter—that sect prevailing at Muttra, as do the followers of Shiva at Benares.

We drove more than once through the native bazaar at Muttra: many houses belonging to the wealthiest of its inhabitants are very large, and finely carved. The fronts of these houses have, as a rule, a grand central archway, with arcades on either side, which are let out as shops. Above these there are projecting balconies supported on quaint corbels, and the whole front of the house is covered with minute stone carvings in a great variety of patterns.

Every city in India has a *specialité* for some kind of work: in Muttra it is that of the stone-masons who, on a daily wage of sevenpence halfpenny, execute lovely designs in work of such fineness and delicacy as few European workmen would have patience to copy; and one can only hope that it may be long before any patterns or ideas from the West may be adopted by them, though their style of carving, being very shallow, is more suited to wood than to stone. To me, the Muttra work, like the later buildings in the fort at Agra, has rather, if one may so speak, an air of effeminacy, as belonging to those who had been long enough established in an enervating climate to learn to love ease and luxury; it contrasts strongly with Akbar's style, which, in its massiveness, has something northern and rude, though, at the same time, grand about it—looking almost as if carved out of the living rock. The Turkish lady's house at Futtehpore Sikri is as highly finished as any of the work at Muttra, but is refined and beautiful without weakness. The house called Beer-bul's would be an illustration of the northern style, somewhat softened, but having lost none of its massiveness.

Many poor people were at that time flocking into Muttra from Bhurtpore and other native states, where little or nothing appeared to have been done by their rulers to relieve the distress caused by the want of rain, and consequent failure of the crops. A good deal of this neglect is no doubt to be excused when one saw how that, even under British rule, it was necessary for a European official to be on the spot daily at the hour of leaving off work, and with his own hands pay each man, woman, and child employed on the relief works, which had been organised to assist them. This pittance, being their only means of procuring their daily food, if not thus distributed, would in great part stick to the fingers of any native employed to pay them; and how much more would not this be the case in a native state where European supervision even would not be possible. Certain houses also had been set apart as poorhouses, where those who were too weak or too infirm to work were fed and lodged. We went over one of those refuges, which was maintained by subscription: about a thousand people were housed in sheds belonging to our banker friend, each individual receiving so much bread per diem, the men, of course, having more in proportion than the women and children. The old people appeared to have suffered the most; some of the children looked comparatively well nourished. On leaving this enclosure we found about twenty poor, wretched, half-famished looking creatures outside waiting for admittance. When their strength has been a little restored they are put upon the relief works, which consist in moving and carrying earth, the men loosening it with their picks, and the women and children removing it in small baskets. For this the men receive what is equivalent to three halfpence, the women to three farthings, and the children to one halfpenny a-day. We visited one set of relief works situated between the magistrates' office and the so-called Damdama, now occupied by the reserves of the district police, but originally one of the series of *serais* erected in the time of the Emperor Akbar along the road between the royal residences at Agra and Delhi. Large mounds had long been observed in the space between these two buildings; these were to a certain extent an inconvenience, and being supposed to be the site of some Buddhist remains, it was resolved to employ these poor people to remove this earth.

As long ago as 1860, when the foundations were being dug for the magistrates' court-house, a number of interesting Buddhist remains were found, which were transported to Agra, but I believe from thence they were moved to Allahabad.

The day of our arrival at Muttra the excavators had been rewarded by the discovery of a very fine Buddhist statue, in red sandstone, a little more than life-size, and in wonderfully perfect preservation. The feet were broken off, but they were found near the statue; one arm and part of one ear were missing. Round the head of the figure is a large stone disc or glory exquisitely carved in geometric patterns, which have much of the character of the later Arabesque work. I also distinguished two birds on the upper part of this disc.

The nose, which is slightly aquiline, is quite perfect; the lips are very full, and the countenance has an air of great repose, as is usual in Buddhist sculptures. The hair is arranged in small curls all over the head, and the statue is draped in waving lines, so disposed as to show the figure, clothed in what must have been intended to represent a muslin robe. The left hand, which alone remains, holds up the bottom of the robe. Near the feet are two very small and mutilated figures, in the attitude of adoration. This statue had a long inscription on the base, which was copied and sent to Mr Growse, who was formerly at Muttra in an official position, and is well known for the interest he takes in antiquarian researches; he deciphers a part of it as follows: "This is the votive offering of the monk Yasaditta. If there is any merit in it, may it work for the good of his father and mother, and for the propagation of the holy faith throughout the world." In the remainder of the inscription there are some letters which do not form any known word. He adds that the meaning of this monk's name is "resplendent with glory." Several fragments of other statues had also been found, but no others of importance; a very small portion of the ground had been excavated up to that time.

It would appear from certain inscriptions found nineteen years ago that these mounds covered the remains of four monasteries. In Mr Growse's memoir of Muttra and its district, he speaks of more than one statue, probably the work of Greek artists, which had been found there at different times—a conjecture in which he goes on to say no historical difficulty is involved, since in the Yuga-Purana of the Gárgi-Sanhitá, written about the year 50 B.C., it is expressly stated that Mathura was reduced by the Greeks, and that their victorious armies advanced into the very heart of Hindostán, even as far as Patali-Putra.

Nearly opposite the Damdama, and in the garden of the house which used to be occupied by Mr Growse when he was joint magistrate, there are many fragments of stone sculpture which are very curious. One especially is Greek in idea and treatment, though its execution is in a debased style; at the same time it is not the least Hindú. On one side is represented a figure in the well-known attitude of Silenus, drinking from a full cup he holds in his hand; a female figure is presenting him with a second draught—she has a jeering countenance; whilst a third, also a female, is looking on with evident enjoyment. On the other side of the same stone Silenus is again depicted, as having finished the two cups of nectar, and leaning heavily on two figures; one of his supporters is a female, the other is too much injured to determine what it was.

During our stay at Muttra we drove one day to Máhában, on the other side of the Jumna. The road, being little used, is very bad—about half a mile of deep sand has to be crossed; this, no doubt, is covered with water when the river is in flood. We passed through the village of Gokul, which is the headquarters of another sect of Vishnuvites. These may be called the Epicureans of the East: they hold the dogma of union with the divine, and believe that every sin, whether of body or soul, and of whatever kind, is put away by union with the Creator.

About two miles beyond Gokul, and six from Muttra, is the village of Máhában. Its temples seemed all very poor and modern: the only building of any interest is the Assi-Khamba—*i.e.*, the eighty pillars. This is a curious remnant of antiquity, which has three or four varieties of decoration, and probably these all belong to different periods. The columns are decidedly Hindú in character, as is evidenced by the horizontal instead of perpendicular lines in their carving; a few pillars at one end are quite plain; and others, again, belonging to the latest period, have been ornamented with numbers of small human figures running round them in bands of decoration. All the heads had been knocked off by the Mussulmans at some time or other. On examining it narrowly, we came to the conclusion that this building, as we now see it, had been put together from the remains of still older ones. One small square of the ceiling had a lovely little dome with horizontal bands of ornament; others, again, were flat; and some had the lotus carved upon them. As it now stands, the Assi-Khamba may possibly date from between the time when Mahomed of Ghuznee destroyed the temples at Muttra and its neighbourhood, in A.D. 1017, and the Mohammedan conquest of Delhi 170 years later.

Bindrabun, which is about six miles from Muttra in another direction, possesses one old and several modern temples, all of large size. This place has long enjoyed a high repute as a place of pilgrimage. The largest temple, that of Govind Deva, was in course of being restored by the Indian Government. It is built of red sandstone; its ground-plan and the groining of the nave put me very much in mind of our English cathedrals. It is in the form of a Greek cross, with a dome in the centre, where the two arms meet. The roof of the nave is a vault of pointed form, made of true arches, like our Gothic churches. The transepts, or side limbs of the cross, are divided into two parts by pillars in the lower part of the building; over these a wall is carried up, pierced with small windows like a clerestory. This temple was built in 1590 by Rajah Man Singh of Jeypore, a friend of the Emperor Akbar, who made him successively governor of the districts along the Indus, of Cábul, and of Bihar; but there is a tradition that Akbar, at length jealous of him, had some sweetmeat prepared containing poison, but ate of it himself by mistake, and eventually died in consequence.

The temple of Govind Deva had originally seven towers, according to Mr Growse in his district memoir. The sacrarium has been utterly razed to the ground and rebuilt in brick, and the other six towers levelled to the roof of the nave. The interior of the building, as at present seen, measures 117 feet from east to west, and 105 from north to south. Beyond the sacrarium, and having almost the effect of a second transept when seen from the outside of the building, are what appear the lower storeys of two towers—one of which the people on the spot called the cook-house of the god, and said some other god had his dwelling in the tower on the other side. This temple is singularly picturesque in its general character. What particularly struck us was, that it combined in the most effective manner the perpendicular lines of a Gothic cathedral with the ordinary horizontal lines of Hindú architecture. In the days of this temple's grandeur, when they heard that Aurungzebe, that great temple destroyer, was in the neighbourhood, the original idol belonging to it was removed to Jeypore; and we were told that for this reason, after its restoration shall have been completed, the Hindús will never again make use of it for religious purposes.

The temple of Rang-ji (one of the numerous names of Vishnu in his different incarnations) was built some twenty-five years ago by Seth Govind Das, at a cost of forty-five lacs of rupees (or £450,000). The Seth himself met us there, and showed us all the parts of the building that any one not of their faith is allowed to visit. At Muttra they seemed to be very much more jealous in this respect than at Benares. The entrance gateway of this temple is a very highly-finished specimen of the Muttra carved stonework; this leads into a vast courtyard, containing a tank and a garden; there are colonnades all round, with numbers of small houses for the Brahmins employed in the service of the temple, and their families. These men all came originally from the Madras Presidency; and to induce them to stay at so great a distance from their homes, the Seth is obliged to give each man ten rupees a-month, or £1, besides a certain allowance of food,—the wife receiving half that sum. Five hundred people—pilgrims and others—are daily fed at this temple.

The temple itself is in the middle of the courtyard: it is in the Dravidian style—a term given to the architecture of the south of India. There are two high gate-towers forming approaches to the most sacred part of all; these are covered with very coarse and inferior sculpture, which did not by any means harmonise or contrast well with the delicate and minute Muttra work of the entrance gateway.

About fourteen miles west of Muttra is another spot accounted by the Hindús to be very holy—viz., Goverdhun, which we passed through on our way to Deeg, a fort and palace in the Rajah of Bhurtpore's territories. The town of Goverdhun occupies a break in a narrow limestone ridge of hill, which rises abruptly from the plain for about four or five miles in length, having an average height of about 100 feet. Krishna is fabled to have held this hill aloft on the tip of his finger, to cover the people from the storms rained down upon them by Indra, when deprived of the usual sacrifices made to him. The people of the neighbourhood have a firm belief that, as the waters of the Jumna are decreasing, so this sacred hill is gradually sinking; and say that, in former times, it could be seen from Aring, a place four or five miles distant, whereas the town now becomes invisible at a distance of a few hundred yards. So holy is this hill esteemed, that not a morsel of the stone is allowed to be taken for building purposes; and even the road, which crosses the ridge at its lowest point, where only a few bits of rock are visible, had to be carried over them by a paved causeway.

Goverdhun is now in British territory, though it formerly belonged to the Rajah of Bhurtpore, who still possesses there a small bungalow within an enclosure, where are two so-called *chuttrees*, or cenotaphs, to the memory of the great-grandfather and the grandfather of the present ruler, who is himself building one to his father's memory. These *chuttrees* are both executed in the finest Muttra stonework, and stand in a garden, each on a double stone platform. A second, and smaller one, with cupolas at each corner, which have domes supported on slender shafts, rises above the first platform. In the centre of each of the sides of the upper part is an elegant little pavilion, with lattice-work of pierced stone: the ceilings of these are painted in small compartments, with representations of English gentlemen and native sahibs driving out, and occupied at home or in the chase. In the centre of the upper platform is a square domed pavilion of considerable size; on its interior walls are depicted various incidents in the life of the late rajah. In the middle of the floor of all these pavilions is a large square piece of marble, on which are sculptured the soles of the feet of Vishnu; also a shell, a serpent coiled up, a rosary, a water-bottle, a lotus flower, the sun, the moon; and in the largest pavilion, in addition to these, there is a shield and a curved scimitar.

At Goverdhun there is also a large tank, having fine masonry on three sides, the fourth being formed by the stones of the sacred hill. Near this tank is the only old building now remaining, the temple of Hari-Deva, built of red sandstone, the foundations being of rough limestone. It was erected during Akbar's reign by Rajah Bhagawán Das of Amber, and is about 68 feet in length by 20 in width, the choir being 20 feet square, and the sacrarium beyond about the same size as this last. The nave has five arches, with a clerestory above; and the cornice is decorated with heads of elephants and sea monsters. It possessed originally a double stone roof, —the outer one a high-pitched gable, and the inner one what seems to have been an arched ceiling. The roofing of the interior was almost flat in the centre, but deeply coved at the sides.

Bhagawán Das was the father of Rajah Man Singh, who built the old temple at Bindrabun already described. Bhagawán's father, who was called Bihari Mull, was the first Rajput who attached himself to the court of a Mohammedan conqueror. Bhagawán Das saved Akbar's life at the battle of Sarnal, and was afterwards made governor of the Punjaub. His daughter married Prince Selim, afterwards known as the Emperor Jehangir.

In the year 1872 the roof of the nave of the Hari-Deva temple (which had till then been perfect) began to give way, and before anything was decided respecting its restoration, the whole had fallen in except one compartment, which would have served as a guide for the renewal of the rest. The Government had it examined, and an estimate was made of the probable cost of the repairs, after which apparently six months were suffered to elapse, and no orders were received to commence the work. In this interim a local native merchant came forward and offered to restore the roof at his own cost. All he did was to demolish the small portion that yet remained of the old roof, break down also some of the cornice, and throw rough wooden beams across the whole, which will render the building weather-tight for a few years: all that was unique has ceased to exist.

About four miles beyond Goverdhun we entered the Rajah of Bhurtpore's territory, and drove on to Deeg, four miles further, where we were lodged in the rajah's palace, and became his guests for the time being. The palace is just outside the fort, and is within an enormous quadrangle, laid out in gardens, intersected with causeways of stone, with numerous fountains in the intermediate spaces. There are various distinct pavilions in this enclosure; the one which we occupied a portion of is very large, and is called the Gopal Bhuwan; the Sooruj Bhuwan, which faces it, is all of white marble. At another part of the garden is the Nund Bhuwan, which the rajah uses as his hall of audience; this last is a very fine building. Besides these, there is a semi-sacred range of buildings, dedicated to Krishna and Nund, his foster-father; also a large reservoir with bathing ghâts. The water is well stocked with fish.

The whole of these buildings were erected about one hundred and fifty years ago by Sooruj Mull, the main founder of the Bhurtpore family, and are all as perfect as if just completed by the stone-mason. The peculiarity in their construction which struck us most were the eaves, which are double: the upper ones being an extension of the flat roof, were supported on brackets; the lower ones were sloping, supported in the same manner, and projected some distance beyond the upper eaves.

These pavilions, taken as a whole, may well vie with those of Akbar's palace at Futtehpore Sikri, though the material used at Deeg is white, instead of red sandstone as there; and these white buildings have more of a Mohammedan than of a Hindú character in their decorations. The buildings at Deeg are perhaps, on the whole, as highly finished as those at Futtehpore Sikri, but, being of a later date, they are less pure in style, and their construction is less massive, but more elegant. At neither place was wood employed in any part, though the hall of audience has *now* a plain, flat, rough wooden ceiling, with iron girders. Fergusson, in his work on 'Indian Architecture,' says "the whole is roofed with stone except the central part, which, after being contracted by a bold cove, is roofed with a flat ceiling of timber exquisitely carved. This wooden ceiling seems to have been considered a defect, nothing but stone being used in any other part of the palace."

We remained two nights at Deeg. During our stay,

the rajah arriving there on his return from the races at Agra, my husband paid him a visit in order to thank him personally for our hospitable reception. One of the rajah's carriages then conveyed us to Bhurtpore, about 21 miles distant, where we took the railway and went on to Jeypore, only 115 miles, but a tedious journey of eleven hours.

CHAPTER XV.

JEYPORE—AMBER THE OLD CAPITAL OF THAT STATE—AJMERE—MAYO COLLEGE FOR NATIVE CHIEFS—MOSQUE SAID TO HAVE BEEN BUILT IN TWO DAYS AND A HALF—MOHAMMEDAN MOSQUE, ITS RICH FOUNDATION—ULWAR—HINDÚ REVERENCE FOR THE PEEPUL-TREE—RAJAH'S PALACE AT ULWAR.

JEYPORE, one of the Rajputana states, is in many respects very advanced and enlightened. It has a college where we were told 800 boys were learning English. A school of art was also established there in 1866; young lads are taught drawing from the round, gold and silver work, die sinking, likewise gold and other embroidery. The public gardens of Jeypore are very large, tastefully laid out, and well kept up, and contain a large aviary, with living specimens of many of the small birds belonging to the plains of India, some of them having very brilliant plumage; there are also numerous parrots, monkeys, &c. The present Maharajah has introduced gas into his capital.

Jeypore dates from about 1728, at which time the seat of government was removed there from Amber. This town was built by Jey-Singh, the most famous astronomer India has produced in modern times. He set up astronomical instruments at Jeypore, Delhi, Benares, and Muttra; but I believe the three first named only are still in existence. It is singular to see what a leaning towards imitation and adaptation runs through the family of the rulers of this state. Thus as Man Singh's temple at Bindrabun is an adaptation of his friend Akbar's style at Futtehpore Sikri, in respect to the use of the arch and general grandeur of its conception, and as the palace at Amber is, in many of its details, an imitation of some of the later work in the fort at Agra, so Jey-Singh would appear to have employed an Italian architect to build Jeypore. This tendency to copy certain of the externals of European civilisation is very marked in the present representative of the family.

The whole of this town is built in a quaintly fanciful style—it looks so unreal, and so unsuited to everyday life, and gives one the idea of having been designed by a theatrical scene-painter. The outsides of the houses are all of stucco, painted in pink and white; below are small shops, inhabited by the poorest handicraftsmen; and the second storey is in most instances merely a sham, being simply a wall with openings in it, affording the women a view of the street from the tops of their houses, on which they can sit and see without being seen. The Maharajah's palace is in the same style—within all is stucco, with wall decorations in brilliant or rather glaring colours.

Amber, the old capital of this state, was founded in 1592 by Rajah Man Singh,—the same who built the temple at Bindrabun. It is situated in a valley about four or five miles from the present town of Jeypore; strong fortifications almost surround it. The palace, which is itself placed on a hill, has other and still higher hills round it and overlooking it; these seem thrown about in wild confusion. From the roof of the upper part of this building Jeypore and its fort are visible through a break in the hills, and towards the north another peep of the country beyond is also obtained. Nestling at the foot of the palace hill is a lake, with two walled gardens on its margin. At Amber the greater part of the interior decoration is also of stucco, but in infinitely better taste, and much higher style of art, than at Jeypore. Many of the designs are almost counterparts of those in the Shish Mehal, and other parts of Shah Jehan's palace in the fort at Agra. One detached building is entirely of white marble, and consists of a corridor supported on pillars, and going round three sides of a central hall, which is about 30 by 18 feet. Behind this, again, is a smaller chamber, with two small octagon rooms opening out of it. All these chambers are panelled with white marble up to a height of about four feet from the ground; each panel is bordered with an inlaid design in black marble, and has bases of flowers in the centre carved in *basso-rilievo* in white marble. Above this level the walls are covered with small recesses, each having a cup or a vase represented upon it in slightly convex glass of various colours. The ceilings are all very much coved, and are covered with a delicate flower-pattern in white stucco, the interstices in the design being filled up with small pieces of looking-glass.

Over the three smaller chambers at the back of this building there is a small pavilion corresponding with these in size, and on various parts of the roof of other portions of the palace there are numerous small pavilions in the same style but less highly decorated. At a lower level, and in a different part of this group of buildings, is the Dewan-i-Khas, or hall of audience, placed in a courtyard and open to the north, no doubt, for the sake of the view. Here, as elsewhere, the Dewan-i-Khas is a large open hall, supported on pillars. In this case there is a well-proportioned coved stone roof, covering a space in the centre about 42 feet by 25; and colonnades all round this, about 10 feet in width. This building has been originally of red sandstone. The pillars, two of which are in their pristine state, have been richly carved in the Hindú style, but afterwards covered over with plaster to represent the ordinary twelve-sided Mohammedan ones, thus making them resemble the white marble columns of the centre part. The capitals of all the pillars have the Hindú bracket form, and each is ornamented with the head of an elephant, which has a lotus-flower hanging from its mouth. On a cornice running round the outside of the building are carved bulls, Brahmin geese, and elephants fighting.

In a portion of this same courtyard, and facing the Dewan-i-Khas, there are some red-sandstone pillars of a very rude character, which may possibly be of an older date than those just described. Generally speaking, at Amber very little old Hindú work is to be found; its architect seems to have indulged in mirrors and bright colours as Akbar never ventured to do. You there see three styles exhibited: that of Akbar, of his immediate successors, and also the stucco-work, which was the direct precursor of the still more debased form now seen at Jeypore.

I have omitted to mention that there is a small Hindú temple, dedicated to Durga, in one part of the palace. Hearing a sound like the clashing of cymbals, I went to look, and I saw a number of men, women, and children, all prostrate in front of this goddess, before whom a brass lamp of curious workmanship, with many wicks, was burning. The worship lasted only a very short time: all rose, the lamp was removed, and handed to each one, who passed his hands over the flames, and then, touching his forehead, seemed to say a prayer.

From Jeypore we took the rail again, and went on to Ajmere, which is the winter headquarters of the Governor-General's agent for the Rajputana states, nineteen in number, including large and small. This official resides in the summer at Mount Aboo. Rajputana is almost the only part of Hindostán which held its own against the Patáns and Moghuls, though the former of these have left their mark in a mosque, to make which they used and adapted the materials of an old Jaina temple.

The Rajputs have always been a very warlike people; and this, together with the hilly and barren nature of the country, no doubt prevented permanent occupation by invading forces. The rainfall generally is very small —about twenty-three inches annually, and very much less than this on the north-western side of the Aravelli Mountains. At Ajmere, and also at Jeypore, owing to this circumstance, they only obtain summer, or wet weather, crops. Part of the Jeypore district is a rich loam; but much of it is pure sand, as is also a good deal of the country round Ajmere.

The first stone of the Mayo College, at the latter place, was laid a short time before our visit. This institution is destined to promote the education of the upper class of natives, and will contain a lecture-hall, class-rooms, &c., and form a centre for various detached houses, each of which will belong to, and be occupied by, the boys of its own state.

We went over the Ajmere house, and there, as in all the others, each lad has his separate bedroom, with its iron cot, writing-table, and chest for clothes. The boys are taught to ride, and go in for cricket, lawn-tennis, and other English games. The principal of the college is an English military man; various other gentlemen assist him, all living in houses near. At that time there were only forty boys, but it had only been established two years, so the numbers will probably increase considerably in time. In the Ajmere house, when I saw it, all the pupils were the sons of Thakurs, who are nobles answering somewhat to the chiefs of our Scottish clans, and owe allegiance to their own princes, of whom, according to Tavernier, who spent some time at the court of Shah Jehan, there were formerly four, a certain kind of feudal service being exacted from them. In Rajputana the Thakurs date from the time of the Patán conquest of Upper India. The Rajputs, being driven out from thence, came with their followers and took possession of the best portions of this hilly district, driving back the aboriginal inhabitants; and, as in Scotland, each man took the name of his chief.

It is little more than eight years since the greater part of Rajputana has been brought into anything like order. This has been principally effected by enlisting into our army the boldest and most enterprising men amongst the aboriginal tribes, the most important of which are the Bheels and the Mhairs. These help to keep their own friends in order, and thus three or four native regiments have been formed. On looking at the map, our territory of Ajmere appears like a little island in the midst of a large sea of native states; but the fact is, it is the highest land in Rajputana, and, in a military sense, commands it. For this reason, no doubt, the Mohammedans seized it immediately after their conquest of

Delhi. The Mahrattas also held it when they were the dominant power. We took it from Scindia, and hold it as the key of our position.

When we were there, the railway had only been opened two years; but Ajmere must in time become one of the great railway centres of India. Ajmere was conquered by the first Mohammedan invaders of India, and the mosque, to which I have already alluded, was built about the year A.D. 1200,—at any rate it is known to have been finished by Altumsh, the second of the Patán slave-kings, between the years 1211 and 1236 A.D.; and the Jaina temple which was made use of is probably a couple of centuries older. According to tradition, this mosque was built in two days and a half, hence its present name Arhai-din-ka-Jhomphra; but probably this only allowed time to knock off the heads of the figures on the columns, and to destroy whatever symbols they may have found of the former worship.

The Patáns erected a screen of seven arches, covered with the richest Arabesque work, joined to Arabic inscriptions in the style of the mosque at the Kutb, near Delhi, built at the same period. At the top of the central arch of the screen are the bases of two minarets, fluted in the style of one portion of the Kutb: these have either fallen down, or may possibly have never been completed. Behind this screen are the remains of a temple, originally built in the richest Jaina style, with innumerable columns. Some of those at the north end, the roof of that part, and also of that nearest to the screen, would appear to be very inferior Mussulman imitations of the old work. There have been formerly five Hindú, or horizontal, domes to this temple, each course of stone in these domes overlapping the preceding one, so that there is no outward thrust. One has entirely disappeared; the centre one was restored with plain stones about eight years before our visit, but three are still tolerably perfect. The pillars which we supposed to have belonged to the original temple are all carved in patterns forming horizontal lines up to the very top, thus somewhat approaching the Chalukian style. The ceilings of the square spaces between each four pillars are all of them carved more or less,—some have exquisite designs upon them, the lotus-flower generally forming the basis, and being treated in various ways.

Both the Mussulman and Hindú portions of this building are beautiful in themselves: in no part of it are there true arches, but the form of the arch in the Mussulman part is given by stones laid upon and projecting beyond each other till they meet in the centre, and thus naturally acquire a pointed form. This mosque was in a very ruined state a few years ago, and had, I believe, long been in disuse as a place of worship. When we saw it, works were in progress to protect what was still intact; and it was intended to collect all the stones and fragments with any carving upon them, and, as far as possible, arrange and place these so as to preserve them.

There is a mosque at present in use at Ajmere which is said to have been built by Shah Jehan, and consists of a considerable pile of buildings having more than one large courtyard. A rich foundation is attached to this mosque, which maintains a great number of attendants. All the buildings are of white marble, with the exception of the entrance archway, which is built of stone. Close to this gateway was a large open hall, supported on columns, and having sloping caves made of great slabs of marble. This hall is of an oblong form, with a dome in the centre.

The mosque proper stands within an inner raised court, with a marble balustrade all round it, and is also of white marble, but has no carving about it—a little inlaid work in black marble being its only decoration. Beyond this, again, and built of the same material, is the tomb of a Mussulman saint—a Haidji, or one who has made a pilgrimage to Mecca. In another court we were shown two enormous caldrons made of plates of iron riveted together, and so arranged that a fire can be lighted beneath them.

During the annual fair, and apparently at other times also, when a rich Mohammedan is seized by a generous impulse with a wish to give a feast to his poorer brethren, these caldrons are filled with rice, *ghi* (or clarified butter), and other condiments, and the contents when prepared are distributed around. The attendants told us that each of these vessels would hold about 1000 lb. of rice; and that, had we remained a few days longer in the place, we could have witnessed this cookery on a large scale, as a fair would take place a week later, to which people would flock from all parts.

On leaving Ajmere we went to Ulwar, to stay a few days with our friend the political agent there. Ulwar is situated in one of the prettiest parts of Rajputana, though, owing to the long drought from which that country had then been suffering in common with so many other parts of India, we did not see it to advantage, as the authorities had been forced to allow the people to cut away all the branches from the trees as fodder for their cattle.

The state of Ulwar was, in the old times, it appears,

more dependent upon the emperors of Delhi than the rest, its rulers being at that period more like governors than independent princes. In March 1878, when we were there, the rajah had only come of age a few months previously and taken the reins of government into his own hands; but before that, during the incapacity of the late rajah and the minority of the present one, his estate had been well administered, and a heavy debt cleared off which had been left by his predecessor. Some new bazaars were built during this period; and the following curious anecdote was related to us in connection with them: The then political agent wished to plant an avenue of trees on either side of the road in front of the shops, for the purpose of giving shade, and had decided to put in peepul-trees, which are considered sacred by the Hindús; but the *bunniahs* (or native shopkeepers), one and all, declared that if this were done they would not take the shops; and when pressed for a reason, replied, "It was because they could not tell untruths or swear falsely under their shade;" adding, "and how can we carry on business otherwise?" The force of this argument seems to have been acknowledged, as the point was yielded, and other trees have been planted instead.

A few days later, when we were at Delhi, I had an opportunity of assuring myself of the correctness of this anecdote. A Hindú merchant brought some goods for sale to the bungalow where we were staying. His wares being very dear, I said to him, "Would you ask so much if you were standing under a peepul-tree?" He replied, "No." I rejoined, "Suppose yourself in that position, and tell me what, under those circumstances, would be the price of the article I require?" The merchant at once named a lower, and I believe a correct, sum.

A good Hindú when on a journey, if he sees a peepul-tree by the roadside, takes off his shoes, walks round it from left to right, and repeats the following sentences: "The roots are Brumha, the bark Vishnu, the branches are the Mahadevas; in the bark lives the Ganges; the leaves are the minor deities. Hail to thee, king of trees!"

The Rajah of Ulwar has a sort of summer palace in the centre of a large walled garden, part of which is laid out with flowers, and the rest planted with fruit-trees. The palace, which is in the native city, is about a mile beyond this, and has a grand background of hills behind it. Some part of the palace was built about forty years ago only, and resembles a little in style the palace at Deeg, in the double eaves of the buildings: some of the same forms are also preserved in the numerous small balconies with coved roofs surmounted by gilt pinnacles. At one end of the courtyard is a raised platform; opening out of this is the great hall, where durbars are held. At the back of the durbar chamber, and on a higher level, is a small but very prettily decorated and well-proportioned room. I should have much liked to have seen this well lit up. The effect must be very pretty, the walls and the ceiling being almost covered with small pieces of glass having various coloured foils; on the walls there are also small mirrors arranged in various patterns. Even by daylight the effect of the reds, blues, and greens was very brilliant. On some parts of the walls were pictures representing incidents in the history of the Hindú gods: these, as we were shown in one which was being made for another room, were all carefully painted on cardboard first, and a sheet of glass laid over them.

There is a very striking view from a window at the back of this apartment: a large tank forms the foreground, on the opposite side of which is a series of small temples, and on the left hand a large *chuttree*, or cenotaph, to the memory of some former rajah. The background to this picture is formed by very rugged and wild-looking hills of a grey colour, and these, together with some of the buildings, are mirrored in the water below. The whole scene, in its still calm, looked so unlike a bit of the common world—so unreal, as seen out of that small opening—so like a stereoscopic view or a panoramic scene—that one almost expected to see it disappear, and another picture take its place.

The native town, and some of the gardens round Ulwar, are supplied with water by two channels of masonry, which were made many years ago, and communicate with the Siliser Lake, about seven miles off. At the point of the lake which is nearest to Ulwar there is a large stone dam. From the top of this there is a lovely view of the whole expanse of water, and also of a summer palace of the rajah's. The locality seems but little visited, judging from the number of water-fowl which we saw. Amongst the larger kinds were the Sarus, or *Grus Antigone*, and the pelican; there were also a great variety of smaller birds, whose names I did not know. We went some distance in a boat in order to get a better view of the whole than could be obtained from the shore. On one tiny island we saw an alligator, whose slumbers we apparently disturbed. He flopped down into the water and disappeared. In Ulwar, too, relief camps had been found necessary. We passed close to one of these on our way to Siliser, where they had made work for the poor people by setting them to bring stones and earth, and make walls to enclose a space where the rajah's young horses could be trained.

CHAPTER XVI.

THIRD VISIT TO DELHI—DESCRIPTION OF VARIOUS TOMBS IN THE NEIGHBOURHOOD—PATÁN EMPERORS OF DELHI—KUTB MINAR—IRON LÂT, OR PILLAR—TOGHLAK DYNASTY—THE CITY OF TOGHLAKABAD—S.P.G.—MISSION WORK IN DELHI.

FROM Ulwar we went direct to Delhi, reaching it on 5th March, spending altogether about ten days there and in the neighbourhood, going once more carefully over all the old buildings in the fort and elsewhere, and also spending four days at the Kutb. About two miles from Delhi, on the road to Muttra, there is a small fort, known by the name of Indraput, or the Purana Keela (or old fort). This spot is said to have been the site of the ancient city of Indraprastha. The present walls and the gates of this fort are the work of the Emperor Humaion, who is also believed to have begun the mosque which is within it—which building was afterwards completed by Shir Shah, and is a most beautiful specimen of the later Patán architecture, being erected in the year 1541 A.D. One distinctive mark of the architecture of the later Patán is that, as time progressed, they seemed to be more able to construct domes which afforded them complete satisfaction, and no longer sought to hide the exterior of them by an enormously high propylon, as at Jounpore, for instance. The domes made by the earlier Patáns were extremely flat and low: they produced a very good effect when seen from the inside, but viewed from without they added neither beauty nor dignity to their buildings. In the case of this mosque, by means of Hindú bracket pendatives, a square is made into an octagon, and this again into sixteen sides, in order to support a dome. The mosque proper consists of five halls, opening out of each other, and covered by as many domes. Exteriorly only the centre and largest dome is visible; the two on either side of this appear (as seen from the interior of the mosque) to be almost flat. The two halls on either side of these last are oblong in form, and have both of them a small dome in the centre, supported on either side by a semi-dome. In the decorations, the lotus-flower, which is the symbolical ornament most frequently introduced in Hindú buildings, is here repeated with various modifications,—the open blossom in the centre of the dome, and the buds forming a chain round the edge of some of the doorways, are the most remarkable instances. I could trace no signs of there ever having been cloisters round the courtyard of this mosque, which seemed to have been as necessary to a Jumma Musjid, or principal mosque, as the central tower was to a cathedral or minster at home. In this case there are also no minars, properly so called: a small column only has been placed on either side of the propylon, which is not of the same grand proportions as in the earlier Patán mosques. Round the arches of the three central entrances to this building, the chief decoration is an inscription, in raised Arabic characters. The middle doorway has, in addition, mosaic inlaid work, in geometric patterns, the principal colours being red, white, and black. Along the top of this mosque, and also on some of the string-courses, there are small round medallions containing the word "Allah," in Arabic characters. Just below the battlemented top there are brackets, of the regular Hindú form, supporting sloping eaves, which run the whole length of the building.

The tomb of Humaion is on the same road, about a mile beyond the Purana Keela. The road thither from Delhi passes through a regular street of tombs even more numerous than those of the Appian Way, near Rome. In fact, from the top of Humaion's tomb, the country, as far as the eye can reach—from Delhi on the one side to the Kutb on the other—appears a sea of old ruins and tombs, these last being nearly all domed and mostly of a large size, some having been originally ornamented with glazed tiles of various colours. The tomb of Humaion is situated within a large walled garden, as were all the larger Moghul tombs. Its exterior is of red sandstone, inlaid with white marble; the dome, which is of the same material, is slightly bulbous: it is said to be the first of that particular form which was ever constructed in India.

This tomb has a kind of double platform, the lower one only about four feet high, on which is a smaller one containing mortuary chambers with many tombs in each; the principal monument is in the centre of the upper platform. In the large domed hall is a single plain tomb of white marble, beneath which are the remains of Humaion. Steps lead up to a large terrace which forms the roof of the building: at the four corners are cupolas supported on shafts of a decided Hindú character. It is noticeable that in this building, wherever pillars and their capitals occur, these last have all the Hindú bracket form. This tomb may be called the earliest existing specimen of Moghul work; for though the Emperor Baber, in his autobiography, speaks of employing a great number of masons, yet none of his buildings have come down to us.

Very near Humaion's tomb, but on the opposite side of the road, is the tomb of Nizam-ud-din Aulia, a very celebrated Mohammedan saint belonging to the fraternity of the Chistís. This man during his lifetime was believed to have a knowledge of future events: even now pilgrimages are made to his tomb from all parts of India, for many natives believe that miracles are still worked there. Nizam-ud-din lived in the reign of the Patán emperor, Toghlak Shah. His tomb was begun under that dynasty, but the dome was only placed upon it during Akbar's reign; and in Shah Jehan's time the building was put into thorough repair. Within the same enclosure are many other tombs, which, no doubt, were placed there in order that their occupants might rest near this holy man. A verandah with marble columns is round the saint's tomb, and a pierced screen of white marble slabs surrounds the sarcophagus. General Sleeman, in his work, is of opinion that this Nizam-ud-din was probably the head of the Mohammedan Thugs, or assassins of India. I believe it is known that for years after his death many Thugs made yearly pilgrimages to his tomb, so it would seem to be not at all improbable that by that murderous trade the saint (?) amassed the great wealth he is known to have possessed, which enabled him to set his sovereign at defiance, and be concerned in, if not an active participator in, his murder.

The poet Khusroo's tomb stands at no great distance from that of his friend Nizam-ud-din. It is related of him that for six months he never ceased to sit and watch by the saint's grave, at the end of which time death released him from his troubles. An inscription in the outer enclosure of his tomb styles Khusroo "the sugar-tongued parrot;" and even now, after an interval of 400 years, his songs are still most popular. Khusroo was born in India, of Turki parents. On the Toghlak dynasty coming into power he rose to high honours.

In this cemetery, among a great many graves of undistinguished people, are the tombs of Mirza Jehangire, Mahommed Shah, and Jehanara Begum. The first-named was the son of Akbar the Second: his tomb, which is of exquisite workmanship, was built as late as 1832. Mirza Shah drank himself to death with Hoffmann's cherry-brandy. When General Sleeman visited him at Allahabad, he said, "This is the only liquor you Englishmen have which is worth drinking; its only fault is, that it makes one drunk too soon." But in order to prolong his enjoyment, he used to limit himself to a large glass every hour, till he became dead drunk.

Mahommed Shah's tomb has also a screen of pierced white marble round it. During his reign, in the year 1739, the Persian conqueror, Nadir Shah, invaded India, despoiled the peacock throne in the fort at Delhi, and allowed his followers to sack the city.

Jehanara Begum, to please whom her father, Shah Jehan, built the mosque near the fort at Agra, showed later on the most touching devotion to him: when Shah Jehan was deposed by his son Aurungzebe, she shared her father's life-long imprisonment, while her sister Rushanara is said to have espoused her brother's cause. Jehanara is said to have been remarkable for her wit and beauty, and to have also possessed many gentle and endearing qualities, though she seems to have hated Aurungzebe,—her warm and affectionate nature resenting most keenly his behaviour towards Shah Jehan, who died in 1665. Rushanara survived him five years, and Jehanara died at Delhi in A.D. 1681. She built this tomb for herself; it stands in a small marble court. The inscription on the headstone, which she is said to have partly composed, is to the following effect: "Let nothing but the green [grass] conceal my grave. The grass is the best covering for the tomb of the poor in spirit; the humble, the transitory Jehanara, the disciple of the holy men of Chist; the daughter of the Emperor Shah Jehan. May God illuminate his intentions."

The Jama'ath Khana Mosque is also not far from the tomb of Nizam-ud-din; it is supposed to have been built about the year 1353 A.D. by Firoz Shah Toghlak. It is of red sandstone throughout, and may be called a very fine example of Patán architecture. It is divided into three chambers; a large dome covers the central part, the side chambers have each two domes, and there is some very pretty stone lattice-work in parts of this building.

The tomb of 'Azim Khan lies to the south-east of the saint's tomb. It appeared to be a very fine specimen of the Patán inlaid work in red, white, and black; but we were unable to see the lower part, or go inside it, and could only get a view of it from some mounds near, over a high wall which surrounded it on all sides, and seemed to have no opening; but a funeral, which was going on close by, prevented us from ascertaining this positively. 'Azim Khan's original name was Shams-ud-din Mahommed, but Akbar gave him this title of honour on the occasion of his victory over Bairam Khan, near Jullunder. When Humaion was defeated by the Patáns at Kanouj, 'Azim Khan assisted that emperor to escape from the field of battle. Later on he was made Governor of the

Punjaub, and, finally, was murdered, A.D. 1566, by Adham Khan, the details of which crime will be given at length when I have to describe the buildings at the Kutb.

About twenty yards from the tomb of 'Azim Khan there is a white marble building, called the Chausat Kambah, or hall of sixty-six pillars. The only thing worthy of notice in it is its pierced marble screen; the pillars have scarcely any decoration. The remains of Mirza Aziz Kukal Khan lie within it: he was a son of 'Azim Khan, and foster-brother to the Emperor Akbar, who took charge of his fortunes after his father's death. His career was a checkered one, being raised first to posts of distinction, and suffering penal servitude at a later period when, after the death of Akbar, he joined himself to the cause of Prince Khusran against that of his father Jehangir. Mirza Aziz died at Ahmedabad, A.D. 1624, but his body was brought to Delhi and buried near the graves of his father and Nizam-ud-din.

On the road to the Kutb, and about six miles distant from the present city of Delhi, is the tomb of Safdar Jung. His real name was Abul Mansour Khan; he was the nephew and successor of Sa-adat Ali Khan, Viceroy of Oudh. Being by birth a Persian, he came to India on his uncle's invitation, who gave him his daughter in marriage. After the invasion of Nadir Shah, when order had been restored in Delhi, he became a favourite at the court, was afterwards made *wuzeer*, and the title of Safdar Jung was bestowed upon him (Safdar means hero). He had a rival in Ghazi-ud-din Khan, who at length compelled him to abandon his distinguished posts; and he ostensibly retired from public life, and lived in a hotbed of intrigue till his death, in A.D. 1753.

His mausoleum is in a garden surrounded by high walls. Over the entrance gateway, and in the centre of the north and south walls, there are apartments which are now used as rest-houses by Europeans. At each of the four corners of the garden there are octagonal towers, which have perforated red-sandstone screens. The principal entrance to the garden is a two-storeyed building. A large hall is in the centre, with a domed roof; and there are four small chambers opening out of this hall. The second storey has a balcony round it, from the roof project sloping eaves, and there are several small chambers in it. The mausoleum in some respects resembles the tomb of Humaion,—many imagine it was intended as a replica of it. It stands on a terrace or platform about 10 feet high, and 110 feet square, the tomb itself being about 60 feet square, and 90 feet high to the summit of the dome, beneath which there is a very highly finished white marble sarcophagus. Surrounding the central hall are eight chambers—four are square, and four octagonal in form—and there are apartments above corresponding with these. The dome, as seen externally, is of a bulbous form. There are marble minarets at each angle of the building, inlaid with lines and patterns in red sandstone. The four sides of the tomb are all decorated with bands of white marble, and in one part is the following inscription: "When the hero [Safdar] of the plain of valour accepted the order to leave this transitory house, the following date was given of it [his departure]. . . . May you be resident of the high heaven."

About eleven miles from Delhi is the Kutb Minar, which, together with the buildings which surround it, occupies a portion of the site of old Delhi, or the city of

Rajah Pithora, which fell into the hands of the Mohammedans in A.D. 1191. At the death of Mahommed Ghori, in 1205, the empire of Ghusnee may almost be said to have been at an end. There were still some surviving members of the house of Ghor; but those princes were unambitious men, thus, consequently, an opportunity arose for two of the imperial slaves, Ildecuz and Kutb, to divide the empire between them. By *slaves* are meant captives and young children bought by kings; therefore the word slave must not be understood in the sense in which we use it, for these persons were highly educated, for the purpose of fitting them to fill offices of state, and at one time successive slave-kings reigned in Hindostán. With Kutb—the second of the two I have mentioned—commenced the Mohammedan empire of the Patáns, or Afghans, in India. He was the favourite friend and servant of Mahommed Ghori: his name has come down to us as a brave warrior, open and liberal to his friends, and courteous to strangers. When quite a child, Kutb was brought from Turkestan to Neshapoor, and there sold by a merchant to Casi, the son of Abu, who, finding him a clever lad, sent him to school. He had already made great progress in Persian and Arabic, when, his patron dying suddenly, he was sold with the rest of his master's property, and passed into the hands of a rich merchant, who paid a large sum of money for him, and then offered him for sale to the emperor, who purchased him, and gave him the familiar name of Eibek, from his broken little finger. He soon attracted Mahommed Ghori's notice by his pleasing manners and behaviour. On the occasion of a festival at court, when a large distribution of presents had been made, Eibek, who had received both gifts and money, instead of keeping it to himself, divided his share amongst his companions. The emperor, hearing of this, asked him the reason. Eibek replied "that his wants were sufficiently supplied by his Majesty's bounty; he had therefore no desire to burden himself with superfluities, the king's favour being a sure independence."

Mahommed, much pleased with this reply, immediately gave Kutb an office near his person, and shortly after appointed him Master of the Horse. In course of time he rose to various military commands, and about the year A.D. 1192 was made Commander-in-Chief, with the title of Kutb-ud-din (or the pole-star of religion). In the following year he defeated the Jits, who were the subjects of the Prince of Narwalla, in Guzerat; and also the Prince of Benares, which latter country Mahommed Ghori took possession of without opposition. Three hundred elephants were captured from the Rajah of Benares, besides other valuable spoils. Their riders had instructions to make all the elephants kneel down simultaneously at a given signal, which they did, with the exception of one white one, whose rider was nearly killed in the attempt to make him pay homage. The emperor presented this elephant to his favourite, and wrote him a letter adopting him as his son. Kutb ever after rode this animal; when he died it pined away and died the third day.

Shortly after the conquest of Benares, news came that some of the independent Indian princes intended to unite their forces and wrest Ajmere from the Mohammedans. Kutb's troops being at the moment much dispersed, he marched against them with the small force that lay at Delhi, in order to prevent certain of them from joining the rest, but was defeated, and carried, wounded, in a litter to Ajmere. In 1202, Tittura, the chief of the opposing army, joined the forces of Narwalla and Guzerat, and sat down before Ajmere. Mahommed hearing of this, sent a large force from Ghusnee to relieve Kutb, which, on its arrival, compelled the enemy to raise the siege. Kutb then pursued and routed them with great slaughter, and after giving his troops a short respite, marched on into Guzerat, took the city of Narwalla, and then returned to Delhi by way of Ajmere. Six years afterwards he made another successful campaign, and took the cities of Calinger and Mhoba. After the murder of Mahommed Ghori, his nephew Mahmood assumed the imperial titles at Ghori, and sent all the insignia of royalty to Kutb, who had previously been made Viceroy of all the conquered provinces in India. Kutb at first was not left in undisturbed possession of his new dignities.

Ildecuz, or Eldose, as he is more generally called, another of the imperial slaves, marched an army against him from Ghusnee. After a severe struggle, Kutb repulsed his forces, pursued the flying troops as far as Ghusnee, was there crowned, and took the reins of government into his own hands. After this, the conqueror gave himself up to pleasure, till the citizens, weary of his excesses, sent privately to Eldose to acquaint him of this and entreat his return. Upon this, Eldose hurriedly and secretly equipped an expedition and advanced towards Ghusnee, taking Kutb by surprise, who, seeing that he had no chance of making a successful defence, abandoned his kingdom and retired to Lahore. On reflection, finding to what he had been brought by his own weakness and indulgence, he entirely reformed his habits, and governed with his great wisdom till his death in 1210, which was caused by a fall from his horse. His reign, properly speaking, lasted only four years, though he enjoyed all the state and dignities of a king for a space of twenty years, if one may date from the time that he took Delhi.

Kutb was succeeded by his son Aram, who, after a reign of one year, being engaged in battle with Altumsh, who was the son-in-law and adopted son of Kutb, lost the battle and his empire.

The Kutb Minar is generally believed to have been begun by Kutb, the first of the Mohammedan emperors who reigned in India. This minar, or tower, is a tapering shaft, about 234 feet in height, and divided into five storeys, being a little more than 47 feet in diameter at the base, and 9 at the summit. The interval between the commencement and completion of the building extended over a period of twenty years—viz., from A.D. 1200 to A.D. 1220. Horizontal bands of inscriptions in the Arabic character run round each storey, so that the building tells its own history. It is cased in red sandstone; some white stone or marble is introduced in the two upper storeys, each of these being furnished with a balcony. The lower storey is formed of alternate angular and semicircular flutings; in the second storey these are all semicircular; in the third, all angular; the fourth storey is round, and has no flutings; the fifth is also circular, and has bands of white marble round it.

Though this minar was begun by Kutb-ud-din Eibek, and finished by his immediate successor Altumsh, it was much injured by lightning in the reign of Firoz Shah Toghlak, as set forth in an inscription by him bearing the date of 1368 A.D., saying "that he repaired this building with great care;" and adding, "May the unknown Creator preserve this building from all dangers." Firoz Shah also added a cupola which is said to have been in the form of a harp: this was thrown down in 1803 by an earthquake and no longer exists.

About a quarter of a mile distant is the unfinished minar of Ala-ud-din Khilgi, who probably wished to make a rival one on a much larger scale: inclusive of the plinth, it measures 80 feet in height. It was begun A.D. 1311, but abandoned on the death of the king. As a native historian somewhat quaintly and tenderly puts it, "His days did not help him; the king finished his life before he could complete his work."

Kutb-ud-din Eibek began to build a mosque as soon as he had conquered old Delhi; and it is said that its cloisters were made out of the fragments of twenty-seven Hindú temples. The courtyard has, as usual, three entrances, and stands on a raised platform. The pillars are very varied in form and design, and have evidently formerly belonged to more than one building, though it is doubtful whether any of them are in their original position, for, from the absence of the arch in the early Hindú style of architecture, each single pillar could be detached from the rest, and its position changed without injury to the building. Fergusson, in his work on Indian architecture, when describing it, remarks: "It is so purely Jaina that it should have been mentioned in speaking of that style;" and he adds, "The pillars are of the same order as those used on Mount Aboo, except that at Delhi they are much richer and more elaborate. They belong probably to the eleventh or twelfth century, and are among the few specimens to be found in India that seem to be overloaded with ornament—there not being one inch of plain surface from the capital to the base." The same author observes, further on : "The history of this mosque, as told in its construction, is as curious as anything about it. It seems that the Afghan emperors had a tolerably distinct idea that pointed arches were the true form for architectural openings ; but being without science sufficient to construct them, they left the Hindú architects and builders whom they employed to follow their own devices in the mode of carrying out the form. The Hindús had, up to this time, never built arches, nor did they for centuries afterwards ; accordingly they proceeded to make the pointed opening on the same principle upon which they built their domes. They carried them up in horizontal courses as far as they could, and then closed them by slabs meeting at the top."

During the reign of Altumsh, the son-in-law of Kutb-ud-din, two wings or extensions were added to the mosque. Sultan Ala-ud-din Khilgi, who ascended the throne of Delhi in A.D. 1295, added a gateway on the southern side. The extensions built by Altumsh have also had cloisters : the southern portion of these is now the most perfect part. These cloisters would seem to have formed an outer enclosure to Kutb's mosque on the north and south at least. Just outside the eastern gateway of this part of the building there is an open colonnade of Hindú pillars, which, from their position, would appear to have had no connection with either of the mosques.

Though the Mohammedans were, as a rule, very particular in defacing or destroying any idolatrous images, yet, on some of the columns, we could distinctly trace some cross-legged figures, and in one instance the head and face were intact.

We are told that Altumsh came originally of a noble

Tartar family, and that his father Elim was a famous general. Being his father's favourite son, his brothers were envious of him, and determined to get rid of him. In order to effect their purpose, one day, when they were out hunting, they stripped him and sold him for a slave to some travelling merchants, who carried him to Bokhara, where they again sold him to some relations of the prince of that country, by whom he was given a liberal education. After his master's death he passed successively into the hands of two other merchants, and was finally carried to Ghusnee. Mahommed Ghori wished much to purchase him, having heard of his talents and good looks, but he could not agree with the merchants about his price; so Altumsh was taken back to Bókhara for a time, till Kutb, after obtaining the king's leave, bought him for 50,000 pieces of silver. Altumsh distinguished himself in various engagements, and Kutb was so pleased with his behaviour that he declared him free, and bestowed many gifts upon him. He at length rose to be Captain-General of the empire, married Kutb's daughter, and upon that king's death, as I have before stated, advanced against the capital, expelled Aram, and proclaimed himself emperor by the title of Shams-ud-din Altumsh.

The Alai Darwaza, or gateway of Ala-ud-din Khilgi, has the date of A.D. 1310 upon it. It seems as if part of the cloisters arranged by Altumsh had been knocked down to make room for it. The back wall of the cloisters is of rough-hewn greyish stone—the same material as was used for the Hindú pillars—while this gateway is of red sandstone. General Cunningham styles it "the most beautiful specimen of Patán architecture that I have seen." It has four entrances: a window of pierced red sandstone is on either side of each of these. The exterior walls are panelled, and inlaid with white marble, and have a battlemented parapet, surmounted by a dome. Inscriptions in Arabic characters form the perpendicular lines of the ornamentation: the horizontal lines are geometric patterns. In the interior, in order to reduce the square to an octagon, there are niches in each corner, composed of five horse-shoe arches, each smaller than the other, made on the principle of the true arch. I should think they must be the earliest instances of the arch in the neighbourhood of Delhi.

Before leaving this group of buildings, I must not omit to notice the iron *lát*, or pillar, which stands in front of the mosque of Kutb-ud-din. It was erected as a triumphal column by a king of Delhi, whose name has been variously stated as Rajah Dáva, Anang Pal, and Chandra. Fergusson says: "My own conviction is that it belongs to one of the Chandra rajahs of the Gupta dynasty—consequently to either A.D. 363 or A.D. 400."

The capital of the iron pillar is entire, and of the reeded or Persian form. Upon this is a square block, forming the summit, on which was probably placed some emblem of Vishnu, who is mentioned in the inscription; but if such emblem or statue there were, it has now disappeared. The inverted reeded cup-like form of this capital exactly resembles what now remains of the capital of the *lát*, or stone pillar, at Bithri—a place situated about half-way between Ghazipore and Benares. The diameter of the iron pillar at the Kutb is over 16 inches at the base, and at the capital, which is 3½ feet high, rather more than 12 inches, and it now stands 22 feet above the ground. In 1871 General Cunningham caused excavations to be made round it in order to ascertain how much of it was underground. It was found to be shaped at the bottom like a flat turnip; and it rested upon eight pieces of iron, which are fixed with lead into blocks of stone, equidistant from each other. This pillar has been variously described as being of mixed metal—brass, or bronze; but Dr Murray Thompson, who analysed a small bit for General Cunningham, was of opinion that it is composed of pure malleable iron. The people of that day may have possessed some secret in preparing iron with which we are unacquainted. This column has now stood for many centuries exposed to the heavy Indian rains, and to various changes of temperature, and yet it is not rusted or corroded in the slightest degree.

The natives say that two unsuccessful attempts have been made to destroy this pillar: Nadir Shah, they relate, caused the earth to be removed from its foundations. The workmen, however, could not proceed: the serpent whom they suppose resides beneath it, shook his head, and a violent earthquake ensued. The Mahrattas, also, they affirm, brought heavy cannon to bear upon it, but these did no damage beyond leaving a mark. There are many curious legends extant regarding it, one of which is, that the rajah who erected it was told that this pillar, having been firmly driven into the head of Sahes-Nág, the serpent-king, his empire would be as permanent as this pillar. The rajah, however, disbelieving this, and being desirous to test a prophecy of such importance to his dynasty, had it taken up, when, to the horror of all, the foot of the pillar was found to be wet with the serpent's blood. All attempts to fix the pillar again, failed: it remained loose (*dhîla*) in the ground, whence the name Delhi, and the serpent was gone. This story is told in various ways, with additions and alterations, but Sahes-Nág figures in all the versions.

The tomb of Shams-ud-din Altumsh, who was the most famous of the slave-kings of Delhi, is close to the mosque, being just behind its north-west corner, and almost touching the present roadway. Some say that this tomb was built by Altumsh himself; others attribute it to two of his children. General Cunningham observes that it is of the same date as the Kutb Minar; he also seems to be of opinion that it was originally covered by an overlapping Hindú dome. It is said to be the oldest authentic Mohammedan tomb in India: its arches are all formed on the Hindú principle, which I have already described. Here, as in the 'Alai Darwaza, the square is formed into an octagon by niches at the four corners, but in this instance there is only *one* arch at each corner: a half dome is thus formed within this space, constructed by each course of stone-work resting upon and overlapping the preceding one. The walls of the interior are quite plain up to a height of about eleven feet; but they have evidently had a coating of stucco. In one corner I could trace on this the remains of a geometric pattern of a green colour. The whole of the walls above this level are most richly carved in red sandstone, with geometric patterns in horizontal lines; the Buddhist bell ornament, and also the lotus, are introduced in the decorations.

There is also another mosque, to the south of these buildings, and distant perhaps about half a mile, of which I could find no account or description in General Cunningham's Archæological Report, or in the book lately published by Mr Carr Stephen. This mosque is flanked on the north by a small courtyard containing several tombs: one of these is in a covered building, which has been used as a mosque as well, for it has the recess, or *kiblah*, on its western side. Externally this little building has originally had tile decoration in three shades of blue, and within it is very beautifully decorated with raised plaster-work in minute patterns, painted in various colours: this is still in a very fair state of preservation. Here too, as in many of the tombs of that period, the square has been made into an octagon, and then into a circle by cutting off the corners. The roof is flat in the interior, being slightly raised by a cornice which runs all round. The mosque is of considerable size, but very plain, both within and without, being built of rubble and cased with hewn stone. It consisted of five halls. My impression, on examining it closely, was that the interior had at some time or other either been stripped of all its decorative work, or—what was perhaps more probable—had never been finished, as the four lateral halls (two on either side of the larger or central one) have no stone casing on their walls, but are entirely of rough rubble stone, from a height of seven feet from the ground, though all was prepared for the outer stonework,—for the form of the bracket pendatives in the upper corners of each hall may be clearly traced.

I have already had occasion to speak of Adham Khan in describing the buildings near the tomb of that great saint (but, I fear, consummate rogue), Nizam-ud-din; but a detailed account of him belongs more properly to the place where we find his tomb. This monument stands at the south-western corner of the citadel of the capital of Rajah Pithora. Adham Khan appears to have been a turbulent man, who more than once incurred the displeasure of the emperor. At length, at the instigation of

M'unim Khan, a minister and influential man at the court of Akbar, he one day suddenly entered the audience-hall at Agra and struck 'Azim Khan (or the Atgah, as he is sometimes called) with his dagger, and then told one of his companions to despatch him with his sword. The emperor could not allow the murder of his foster-father to go unpunished, perpetrated as it was almost in his very presence, though Adham Khan, trusting in the favour and kindness usually shown him by the emperor, went out and stood at the door of the harem. Akbar rushed out, sword in hand, ordered the assassin to be bound hand and foot, and then to be thrown over the parapet, which was done; after which, according to one author, a spark of life being still left in him, the emperor commanded him to be hurled over a second time. Adham Khan's mother, Maham Ankah, hearing something of the broil, but not knowing what had happened to her son, though herself ill at the time, went from Delhi to Agra. On seeing her, Akbar said, "He has killed my foster-father, and I have taken his life." "Your Majesty has done well," she replied, and left the hall; but forty days afterwards she died of grief, and was buried near her son at Delhi, in a tomb which Akbar built for this purpose: we may therefore conclude that it was begun A.D. 1566, the year of 'Azim Khan's and Adham Khan's death.

This tomb is placed on an octagonal platform about seventeen feet above the level of the road; on this is a colonnade of the same form, supported on massive pillars, forming arches and surrounding the central hall, which is also eight-sided, and has a fine domed roof. The sarcophagus has been removed into the colonnade, and a part of this enclosed to form bedrooms. Some furniture has also been placed in the building, so that any one bringing their own servants and supplies can inhabit it by paying the same fees as required at a *dák* bungalow.

Whilst we were staying at the Kutb we devoted one afternoon to seeing the fort of Toghlakabad, situated about four miles to the east, the road to it from the former place being about the roughest and worst cross-country one I have ever seen, even in India. Our only way of going thither was to hire a small country vehicle without springs, and drawn by a couple of bullocks. This cart—for I cannot dignify it with the name of a carriage—is very commonly used by the natives, and is not unlike an old-fashioned four-post bedstead, with a canopy and curtains all round, placed on two wheels, only that this conveyance would be about of suitable dimensions for the bed of a good-sized doll. The bullock-driver sits astride on the pole to which the oxen are yoked, making himself a saddle with a sort of wadded quilt. It is astonishing in what a small space the natives of India, both men and women, contrive to sit. I have myself often seen at least four women and a couple of children sitting in a similar cart, who all seemed perfectly at their ease, though my husband and I, being both of us tall, found it a tight fit with our English mode of sitting. There is hardly any iron about these vehicles, the wheels being of wood; and the whole concern is kept together by a most wonderful and complicated arrangement of cords and ropes. The absence of springs to this cart, and the bad road we had to pass over, made our seat anything but a bed of rose-leaves; but the sight of the fort amply repaid us for the inconvenience.

Toghlakabad is about twelve miles south of the modern

Delhi, and was the fourth city which became in succession the capital,—the first being old Delhi, or Kila Raj Pithora; the second Kilokheri, or Naid Shahr, on the banks of the Jumna; the third Siri, about six miles distant from the present Delhi, in the direction of the Kutb. Ghiyás-ud-din Toghlak, the first of the dynasty, was the son of a slave. His son, Sultan Muhammad, was the most accomplished prince of his age. He made expeditions against both Persia and China, but was unsuccessful. His conduct in later life was such that only the plea of insanity could justify it. He used to assemble his army as if for a great hunt, and the troops gradually closing towards a given centre, all within that area were massacred. This was more than once repeated: many of the inhabitants of Kanouj were slaughtered in this manner. None of his whims caused so much distress and misery as that of moving his capital from Delhi to Deogiri (the present Dowlátabád). Twice the people were allowed to return, and twice made to leave it again. His finances being very much involved, and having heard that they used paper money in China, he introduced it, giving copper tokens for paper. But as foreign merchants refused to take these notes, all was confusion and distress. Upon the death of Muhammad in 1351, Firoz-ud-din, his cousin, who is commonly known as Firoz Shah, was raised to the throne.

According to a native historian, Toghlakabad was commenced A.D. 1321, and finished two years later. The fort has a circuit of nearly four miles. The walls slope rapidly inwards; some of the bastions are still in a fair state of preservation. The whole has a massive appearance, though in parts it is rugged and much broken, so that, when viewing it from a distance, we thought it was the ridge of a hill, and that we must have mistaken the position of the fort. The whole of the interior is now in such a ruinous condition that it is difficult, if not impossible, to make out the ground plan or the situation of the buildings which were originally within it; but there are still some underground apartments on a level with large wells or water-tanks which are faced with stone. The emperor is supposed to have inhabited eight circular rooms in the citadel, with apertures in the roof for the admittance of light.

The citadel is believed to have had three gates, and was difficult of approach; and at its foot was a large tank, from which the garrison could be supplied. The upper part of the fort seemed a mass of ruined houses and fragments of masonry. Though time did not suffice for us to examine it carefully, yet from a high point to which we climbed no entire building could I see, except one small one, which had either originally been a mosque or had since been converted to that use. Outside the western gate by which we entered is a long stone causeway supported on arches, but now much out of repair. It leads to what may be called a fortified outpost to the fort, and is a complete fortress, having bastions at intervals and battlements all round, formed of loose stones of large size, with spaces between each. No doubt they were thus arranged in order that they might be used as missiles to hurl down upon an attacking force. There are small loop-holes at intervals in the outer walls, and an arched passage runs all round the inside of them, so that the besieged would be protected when firing upon an enemy.

Within this little fortress is a massive structure of red sandstone, which is turned obliquely to the outer walls, probably with the view of making its western side point towards Mecca, and thus render it a mosque as well as a tomb. This building is of a considerable size at the base, and narrows gradually till it is crowned by a white marble dome. A band of the same material is carried round it about half-way up, and slabs of white marble are introduced in other parts. It seemed in its massive grandeur a fit resting-place for the remains of a great warrior like Toghlak Shah. His tomb, and that of his son, Muhammad Shah, who succeeded him, are side by side.

When on his way back to Delhi, A.D. 1325, after a successful invasion of Bengal, Toghlak Shah was told that certain wise men and astrologers had prophesied that he would never see Delhi again—the chief amongst these being that so-called saint, but in reality arch-rogue, Nizam-ud-din Aulia, who had long been at enmity with him, and in league with his son Muhammad Shah. Toghlak said, "Let me only reach Delhi, and this fiend-priest shall be humbled." Nizam-ud-din's friends hearing of this threat, implored him to leave the capital; but all he said was, "Delhi is still far off."

Arrived at a distance of about six miles from Delhi, Toghlak Shah was lodged in a temporary wooden palace, which his son had caused to be built in three days, it being given out that his intention was to rest there, and the following day make a triumphal entry into his capital. The popular account is, that this wooden building had been so arranged as to fall down with a crash when the elephants touched it at a certain part. The sultan stayed there; and after he had feasted the people, his eldest son and heir-apparent asked leave to parade the elephants before him. The emperor's favourite son, Mahmúd, was seated by his side, and when the elephants passed by, the building fell down upon them both. Muhammad, the heir, then called for shovels and pickaxes to dig out his father and brother; but, by a sign, delayed their arrival for some time, till at sunset the sultan was taken out dead, having bent over his son in order to save him. Others, again, maintain that Toghlak Shah was taken out alive, and an end made of him, the body being transported at night to the tomb he had built for himself at Toghlakabad and there buried.

Muhammad Shah, who then became sultan, was the most inhuman and tyrannical of all the Patán sovereigns of India: of this I have already given some examples. His cruelties were, many of them, witnessed by his cousin and successor Firoz Toghlak, who, when he came to the throne, sought by a most singular method to cancel some of his predecessor's sins. The words of Firoz himself, as related by Ferishta, the Persian historian, who took them from an inscription on a large mosque at Firozabad, are as follows: "I have also taken pains to discover the surviving relations of all persons who suffered from the wrath of my late lord and master, Muhammad Toghlak, and having pensioned and provided for them, have caused them to grant their full pardon and forgiveness to that prince in the presence of the holy and learned men of this age, whose signatures and seals as witnesses are affixed to the documents, the whole of which, as far as lies in my power, have been procured and put into a box and deposited in the vault in which Muhammad Toghlak is entombed." These papers were to act as vouchers of free pardon from all whom the dead man had deprived of a nose, a limb, or of sight, &c.; and were placed near him in order that he might pick them up at the last day; for, according to the Mohammedan sacred laws, every offence has a double aspect—in its relation first to GOD, and then to man; in the latter case, pardon given by the injured one is believed to reduce some portion of its punishment. These documents would be interesting to read; they are probably still quite safe within the sarcophagus, which is in good order, and appears never to have been disturbed.

Toghlakabad formerly belonged to the principality of Balabgurh, but the British Government annexed it in 1857, on account of the complicity of its rajah in the rebellion at that period. It is now an insignificant Gujar village. The Gujars are a distinct tribe of people, belonging principally to the Punjaub, who possess cattle, and wander with them in the summer and autumn in search of pasturage. Whilst we were in Kashmir we saw some of these people at a place called Killan, 9000 feet above the sea; and as the season advanced we were told they would go down and take possession of the huts which the English had erected and vacated at Gulmurg, about 2000 feet lower down, till the weather forced them to move again.

Nizam-ud-din's prophecy respecting Toghlakabad has thus come true. He said of it, "Thou shalt either be inhabitated by Gujars, or be abandoned."

After leaving the Kutb we stayed two or three days with a friend in Delhi, and I had an opportunity of hearing and seeing somewhat of the S.P.G. work in their St Stephen's Mission there. The converts they make are principally, if not entirely, Hindús. A Mohammedan rarely becomes a Christian. The Hindús they gain over are, for the most part, of the lowest caste—such as *chumárs*, or workers in leather. These, when they embrace Christianity, do not sink or lose caste in the eyes of their relations or equals. Attached to the mission is a German lady, who has regularly studied medicine and surgery, and passed the necessary examinations. She of course is admitted into both Mohammedan and Hindú houses, where a medical man would not be allowed to enter—though she told me that frequently she is not sent for till some of their ignorant old women have resorted to all kinds of means and nostrums, so that very often she arrives too late to save the patient's life. This lady attends daily from twelve till two in her dispensary, giving advice and medicine to women and children, who come in considerable numbers to consult her. Books are kept in which the caste, name, and age of each applicant are entered, their complaints, and what remedies have been given. These are from time to time submitted to the medical authorities.

The number of converts made at Delhi is said to be very considerable. The missionaries are careful to hold out no temporary advantages as a bribe for their conversion, therefore it may fairly be assumed that their profession of Christianity is genuine.

CHAPTER XVII.

MEERUT—RED-SANDSTONE TOMB THERE—SIKH FESTIVAL OF THE NEW YEAR AT AMRITSAR—BAPTISM OF SIKHS—REQUIREMENTS OF THEIR RELIGION—ORIGIN OF CITY AT AMRITSAR—GOLDEN TEMPLE—HINDÚ FESTIVAL OF THE DIWALI.

LEAVING Delhi on the 18th of March, we went on to Meerut to stay with other friends there. Though the column of Asoka, now on the ridge at Delhi, but originally brought from Meerut, shows that this latter place was most probably the site of an ancient city as long ago as 250 B.C., yet no vestige of this now remains. The only old building we could find, or hear of, was a tomb just outside the present native city. It belonged, we believed, to the Moghul period, though some work in the Patán style has been used in the interior decorations. This monument stands on a platform about nine feet in height. At the four corners and centre of its sides have been projecting cupolas; the pedestals which supported their shafts are still remaining. A colonnade has been carried all round the tomb; a small portion of it is still intact, and has been propped up with masonry to preserve it, so that one can clearly see that there has been a small dome between each four pillars of the colonnade. Every arch of the colonnade and of the tomb itself is formed of two large, almost triangular, stones meeting in the centre; those in the colonnade have been richly carved. Projecting from it are some brackets of the Hindú form, which no doubt originally supported sloping eaves. The whole building is of red sandstone. The domes, both of the roof itself and those belonging to the colonnade, have been of rubble, plastered without, and faced with red sandstone within. The exterior of this building is covered with rich carving, which is not deeply cut, and in that respect resembles the Muttra work.

Outside, and near the ground-level, are carved water-vessels in *basso-rilievo*, by which it would appear that it was used as a place of feasting during the lifetime of its founder. Within it is about thirty feet square, and highly decorated. Up to the height of the top of the doorways there is inlaid work in white marble, in the Patán style, as seen in the mosque at the Purana Keela and other buildings near Delhi. On the walls at the upper part near the dome are vases of flowers carved in red sandstone. These are not unlike in form to some decorations used by Shah Jehan, so that there is much probability that this tomb was of that period. Here, too, as in many other instances, the square hall has been made into a circle in order to place the dome upon it by means of arches cutting off the four upper corners of the building. But in this case there was this peculiarity, that the light-looking shafts which support these arches spring from the ground. These shafts are carved in horizontal zigzag lines—a design which we had seen elsewhere in work evidently of an earlier date than this specimen, where the styles and work of several periods seem to have been mingled together.

From Meerut we went on to Lahore, where we were detained some time by the non-arrival of a portion of our luggage. Consequently, the 10th of April finding us stil there, and hearing from a friend that the *baisakhi*, or Sikh festival of the New Year, would be celebrated at Amritsar on the 11th, we went over to see it. There are four divisions of Sikhs—the Nanuk Sikhs, the Akalis, the Nihungs, and the Nirmulas. The form of worship used by all of these is the same as regards the following particulars. They rise at daybreak, read certain passages in the Adi-Granth, which is their scriptures; repeat an evening prayer called Rat-ras, or straight road; and on going to bed must again read certain portions of the Adi-Granth. The morning devotions are much insisted upon by the Nihungs; the others do not lay the same stress upon them, but perform them if they have time. According to Sikh traditions they have had ten *gurus*, or teachers. The first of these, Nanuk, was born A.D. 1469; the last, Guru Govind Singh, died in 1708. The Granth is said to have been partly composed and compiled by one of the *gurus* named Urjoon. The book itself is worshipped by the Sikhs, it being to them not only a sacred book, but they bow before it, and bring offerings to it; so that to them it is no guide to God, but rather an agency by which they can propitiate both God and Mammon.

The principal distinguishing mark of all Sikhs is their unshorn hair and beard. Five tokens are essential: these are called the five K's, as they all begin with this letter in the vernacular. These signs are,—1st, a nether garment of a peculiar form; 2d, a knife with an iron handle; 3d, a comb; 4th, long locks; 5th, an iron bangle on the wrist. Sixty-four precepts have been enjoined upon them in regard to their moral behaviour. In these they are strictly ordered always to speak the truth. Smoking and the use of razors are forbidden; but they are allowed to eat animal food. Their marriage and funeral ceremonies are the same as those of the Hindús, except as regards about one hundred Sikhs at Nadersh, who still retain the manners and customs of Govind Singh's time, and follow no Hindú observances or ceremonies: their widows also are permitted to marry again.

The Sikhs of the Punjaub have allowed their religion to be much contaminated with Hindúism. One tomb we visited near the Golden Temple had recesses all round the walls in the interior, in which were statues of Ganesha, Rang-ji (one of the incarnations of Vishnu), and other Hindú gods. One of the natives who accompanied us in our rounds told us that the Sikhs worshipped these idols, whilst another said they were only placed there for ornament.

According to Sikh tradition, it was revealed to Ramdass, the third *guru*, that there was a holy spot, somewhere to the west of the village where he lived, which the deity intended to be their most sacred place. Accordingly he directed his son-in-law, who was afterwards his successor, to go and find this spot, and dig a reservoir there, which was to be called Amritsar, or "the pool of immortality." After some search, his man found a small pool in the jungle, in which, it was told him, a leper had just bathed and been cured. This leper had a pretty wife, who was very faithful and attentive to him, carried him about on her shoulders, and begged alms for his subsistence. One day, when about to go and procure means to supply his wants, she put him down in the jungle near this puddle, and whilst sitting there he noticed that a crow, which dipped its wing in that water, became white. This induced him to try its efficacy on his diseased members, the result being that they became perfectly sound. The wife, on her return, could not believe in such a transformation, but thought some man had killed her husband and clothed himself in his rags; was very indignant, and refused to acknowledge his identity. Ram-dass's son-in-law, hearing her tale, was certain that this must be the spot he was in search of, and at length succeeded in persuading the woman that the fine healthy man she saw, really was the husband who, when she parted from him, was such a miserable object.

There is more than one version told of this story; but the real truth would seem to be that, up to the time of Ram-dass, the Sikhs had no fixed seat—their *gurus* lived and died at different places; that, possibly, Akbar granted him a piece of land on which he and his followers might live and employ themselves in farming; and that, in order to render the place sacred, they laid the foundations of the reservoir—it being customary for religious men to make gardens and excavate tanks and wells near their dwellings with this object.

The Akalis and the Nihungs have kept themselves more free from Hindúism than the other two classes; they may be distinguished by their blue turbans, and are never without the five K's. The former are looked upon as their priests, are maintained by public charity, and, as a rule, lead a monastic life; they also use certain peculiar modes of speech, one of which is that they always speak in the masculine gender. They wear in their turbans two or three different styles of ornaments: these are invariably of iron, which they consider possesses very sacred properties. Some have a row of small instruments stuck in the front of their head-dress, much resembling spillikens in form and size; others, again, have iron rings, of the quoit shape, round the head. Some have an iron torque worn in the same manner, or a large round brooch in the centre of the front of the turban. The Nirmulas, the fourth denomination, are Sikhs in name only: they do not care for the five K's; initiation, or the Sikh baptism, is not compulsory with them; and their teaching is much more like that of the Hindú Shastras and Vedas than the religion of the Granth.

The Sikhs do not seem to have become a warlike sect till the reign of Aurungzebe, when the father of Govind Singh, who was their tenth and last *guru*, was butchered by that emperor's orders; from which time Govind Singh's teaching took a politico-religious turn, and the race of fighting Sikhs sprang up, whose great principle was antagonism to the Mohammedans, the *guru* telling them that only those would be accepted of God who fell in the field when fighting against the Mussulman. It was this same Govind Singh who introduced monastic distinctions amongst them.

For the substance of this brief general outline of the religious tenets and practices of the Sikhs I am much indebted to a gentleman, through whose kindness I was enabled to read some valuable notes on the subject, which he had received from a native source.

I must now describe the Golden Temple at Amritsar, before giving an account of the special ceremonies we witnessed. This temple is one of the best specimens of the modern Indian style. Soon after our conquest of the Punjaub, and at a time when our rule was not as firmly established as at present, the British Government issued directions that all Europeans desiring to make a tour of its sacred precincts should be attended by one or more policemen, and must likewise remove their leather boots or shoes, and put on felt slippers provided for this purpose. This order is still in force. We were accordingly thus equipped, and were then allowed to descend a flight of steps, at the bottom of which was a platform of white marble, about fifteen feet wide, going round the four sides of a large square, which had a tank in the centre; and in the middle of this tank is the Golden Temple itself, with four entrances, each approached by a marble causeway, with a balustrade. A similar causeway also runs right round the exterior of the building, and is bordered by a light trellis-work of the same material.

The exterior of the temple is of white marble, carved in pierced work and various other pretty designs up to a height of perhaps twenty feet; above that height the walls of the building, the large central dome, and the smaller ones at the four corners, are all richly gilt. The interior walls are covered with Arabesques painted in brilliant colours. The space beneath the central dome is enclosed by a wooden balustrade about a foot high; within this space is placed the sacred book, the Adi-Granth.

The religion of the Sikhs, as I have before said, enjoins early rising upon them, so we were recommended, if we wished to see the *baisakhi* properly, to be on the spot as early as possible. We accordingly reached the temple about 6 A.M., and even at that hour found great numbers of people bathing in the tank (the women have a part of it walled in for their use). Such a crowd of people were pressing into the temple, and lining every part, that our guide made way for us with much difficulty. Within the enclosed space, and near the holy book, sat a priest. The ever-moving and changing crowd made offerings of sweetmeats, flowers, cowries, and small coins, and were then caused to "move on" (rather by blows than words, I fear) and give place to those behind.

At one side of the large square is a smaller one paved with marble. At the further end of this, and facing the temple, is a building with a marble balcony raised about ten feet from the ground, where were seated some of the heads of the Sikh community, with some of their Akalis, or priests, whose special business it is to perform initiation, or Sikh baptism, which, I believe, can be conferred at any time of the year, though the New Year is their favourite season for the ceremony. One of the Akalis, specially chosen for this purpose, had before him a large metal basin tied to the front of the balcony; the candidates, who must present themselves five at a time, stand on the ground below. Out of this basin the priest gives each of them water to drink in their two hands; and performs the baptism, or ceremony of initiation, by sprinkling water three several times on the crown of each man's head. The neophyte is then required to go and bathe once more in the tank, and put on a new turban, which must be arranged in the Sikh fashion. To enable them to make this part of their toilet to their satisfaction, a good many men are stationed near the tank holding looking-glasses.

On inquiry, we were told that even the son of a Sikh is not born one, but must be made so by means of this ceremony, which costs about five shillings English money, and can be paid up by instalments afterwards; but their priests impress upon them that their sins are not washed away till the whole demand has been satisfied. I believe an orthodox Sikh only marries with his own people:

their women appear to wear their hair rolled up in a coil at one side of the head, though I could not see exactly how it was dressed, as a square veil of some bright coloured stuff, in many cases richly embroidered with coloured silks, enveloped the head and the greater part of the person.

Opening out of the large square where the temple stands is a narrow passage between houses leading to a large garden, which is also considered sacred ground. Here we saw a great many religious mendicants of the class called Nangas, or *jogis.* They are ascetics of the most rigid kind, and are Sikhs inasmuch as they read the Granth, but in other respects more resemble Hindús, we were told. Nearly a dozen of these *jogis* were seated on the ground at one spot in this garden: some quite young boys were amongst them, and they had lighted a small wood-fire. They are most wild-looking objects, their hair being left to grow long and matted together with mud; and their faces and the exposed parts of their bodies being smeared over with wood-ashes, gives a most ghastly look to the dark oriental skin. Whilst we were standing by, some one brought them a quantity of a kind of native sweetmeat, and laid it on the ground near them. One of their number took a small portion of this and crumbled it over the burning embers, and the remainder they then divided equally.

At no great distance from the Golden Temple are several tombs, some of which are in buildings of a considerable size. Regarding one of Baba Utal (or child Utal) they have a curious legend. He was the son of a *guru,* and a clever boy, and they say that had he lived he would have perhaps been equal to Nanuk, the first *guru.* Hearing one day of the death of one of his playfellows who owed him a game, he went to the house and addressed the dead child, saying, "It was not fair that he should die without clearing his debt," and went on to say, "Pay me what you owe, and then you may go;" on which the dead boy got up, and began to play with him. Such an extraordinary occurrence of course made a great noise in the town. When Hur Govind, Utal's father, heard of it, he said, "Two swords cannot rest in one sheath"—meaning that two prophets could not exist at the same time in one community; on which the lad went and laid himself down on the spot where his tomb now stands, and then expired.

We visited the native bazaar at Amritsar, and examined the shawl embroidery which is carried on there; and also drove to the Ram-bagh, or civil gardens, which are laid out with great taste, and very carefully kept. The *diwali*, or festival of lamps, is observed equally by Sikhs and Hindús. It takes place in the autumn, and may be said to symbolise the death of vegetation, as the *baisakhi* typifies its birth. I was at Saugor in the autumn of 1877 when this feast was celebrated, but was unable to witness it, as cholera prevailed at that time in the native city, and we were advised not to enter it.

The traditional origin of the *diwali* is as follows: When Rama, King of Ajoudhya (the modern Oudh), was returning to his kingdom after gaining some great victory, he ordered the capital to be illuminated in his honour. Whether by intention or accident, or because a sufficient supply of oil was not at hand, all the lamps went out by midnight, except those in one house belonging to a *bunniah*, or native grain merchant, who was a God-fearing pious man. Rama's wife, Queen

Sita, charmed at this attention to their commands, went and knocked at the *bunniah's* door, but in vain she sued for admittance. He refused to open it, saying that all respectable people ought to be in bed at that hour. However, her importunity at length prevailed, and she was let in. The inmates then asked her who she was. She replied, "I am Lakhsmi, the goddess of wealth;" whereon the *bunniah* and his wife and family fell down and worshipped her. On her departure in the morning a pile of gold was found where she sat. When she returned to her husband he instituted this feast in honour of Lakhsmi, and commanded that it should thenceforth always be observed in remembrance of this miracle. This is, of course, a festival more especially celebrated by the *bunniah* class, who at this time make up their accounts, and call in all outstanding debts.

CHAPTER XVIII.

KASHMIR CLOSED TO TRAVELLERS — CONSEQUENT CHANGE OF PLANS—DALHOUSIE—CHUMBA—VISIT TO NATIVE LADIES—DHARMSALA—OLD TEMPLES AT BIJNATH AND HARRA-BAGH—NATIVE STATES OF MUNDI, SUKÉT, BILASPORE, AND ERKI—SINGULAR MODE OF PUTTING CHILDREN TO SLEEP—SIMLA.

We had intended going once more to Kashmir, but we were strongly advised not to do so by a friend just returned from there, who gave us terrible accounts of the famine then raging in that country. Immediately upon this we saw in the newspapers that all the passes into it, except one, were closed by order of the British Government. The only one open to us being very high, would have been impossible to traverse till some weeks later. Having engaged our servants, and bought tents and camp furniture, we still hoped to be able to penetrate into Kashmir later on in the season, when their summer crops had been got in; and in the meantime we proposed to visit some of the hill stations. Our servants and baggage having started with bullock-waggons some days previously, we ourselves left Lahore on 6th May, and went by train as far as Amritsar, where a *dâk gharrie* (a conveyance furnished by the post-office) met us at the station, and we reached Patánkote, a distance of sixty-seven miles, the same day.

On leaving Amritsar, for some distance on either side

of the road there were fields of roses, grown for the purpose of making the attar. After a time the land seemed mostly to be used for grazing purposes, though a certain amount of wheat cultivation was carried on. Babool-trees (the wood of which is used in dyeing) formed an avenue through which we passed. These were succeeded by mulberry-trees of two or three different varieties: the fruit being ripe, men, women, children, and *dogs* had all turned out to take their fill. The whole country was fairly well wooded. In one or two places we passed through thick copses; and though here and there I saw old trees, yet the majority were not more than twenty or thirty years old. The sheshum-tree was the most common; the Bombay black-wood furniture is made from its timber. During the latter half of the road white ants' nests were numerous. They were very curious, the little animals building their nest (which is of earth) round the stem of a species of cactus, or round the stalks of a tall kind of grass, not unlike the pampas-grass. These nests are broad at the base, and taper to a point at the top; they vary from three to four feet in height, and are deeply furrowed all round. As soon as it began to get dusk the fireflies surrounded us in myriads.

We did not see anything of Patánkote itself, as we only arrived there after dark, and left it at 7 A.M. the next morning. The carriage-road ceasing at Patánkote, I started for our march of eighteen miles, mounted on a Yarkundi pony, which we had bought at Amritsar some time before; and my husband walked, as he had been unable to procure a second animal. The first part of the road was a gentle rise; but after going about five or six miles we came to a low range of hills, and the remainder of the distance was a continual ascent and descent, winding round the spurs of these hills, which were intersected with numerous ravines, rendering the road a very tortuous one. The whole of this march was through a well-wooded district; flowering shrubs covered the ground, and large trees rise at intervals in the midst of these. The branches of one tree—I do not know its name, but it is a very common tree in the jungles—looked like gigantic masses of coral; for its flowers, which are of a bright red colour, come out before the leaves, and encircle the branches. The oleander also grew in great profusion, and was in full bloom. The last two or three miles of the road up to the bungalow at Dhar was through a wood of the *Pinus longifolia.* The march from Dhar to Dunera was only eleven miles. The road wound round the hills much in the same manner as before, but the ravines were less steep and abrupt; and on approaching Dunera some cultivation is possible in them.

The following day we marched to Mamúl, starting at 6 A.M. On leaving Dunera the road enters upon the higher mountains. This day I saw very lovely *trees* of *Spiræa*—many of them at least 20 feet high, and white with bloom. Also a species of cactus, growing to a height of 12 or 14 feet, with stems 6 or 8 inches in diameter, whence issued stiff branches, giving it a resemblance to a candelabrum. About two miles before reaching Dunera a road turns off on the right, leading to the military depot of Bukloh, where a regiment of Goorkas is always stationed. The *dâk* bungalow is on the spur of a mountain and in the midst of a pine-wood. Bukloh is on another summit, which perhaps may be a mile or more distant as the crow flies, yet I could, from where we were, distinctly hear the tunes played by the military band when they were practising, soon after our arrival.

The mountain-slopes round Mamúl are of great depth, and have most of them been very skilfully terraced with stones: that, and the general aspect of the scenery, reminded us very much of some of the southern slopes of the Alps. The following morning we left for Dalhousie, a distance of thirteen miles, our road again taking a course round the sides and over the shoulders of some mountains, and necessarily winding to such an extent to avoid descending into the ravines below, that we saw some of the houses at Dalhousie two hours before we reached the place. We here first saw rhododendron *trees* (I use this word advisedly, for not a few specimens were between 30 and 40 feet in height, with trunks of proportionately large diameter). Though it was too late in the season to see the grand effect of the whole mass in full bloom, yet individual trees had still many bunches of flowers upon them, all of the dark crimson variety; but I heard that, at a still higher elevation, those with white blossoms are not uncommon. Amongst other trees we saw gigantic ilex (the evergreen oak), and a species of horse-chestnut, differing slightly in the form of its leaf from our own well-known kind, but exactly the same as a variety we had met with in Kashmir. Of smaller shrubs and flowers I observed the two kinds of berberis which are common at home; also kalmias, and a tiny mauve auricula which I have often found in the higher Swiss mountains, and the modest violet.

On the previous march we had caught glimpses of snow-tipped mountains in front of us, but it was not till we had climbed up to the top of what appeared from below to be a small level ridge between two hills, had turned round a corner, and were fairly in Dalhousie on that part of it called Teera, where the friend resided whom we were going to stay with, that a most glorious panorama burst upon our view—a chain of snowy summits forming the background of the picture. The selection of a site for a sanitarium, which was afterwards called Dalhousie, was made by Lord Napier of Magdala in 1851, and five plateaux at different elevations on the mountain were chosen on which to build, and were finally marked out in 1854. These are now called respectively Kuttullaugh, Potrain, Teera, Bukrota, and Bhungora. In 1866 a plateau called Baloon was selected, instead of the first named of these, as a site whereon to build barracks for convalescent soldiers; and on Bukrota there is a military cantonment. Since this last date a number of detached villas have been built by private persons and others on the various plateaux. Some of these are built in the Swiss *châlet* style, with high-pitched roofs, projecting eaves, and casement windows. Teera, the hill on which we lived, is 6820 feet above the sea; Upper Bukrota, the highest part of the whole station, is 7687 feet. Potrain and the other sites named are at a lower level.

We left Dalhousie for Chumba on the 16th of May, taking the upper road, which is a rather difficult one, but was considered far more beautiful than the lower one. On leaving Dalhousie we had to mount Bukrota hill and reach a still higher point, whence there was a descent mostly through thick woods to Kejeár, where there is a pretty little bungalow situated on a grassy meadow of some extent, having a tiny lake with a floating island in its midst. The following morning we went on to Chumba, the principal town in the native state of that name. This was a rather fatiguing though a very lovely march. After accomplishing about half the distance, we came to a high ridge or gap between two mountains; from this point we had a view of the town of Chumba and the course of the river Ravi at its foot. During the first day's march the vegetation was much the same as at Dalhousie; but on the second, in addition to the rhododendrons, &c., there were more deciduous trees, a greater variety of ferns, and a small species of bamboo, which was very graceful, and grew from three to four feet high. I also noticed some of the same flowering shrubs which we had seen in Kashmir, and a clematis, with large star-like white flowers, which is very common in parts of Algeria.

On approaching Chumba we crossed the Ravi by a suspension-bridge, and then had to mount some 500 feet to reach the plateau on which the town is built, and where is also the house of the Political Agent, whose guests we were going to be. Two rivers meet near Chumba—the Ravi is joined by its tributary the Sao. The valley is surrounded on all sides by grand mountains; at the southern end a lofty snowy cone bounds the view. The *maidán*, or plateau, where the town is situated, is about 500 paces in length by 80 in breadth: it lies about 3000 feet above the sea.

The state of Chumba extends about fifty miles in a straight line from north to south, and somewhat less from east to west. The natives' houses are all built of wood, with roofs of the same material (even the rajah's palace was no exception to this rule, except that its foundations are of stone); many of them much resemble Tyrolese or Swiss *chálets*. The houses of the Political

Agent, and those occupied by the medical missionary, engineer, &c., are more solidly built, and have slate roofs. The rajah abdicated about three years before our visit in favour of his son, who, when we saw him, was a lad of about twelve, but very small of his age. From all I could gather, the old rajah, who lives somewhere in the state, though not in the Chumba capital, was a good riddance; for, amongst other peccadillos, he terribly ill-treated his wives, the two ranees, who are twin sisters. I paid them a visit; for, unlike many native ladies, these, I was told, are always pleased to see Europeans. One sister has no children, but the other is the mother of the young rajah and his little brother. Of course they pass what would be to us a most terribly secluded life, rarely leaving the house; if they do go out, it is only in a closed palanquin: but there is a fine view from some of the latticed windows, behind which these ladies can sit and see without being seen. On one side is a mountain gorge and pass; and on the other they have a view of all that is going on in the green meadow below, whither the little prince and his brother constantly resort to play at cricket. The elder boy is not at all a bad performer at this game, or at badminton, which he seemed thoroughly to enjoy. A European gentleman who, a few years ago, temporarily filled the post of Political Agent, gave the queen-mother a binocular glass, which is a great delight to her. That lady could not be more than twenty-six or twenty-seven years of age when I saw her: she had a sweet but very sad expression of countenance. Her movements were graceful, and she had remarkably pleasing manners.

The royal family of Chumba are Rajputs of the highest caste. They and other mountain rajahs are known and distinguished by some appellation which either has reference to their state or to the founder of their family. Those of Mundi are called Mundial, and of Chumba, Chumyal, from a distinguished Rajput. The boy-rajah of Chumba has an English tutor, and a Hindú pundit (all the people in Chumba are Hindús) teaches him Sanscrit and other native languages. His small brother, and three other boys, sons of his officials, are educated with him, and are his constant companions. One of these last is extraordinarily stout, and seemed to be the butt of the whole party, being known as the fat boy, and the muff, because he could not run, or bowl, or catch a ball like the rest; but he appeared to take all the chaff in good part.

During our stay in Chumba I also visited five other ranees who live in another palace in the higher part of the town. They are all the widows of a former rajah who had died about eight years before. He was the brother of the man who had abdicated, and consequently the uncle of the present boy-ruler. The ages of these widows vary from twenty-two to perhaps twenty-six years, the youngest was thus a widow at the age of fourteen. Since their widowhood, custom has obliged them to leave off wearing jewels, to dress entirely in white, and to abstain from eating either meat or fish. Two of these ladies were rather short, plain, and uninteresting-looking; the other three appeared very intelligent, especially the youngest, who was the chief spokeswoman. These last all said they could read Hindí. The youngest exhibited some very beautiful embroidery she had been working with floss silks. She told me she was a Kashmiri, and, as a child, had been educated by a pundit who lived in her father's house. It made me very sad to think of the life of perpetual seclusion to which such an intelligent young lady is condemned by Hindú prejudices; as, from what I saw of her, I could well imagine she might become a useful and happy member of society if only it were possible to emancipate her.

On 22d May we left Chumba for Dharmsala in the Kangra district. It is four marches—the first, to Chohari, 17½ miles over the pass of that name. For the first nine miles the road was a continual steep ascent; we had to mount nearly 6000 feet to reach the top of the pass. When about half-way down on the further side, to our great surprise, we had a view over the lower ranges below us, down to the plains of India. Between Chohari and Sihanti (16 miles) we had to descend and ascend three steep ravines, which made the march a fatiguing one. The following day, from Sihanti to Shapore (14 miles), our road was a very undulating one, though at the latter place the aneroid marked only 2000 feet. As soon as we got into British territory, which was about a couple of miles before reaching Shahpore, we saw the first tea-plantations. The next morning, soon after we started, we could distinguish some of the houses at Dharmsala, dotted about on the slopes of the mountains some distance above us. It was a good pull of 14 miles up to the house of the friend we were going to visit.

At that point we were at a height of about 6200 feet above the sea; from thence we had a grand and extensive view of the lower hills and the plains beyond. As at Dalhousie, rhododendrons abounded on the sides of the hills. The church is a well-built stone one: its enclosure has a special interest, in that it contains the grave and monument of the late Lord Elgin, who died at Dharmsala in 1863. On 28th May we again started off on our travels, in order to go to Simla, the distance being 161 miles, or fourteen marches. We had of course to descend considerably, and reached Palumpore the second day: that place is the great centre of the Kangra valley tea-plantations. At Bijnath, our next stopping-place, there are two old temples: both of them have much ornamentation, and are dedicated to Shiva. The larger and more highly decorated one is in the middle of the village, and consists of a square walled enclosure, in the centre of which is the ante-temple, with a Hindú ceiling supported on four columns. There are window-like openings on either side, having small projecting balconies at a height of about seven feet from the ground. The roof of the shrine is of the usual curvilinear pyramidal form, such as is almost universally found in the old Hindú temples of northern India. In the courtyard is a Brahmini bull carved in stone, all worn into holes by the oil which has been burnt upon it by devout pilgrims and others.

At Dailoo we entered upon the territory of the Rajah of Mundi, who keeps up several bungalows for the use of travellers passing through his state, and supplies these houses with servants, crockery, and furniture on the *dâk* bungalow principle; but, unlike those establishments, the rajah's accommodation is free. About three or four miles beyond Dailoo, in the middle of a large wood of *Pinus longifolia*, and a few hundred yards below the road, is the little village of Harra-bagh, where there is a curious and interesting old Hindú temple, which is richly decorated both within and without, and had recently been restored without any unnecessary injury to the original character of the building. A spring of water rises from under it and forms a small tank. On mounting a few steps a platform is reached, which is surrounded by a wall about 12 feet high. The temple in the middle of this courtyard consists of a square hall of about the same dimensions as the ante-temple at Bijnath, and constructed in a similar manner. In the centre of the space between the pillars is a Brahmini bull carved in stone. A female figure is holding the tail of the animal, and the bell which hangs from its neck rests upon the head of a cobra. On slabs of stone resting against the walls of this chamber are carved representations of Hanuman, Gunputi, &c.; and also on either side of the door-posts leading to the inner shrine is a male figure. One of these bears a club, no doubt to show his authority in civil matters, and is most probably intended to represent Shiva as Baironath; the other, a military official, is armed with a sword, and has a couple of fierce-looking dogs at his feet. Inside the shrine is a dark-coloured female goddess—a life-sized figure dressed in a white robe, and carrying a still blacker infant on her left arm. On inquiry, we were told that she was Bhavani—the name for Durga, as the goddess of nature and fecundity.

The men and women, in the part of Mundi we passed through, wear a sort of loose dress of white woollen stuff, with a band or rope round the waist. The former wear a high cap of the same material, shaped like a bag. The women's head-dress is of the same form as that of the men, but made of a dark-red cloth: they roll up the lower part, so that it looks like a kind of turban. The young and pretty ones stick this cap coquettishly on one side of the head, and occasionally adorn it with a bunch of wild flowers. The women's hair is all gathered into a single plait, left hanging down the back: the natural growth is added to and lengthened by having black sheep's wool plaited in with it, so that the tail of hair almost touches the ground. Both men and women carry loads of salt and other things in a basket resting against the back, and supported by ropes round the chest or arms. These baskets were very similar in shape to those in use in some parts of Switzerland. I often could not help smiling to see the use to which the women put them: they seemed to find them a convenient receptacle for their long tails, which sometimes lie coiled up like a snake within their baskets.

About half-way between Dailoo and Jitingri there is a salt-mine on the left hand. Shortly after passing this we entered a forest of deodaras, which seemed to contain very few old trees; but the contrast of colour between their foliage and the wild climbing white rose-trees, which reached the summit of many of them, and hung down a mass of white blossoms, was very striking. The vegetation changed the latter part of the way, and we went through a wood of ilex and rhododendron. The bungalow at Jitingri is placed on the crest of a spur of a mountain-range: the aneroid indicated a height of 6200 feet.

The following march, to Drang, was a hot and fatiguing one of fourteen miles: it was necessary to ascend some 500 or 600 feet, and ride for ten miles up and down steep pitches. The last four miles was a stony descent, steeper than the roof of an ordinary house, and a mass of rolling stones. At Drang, also, there is a salt-mine—or, rather, the salt seemed to be quarried, like so much stone, out of the side of a mountain.

Our next halting-place was Mundi itself, the capital

of the state. The celebrated traveller Vigne, who passed through Mundi nearly fifty years ago, states that the then rajah told him that this name was taken from that of a holy man, one of his ancestors; and added, that Guru Govind Singh, disguised as a fakir, arrived at Sultanpore, in Kulu, whose rajah, a pious Hindú, asked him to perform a miracle. The pretended fakir took hold of his own beard, and drew it out to a great length; but the rajah showed him a miracle in return: he breathed forth a flame which consumed the fakir's beard; and then, still further to show his power, imprisoned the *guru* in a cage—upon which this last caused himself to be borne through the air to Mundi, cage and all. Its ruler treated him with much kindness, and in return begged the *guru* to decree that no stranger should ever invade his country. The *guru* replied that the rajahs of Mundi must give tribute to the Sikhs, but that these should never enter their capital. This rule was still in force in the time of Ranjit Singh —no servant or official of his having ever entered Mundi, the officer appointed to receive the revenue always residing outside the town.

The rajah had received a private letter beforehand to tell him that we were coming through his territories; and as soon as we arrived he sent down an official to ask my husband to pay him a visit. C., on his return, said he found him very pleasant and agreeable, and that he spoke English remarkably well. On taking leave, my husband was presented with a small case of particularly delicious orange pekoe, grown and manufactured in the state of Mundi. The Beas has become a considerable river by the time it reaches this point, and is crossed by a good suspension-bridge.

The following day, after having left Mundi about a mile behind us, we saw, by the roadside, a singular collection of upright stones, which must have been upwards of one hundred in number. There were, perhaps, about four or five large ones about 12 feet high, on which were sculptured a man on horseback, with a sword in his hand, his steed being fully caparisoned; also figures holding *chauris* (or fans of yaks' tails) to drive away the flies. The smaller stones, which varied perhaps from 4 feet in height down to 12 inches, had all of them female figures sculptured upon them. We were at the time much puzzled to understand the meaning of this singular collection of stones; but on afterwards turning to one of the Government records compiled by Major Harcourt, who was for some time Assistant Commissioner in Kulu, I saw that he mentioned having observed similar rows of stones at Nuggur, in that valley, and that there the report was that such stones were placed in position at the death of every sovereign, and that the female figures were the effigies of such of his wives as had performed *suttee* at their lord's death. If this was the case, what a fearful number of victims must have perished on each such occasion!

Our next march was to Sukét, the capital of a small native state. Its rajahs are believed to be one of the oldest, if not the oldest, of the Rajput hill-families. On approaching the town we were met by some of the officials of the state, the Rajah of Mundi having sent on a messenger to apprise them of our coming. These officials escorted us to the bungalow, near which, standing beneath an umbrella of state, was a young nephew of the deposed rajah, who bade us welcome. His uncle had been deposed about a couple of months previously, he having, by his oppressions and misgovernment, brought his people into almost open revolt; upon which the English Government sent an officer to remain there for a period and arrange matters; and accordingly the rajah's eldest son, a lad of fourteen, was made rajah, and his uncle appointed regent during his minority. Later on in the day the regent also came to see us, and made us all manner of civil speeches; and in the afternoon, at his invitation, we went to his durbar-room, and there saw several of the old rajah's younger children: the little rajah himself was ill, and unable to see us. Since then we have heard of his death, in a deep decline, and the brother next in age will succeed him: the younger ones being half-brothers only, and not by a Rajput mother, are not strictly legitimate, and are incapable of succeeding.

From Sukét we went on to Bilaspore, another native state. This was a long and fatiguing march of twenty-two miles. Having to cross the river Sutlej by a ferry, our servants and baggage were so much delayed that some of them did not arrive till the next day. My Yarkundi pony was very resolute in his determination not to enter the ferry-boat, and for half an hour resisted all the efforts of four or five men to persuade him to change his mind; but at length, a rope being fastened to one of his fore-legs, that foot was dragged by main force into the boat, and the rest of him was then forced to follow. Our cook and his provision-baskets did not arrive at Bilaspore till 10 P.M., so that we should have had to go dinnerless to bed had not the rajah sent us in a native dinner, consisting of two kinds of meat, one vegetable, rice, sweet cakes, sugar, butter, sweetmeats, and *chupatties*—which last are the native substitute for bread. Each *plât* was in a separate little dish, made of the leaves of some tree, pinned together with the thorns of a plant. So artfully are these dishes constructed, that not a drop of the gravy seems to escape. The Hindús adopt these leaf-dishes, because by their religion they may not eat out of any vessel which cannot afterwards be cleaned by scrubbing it with sand; and therefore they either use brass utensils, or else such dishes as I have described made of leaves, which, after being once used, are thrown away.

The following morning the rajah sent word to say that he hoped we would pay him a visit towards evening, when the heat of the day was a little past. So accordingly, about 6 P.M., we went to a garden near the bungalow, where preparations had been made for our reception; and we sat some time conversing with him. We had hardly returned to the bungalow again before that prince sent us some very pretty boxes made of leather; the sides ornamented with medallions of the same material, in various colours; and the top embroidered in a kind of satin stitch, worked with finely-split porcupine-quills, and having a very silvery effect. I had before seen some specimens of this work in private houses, and have since heard that it is made at Jutogh, near Simlà. In India, each town, each state, each little district almost, seems to have its different manufactures, and special varieties in the styles of its jewellery and ornaments, which it is frequently impossible to procure except in their own particular locality. The ornaments worn by the native women, as well as the style and material of their dress, vary immensely in design and shape in different districts, so that the eye has to be perpetually on the watch to grasp the new forms which sometimes are met with at short distances from each other.

From Bilaspore we took the upper road to Simla, which had two advantages, in that it was shorter than the other, and also kept along a higher level, which at that time of year was a great point gained. Since leaving Dalhousie we had already been obliged to descend twice almost down to the plains of India, and found it no joke to be out in the heat of the day during the month of June. The mountain road which we followed from this point had been described to us as a bad and stony one, with steep ascents and descents, but we found it no worse than much we had traversed before. We had to pass through another small native state—that of Erki—where, as before, we were met at the frontier by an official, and, on entering the town, by a near relation of the rajah's. We only remained one night there; and soon after our arrival we went up to the palace at the rajah's request, to pay him a visit. The palace at Erki is much larger and more solidly built than those of any of the small states which I have just been describing. This rajah, who only succeeded his uncle about ten months before our visit, keeps up more parade and show than the other chiefs whose territories we had passed through, though his estates are smaller in extent than those of the rajahs of Mundi and Bilaspore. The ruler of Erki is a fine-looking man, of about thirty years of age, with dignified manners. He received us in a very pretty painted chamber, closed on three sides, and supported by pillars on the fourth. From this apartment we had a view of Subathu, and the hills near and round Simla. The rajah had a very magnificent ornament in his turban: the central emerald was considerably larger than a five-shilling piece, and was surrounded with diamonds. Round his throat were two strings of large pearls; from one of those depended a jewel composed of a fine emerald.

Not far from Erki we witnessed a singular custom, which is peculiar, I believe, to the natives of that part of the hills,—in fact, visitors to Simla, I was afterwards told, are in the habit of going to a certain village not far off, where it is improvised for their amusement. Whilst on the march, on seeing a likely spot near a spring where we could eat our luncheon, we dismounted. Hearing the sound of an infant's voice under a tree, I went round it, and discovered a young child lying in a sort of natural bower, formed by the roots of a large tree, over which branches had been placed so as to screen it effectually from the sun. Its sleeping-place had been so arranged that a half-tube of bamboo caused a small streamlet of water to flow perpetually against the crown of the infant's head without wetting its clothes or any other part of its body. Two or three other children were reposing with a similar apparatus over them: one little fellow of four or five years old came and laid himself down in the proper position to receive the full benefit of another runlet.

We reached Simla on 11th June, and were very thankful to find ourselves at the house of our kind friends there, after having had a most trying march of nearly twenty-five miles. There was so much delay, owing to the change of coolies on passing from native to British territory, that our baggage did not arrive till the following morning. Our friend's house was situated on a hill called "Jacko," and there was a splendid view from it. In the foreground were steep ravines, formed by the lateral spurs of the hills; beyond these a well-wooded range of high hills, on one of which is Mashobra, where the Viceroy has a summer residence; and in the extreme distance there was a grand snowy chain of mountains bounding the view on the north. Simla is best seen on approaching it from Jutogh, whence the whole has the form of an arc, with houses dotted all along it. In some parts the hillsides are thickly covered with bungalows. Peterhoff, the Viceroy's residence, may be called the north-western, and Chor View the south-western, point of the semicircle. The church is almost in the centre of the bow. The different parts of the station have various names, such as West End, Chota Simla, Burra Simla, &c.

During the summer season the place is very crowded, for all the Government offices, with their staff of *employés* and clerks, come up from Calcutta; the Commander-in-Chief and his staff are there likewise. The Lieutenant-Governor of the Punjaub was also at Simla at the time of our visit; it was said that he would for the future make that place his summer headquarters instead of Murree, as heretofore.

CHAPTER XIX.

MARCH FROM SIMLA TOWARDS KULU—JALOURI PASS—OLD TEMPLE AT BAJOURA—SULTANPORE—VISIT TO RANEE—TEA-CULTIVATION IN KULU—NUGGER, THE OLD CAPITAL—MANĀLI, AND CURIOUS WOODEN TEMPLE NEAR ROTANG PASS—LAHOUL—SHEEP AND GOATS USED AS BEASTS OF BURDEN—GERMAN MISSIONARY ESTABLISHMENT—PROPHECY IN THIBET RESPECTING QUEEN VICTORIA—SNOWED UP IN TENTS AT NEARLY 15,000 FEET ABOVE THE SEA—PASSES INTO KASHMIR AGAIN CLOSED—RETURN TO KULU.

We did not quit Simla till 12th July. A good fortnight was taken up in repairing the damages consequent on our twenty-four previous marches, for the Indian workman is slow in his movements; then an attack of fever delayed our departure for some days; after which the monsoon set in, so that all advised us to wait for a break, which came at last.

The first march of eleven miles to Fagoo is a very lovely one. About two miles out of Simla the road passes through a short tunnel, and then continues winding up and round the spurs of the mountains, so that some of the houses on "Jacko" were visible for a long time. The following day we made a double march of eighteen miles to Mattiana: the scenery in itself was not so striking as on the preceding one, but there was a greater abundance of wild flowers. The next march, from Mattiana to Nagkunda (or the shoulder of the snake), was a very beautiful ride of eleven miles. When close to the bungalow at Nagkunda, on turning round a corner, there is a glorious panorama of snowy mountains—the same range that we saw from Simla and Fagoo, only that we were much nearer to them.

We remained a day at Nagkunda in order to ascend Hattoo, 10,646 feet above sea-level. This mountain was about six miles distant. From its summit a splendid view is at times to be obtained; but alas! we were not in luck, for when we got there clouds obscured the distant mountains. It is impossible to ride the whole way either up or down Hattoo, as, for a considerable distance, the road is very steep and stony.

From Nagkunda we went to Dularsh, seventeen miles: this I thought the most fatiguing march, both for man and beast, which we had ever experienced. For the first nine or ten miles the road was a continual descent —the last five of these were much too steep and rough to ride down; so, shortly after passing through the little capital of the native state of Komarsen, I had to dismount, and walk down to the river Sutlej — and a terribly hot and trying walk it was. The Sutlej is there crossed by a fragile-looking wooden bridge; and after passing this we commenced to ascend a mountain very steeply zigzagged in some places. As the Sutlej valley is a mere deep ravine, we had to climb up to the very top of the mountain, whence we had a view into a different valley, and a mile and a half's skirting along the ridge at the top brought us to the rest-house, which was truly properly so-called in our case: we were so tired as absolutely to need a day of repose. The march in the heat, down to so low a level, and the absence of shade made it most trying.

On 18th July we went from Dularsh to Choi, a

distance of only eight miles. It was necessary first to ascend a small pass called the Kanda Ghae: the descent on the other side was through a pine-wood. We then ascended considerably and skirted round the spurs of some mountains. On the following march, from Choi to Kot (eleven miles), the scenery partook of much the same character, but the flora was more varied. I observed a species of *Canna* growing wild, also some common holly, and many ferns which I had never before seen in India. Amongst these were the *Osmunda regalis,* and a very diminutive variety of the holly fern.

At Kot a small excitement was produced by the *lumbadar* (or head-man of the village) applying to us to punish a fakir who had, as he said, been insulting some of the villagers. They were all Hindús, he added; and this fakir, a Mohammedan, had made his way into several of their houses. According to their notions this was a most unwarrantable proceeding. I think our servants were partly to blame, as they had encouraged this man to hang about our encampment at Choi, and he had followed us from thence. The greater part of the population of the village then led or drove the fakir up the hill, and they all disappeared round a corner, he calling out all the time, "Do not whip me! do not whip me!" In a few minutes, however, the matter seemed to have been settled in some manner, for the fakir came in sight again, collected his small bundles of food, and started on his way. On further questioning our servants, I learnt that this fakir was originally a Hindú, who had turned Mohammedan, which, I conclude, made our people (who were chiefly Mussulmans) favour him.

The following day, between Kot and Jibhi, we crossed

the Jalouri Pass (10,500 feet): and this we both considered the most beautiful march we had so far made since leaving Simla. The first part of the road was a long but not excessively steep ascent, partly through woods of spruce-fir. On reaching the summit of the pass we had a view of one grand snowy mountain (clouds, I think, must have obscured others). A short way down the northern face of the pass a considerable extent of ground was covered with low bushes of rhododendron, about the size to which they grow in England, and no longer *trees*, like those at Dalhousie. The descent was tedious, and in some places steep. We had to go down to the level of the valley below before reaching the bungalow at Jibhi, which was very picturesquely situated in a forest of gigantic deodaras.

The road from Jibhi to Manglaor was a rapid descent, the valley becoming narrower as we advanced. Between Manglaor and Larji the valley became still more contracted, and was a mere gorge, with the river flowing through it. Our path, cut out of the side of the mountains, was sometimes high above the stream, and occasionally descended down to its level, and thus was a series of perpetual steep pitches and ascents. On leaving Manglaor there was a steep ascent for about three miles, after which, descending gradually, we found ourselves in the valley of the Beas. As we advanced this valley enlarged, till it was perhaps over a mile in width. At about nine or ten miles from Manglaor we crossed the Beas by a wooden bridge; and from thence the road to Bajoura, five miles further, was good level cantering ground.

Not far from the *dâk* bungalow at this latter place there is an interesting old temple of the pyramidal form, which has a good deal of carving on the exterior. There is only one entrance to the temple, which is merely a small cell, and contains the usual emblems of the worship of Máhádéo. On the other three sides are recesses within which are carved *bas-reliefs* in stone. Gaṇeshạ, the elephant-headed god, occupies one of these; in another, a mutilated statue, which I believed to be a female figure (probably Durga), has eight arms. One hand holds the trident of Shiva, and is in the act of transfixing a male figure which has fallen on one knee at her feet; another hand grasps the same warrior by the hair of his head; the other hands hold respectively a sword, a bow, an arrow, and a cup; the eighth hand also held something, but I could not clearly make out what. In the third recess is a male four-handed figure.

At Bajoura there is a tea-plantation belonging to the Kulu Tea Company, who possess four or five other gardens. This particular one, though small, is said to produce the best tea in the whole of the Kulu valley. From Bajoura our next move was to Sultanpore, now the capital of the district,—Nugger, a place about twelve miles further up the valley, was the old capital. The last regnant chief of Kulu, Jeet Sing, was driven from his throne by the Sikhs in 1840. At his death, Shere Sing gave his *jaghir* (or estate held on a species of feudal tenure) to Thakoor Sing, his distant cousin. It is now held by Rae Duleep Sing, the grandson of the last named, who, when we saw him, was a boy of sixteen, and had been married a few months previously to a daughter of the Rajah of Nadaon—a petty state on one of the roads between Dhurmsala and Simla. The province of Kulu fell into the hands of the British Government in 1846.

Whilst we were in Sultanpore I was asked if I would

care to go and see the ranee, a widow of the late rajah, but step-mother to the present one, whose own mother died some years ago. The customs in Kulu as regards widows differ slightly from those I have already alluded to as existing at Chumba; for at Sultanpore the widowed lady was dressed in bright colours, and wore jewels—though the prohibition regarding eating meat and fish applies equally in both cases. The Kulu ranee made great demonstrations of delight on seeing me, and I believe she really felt much pleasure, as my visit was an event which would beguile the ordinary monotony and tediousness of her secluded life. She told me she had never seen a European lady's face since she married twenty-six years previously, and kept hold of one or both of my hands all the time our interview lasted.

After a time, as the ranee had business matters to talk over with the Deputy Commissioner, she and I moved into another room, which was almost dark. In a corridor outside this were seated my husband and the British official; a sort of screen was between us and them: we being in the dark, the gentlemen could not see us, though we could see them perfectly. In Kulu, as in Chumba state, the ranee had female attendants, and in both instances the term "slaves" was applied to them,—and such they really are. Though they are women of low caste, who ordinarily would walk about freely unveiled, yet when once they enter a ranee's service—which they very often do when they are quite children—they are quite as much secluded from the public gaze as that lady herself.

After staying a couple of days at Sultanpore we went on to Raesun, eight miles further, where we stayed two nights with Mr M., the only tea-planter in Kulu, who is manager and part owner of plantations there, and at Bajoura. On leaving Raesun, which is situated on the right bank of the Beas, instead of going direct to Dwara, our next halting-place, we crossed the river in order to see Nugger, the ancient capital of the district. The old castle there is a prominent object, for it is a large building standing rather apart from the village. Its construction is singular, the walls being made of large slabs of deodar-wood, alternating with courses of stones of various sizes neatly fitted together without mortar, except in one small portion, which is composed entirely of stones. A short distance below the castle there is a collection of upright stones similar to those I have already described near Mundi, but in a very inferior state of preservation. No doubt in both cases they were erected with the same object—that of commemorating the death of a rajah, and the number of his wives who committed *suttee* at the time of his obsequies.

On leaving Nugger we recrossed the river, and passed the night in the bungalow at Dwara. The following morning we rode on to Manāli, about fourteen miles, where we were the guests of Colonel S., a forest official, who had pitched tents for us near his house, his own accommodation being too limited to admit of his giving us rooms in his bungalow. Our friend's house, standing in the midst of a forest of deodaras, was situated on a natural terrace on the side of a mountain about 500 feet above the level of the river Beas, and from this position we had peeps of snowy mountains. The valley, which is very wide at Sultanpore, begins to contract at Raesun, and became very narrow before we reached Manāli. The scenery between Sultanpore and Manāli has, much of it, the character of an English park, the greater part of the road being carried through woods composed chiefly of deciduous trees,—clumps of alder fringing the banks of the river in many places.

Not far from Colonel S.'s house, and buried in the deodar forest, there is a most curious wooden temple, in form resembling those I have seen pictured as existing in Nepaul and Burmah. It is square in form, with overhanging eaves, surmounted by an ornament like a large umbrella. The temple occupied an area of perhaps 60 feet square, but more than half this space was filled up with a huge rock which reached to the roof, and formed the back wall of the inner chamber. A priest came and unlocked the building. Within it was a large horizontal slab of stone about 10 feet by 8, evidently a piece of rock *in statu quo.* Beneath this slab there was a large hollow, and in one corner of this was placed a small brass four-armed idol, which the attendant priest named Hurimba. He also told us that, in another hole close by, the blood of a hundred sheep was sometimes poured, on certain occasions when a rajah or some rich man came and offered sacrifices. The principal front of the temple was covered with rich carvings in wood. On one of the door-posts was a short inscription, which, we were informed, had never been deciphered.

We were detained at Manāli by bad weather, so that we did not leave our friend's house till 5th August, when we marched to Rahla (eleven miles). Between Manāli and Rahla we saw some enormous alder-trees ; one of these measured 12 feet round at a height of 5 feet from the ground. Near Rahla there were also sycamores. On this march we deviated somewhat from our road in order to see the hot sulphur-spring at Beshist, which the natives are said not to prize for its healing properties, but simply regard it as a sacred spot. The water flows into a small enclosed tank, which has various gods sculptured in *basso-rilievo* upon its walls.

The Rotang Pass, 13,500 feet, which we had now to cross, is ordinarily free from snow early in June; but so great had been the fall the previous winter, that, on 6th August, it was not yet free from it. We went over at least eight snow-slopes before reaching the summit, and found there a snow-field which must have been upwards of a mile in length. When we had traversed about two-thirds of the distance, partly on horseback and partly walking, being obliged to pick each step with the greatest care, a dense mist came on, and we were obliged to make a coolie walk a yard or two in advance to show us the way. The beauty of the Rotang consists mainly in the number of jagged snowy peaks which tower around and above it on all sides. From Rahla up to the summit there was a perfect garden of wild flowers, which even there were beginning to spring up wherever the snow had melted; and likewise, on descending to Koksir, 10,800 feet, I observed many wild flowers common to both England and Switzerland.

These became still more varied and abundant on the next march from Koksir to Sisu, though several snow-slopes had to be passed that day also. Just before reaching the rest-house at Koksir we had crossed the Chundra river, which, about twenty-seven miles further on, half-way between Gondla and Kyelang, joins the Bhaga river, and the two thenceforward are called the Chenab, one of the largest of the five great rivers of the Punjaub. The moment we crossed the Chundra we were in Lahoul, and from this point came amongst a Buddhist population, and saw the first *manes* and *chodtens* or *dungtens*, such as are common at the approach to each village in Thibet; but as I have already described these in my account of our visit to Ladakh in 1876, it is unnecessary to enlarge upon them in this place.

During the ascent of the Rotang we first saw sheep and goats used as beasts of burden, and afterwards met large flocks of these animals, each with two small bags slung over its back, and kept in position by ropes, which passed across the chest and beneath the tail, and were attached to the bags on either side. They are chiefly employed in the transport of salt. Each animal carries a weight of about 24 lb. In Lahoul the women not unfrequently act as coolies: they were often employed in carrying our baggage, and seemed to be able to take almost, if not quite, as heavy a load as the men.

The fair sex in Lahoul have a curious mode of dressing their hair. They arrange it in a great number of small plaits, which all (with the exception of three on each side) hang down the back, their length being supplemented with black wool. They are united at the waist, and confined with an ornament made of a piece of some large shell, fashioned somewhat in the form of a tortoise. These ornaments are sometimes plain, but more often engraved. The three plaits remaining on either side are brought forward close to the face, and fastened together on the top of the head with a large silver ornament. The villages in the Chundra valley are very singular: they are built of stones roughly squared and mortared together. Each village resembles a fort, the whole forming to the eye but one building—for every house is joined on to some other one. All have flat roofs and square walls, with loop-holes in them here and there. These villages seemed to be as populous as an ant's nest, judging from the numbers that came out to have a peep at us as we rode by.

On the march from Sisu to Gondla (eight miles) we also followed the valley of the Chundra, still remaining at a height of about 10,000 feet above the sea; yet there were mountains on either hand which towered 10,000 or 12,000 feet above us, on which were glaciers, whence mountain torrents descended, forming innumerable waterfalls. The scenery of that part of the valley was extremely grand and beautiful. At no part did it appear to be more than half a mile in width; consequently the mountains rose almost immediately from where we stood. Their sides were so precipitous as to be almost perpendicular, and their summits very serried in their outline. It was a view which, in singularity and wild sublimity, I have never seen equalled.

From Gondla we went up the Bhaga valley to Kyelang, where there is a settlement of Moravian missionaries. We found two of these pastors there, with their wives and families, living quite in the German style, as far as their household arrangements were concerned. One of these clergymen had been there twenty-five, and the other six, years. They seem to have gained considerable influence over the Lahoulees, who come to consult them in differences amongst themselves, and also to obtain medical advice in cases of sickness: thus, to a certain extent, they have obtained a degree of moral influence over the natives, though not a single convert to Christianity has been made in the valley.

The Lahoulees practise polyandry. This custom would appear, from all we heard, to have a most debasing effect upon the morals of a people. The missionaries have gathered round them a small colony of Ladakhis and Thibetans, whom, together with their families, they have converted to Christianity. One of these men had formerly been a lama. Considering that for many reasons it would be advisable to remove the mission-house to Leh, they have more than once applied to the Maharajah of Kashmir for the necessary permission; but this has been strenuously withheld, his Highness being, according to all accounts, a Hindú bigot, who would like to force the Buddhists of Ladakh to conform to his own faith.

As a rule, the British Government in India hold a neutral position in respect to religious matters; but in Lahoul the representative of the English Government (who is a native) exerts all his influence to excite the people against the Christian missionaries; and as, for a period of four months in the year, that district is entirely shut off from the outer world, owing to the Rotang Pass being utterly impassable in winter, during that time this individual's power is unrestrained by European influence. Amongst other things he is seeking to introduce *caste*, which had hitherto been unknown in Lahoul.

In many of the villages are buildings still in use, dedicated to demon-worship, which was the aboriginal religion of that people before Buddhism was introduced, and has now become mixed up with it. On the roof of such buildings is an erection much resembling an ordinary chimney in form, but made of singular materials—viz., ibex-horns, laid one upon the other; these being a good deal curved, a tolerably round form is thus obtained. It is said that the people not uncommonly find the remains of those animals in the spring, which have been killed and their bodies brought down by avalanches at the time of the melting of the snows of winter.

We were much interested in the useful work going on at Kyelang. The two missionaries have made themselves masters of the Thibetan language, and have translated certain prayers and hymns into that tongue. They hold regular services for their converts twice every Sunday, and each morning have short daily prayers. Their congregation consisted of about twenty grown-up persons. These clergymen, who are both of them highly educated and intelligent men, seemed to have entirely devoted their lives to the work in that spot,—indeed, unless in a case of utterly broken-down health, they never return home again. Their children, when of an age to require more education than they can give them, are sent to Europe at the expense of their society, and there trained to become missionaries, or missionaries' wives; so that these parents, when once they part with a son or daughter, have little or no chance of ever seeing them again.

Kyelang lies at a height of at least 10,000 feet above the sea, yet we were told that wheat ripens upon a portion of the mission farm, which is 2000 feet higher. One or other of the missionaries visits Ladakh every year. They related to us a curious fact which they had heard from the people there, not once but several times, that they believe Queen Victoria to be an incarnation of Durga, the wife of Shiva, and that Buddhism is soon to be at an end, when she will be their patron and protector.

On lately reading Lieutenant-Colonel Prejevalsky's tour in Mongolia during the years 1870, 1871, and 1872, which has been translated from the original Russian, I was much struck by seeing that a somewhat similar idea prevails amongst the Mongols in the province of Ala-shan, which lies to the north-west of China. In a conversation Lieutenant-Colonel P. had with a lama named Sordji, who was the confidential adviser of the prince of that district, the lama related a prophecy respecting Shambaling, the promised land of the Buddhists.

Shambaling was, according to him, an island lying far away in the northern sea. Gold is plentiful there; and corn grows to an enormous height. Poverty is unknown,—in fact, Shambaling is a second land of Canaan. The Buddhists' migration thither should take place 2500 years after the date of the prophecy—450 years of this term are unexpired. Its accomplishment will be as follows: In Western Thibet there is a living Buddha who never dies, but only passes from one body to another. Not long before the time appointed for the fulfilment of this prophecy, this saint will be born in the person of the son of the King of Shambaling. In the meantime the Dungans (Chinese-Mohammedan insurgents, who mostly live by plunder, and are the terror of passing caravans) will have become more troublesome than ever, and have laid waste all Thibet. Its inhabitants, under the leadership of the Dalai Lama, will then abandon their country and start for Shambaling, where they will be received by their saint, who will have succeeded his father on the throne, and have lands given to them. The Dungans, grown still bolder by their successes, will subjugate the whole of Asia and Europe, and invade Shambaling. The saint-monarch will then assemble his forces, defeat the Dungans, drive them back whence they came, and make the Buddhist faith supreme in all countries under his rule.

On being asked if he knew where Shambaling was, Sordji replied that in that country there was an enormous city wherein lives a queen, who, since the death of her husband, has ruled her subjects. Lieutenant-Colonel P., on this, suggested England; when the lama exclaimed, "That must be Shambaling," and begged to be shown that country on the map.

On leaving Kyelang we went on to Kholang (eleven miles), and thence to Darcha, a distance of only eight miles under ordinary circumstances; but a bridge having broken down, we were forced to make a *détour* of four or five miles, which, from the nature of the ground we had to go over, took us upwards of six hours to accomplish. The missionaries had most fortunately lent me a *dandi* (which is a small boat-shaped machine lined with carpeting, in which a lady can be carried), thinking I might require it to cross the Bara Lacha Pass. Not anticipating that we should want it so soon, it was carried empty by two men only. Most fortunately, on reaching the broken bridge we found the civil engineer who was about to restore it already at the spot, and he lent us additional men to assist, so that there were sixteen in all; four to carry me—others to relieve these, and to help the bearers along the more dangerous places. The men scrambled like cats almost (thanks to their shoes made of twisted grass) along ledges where there hardly seemed to be a safe foothold, and where a single false step might have precipitated me down a sheer precipice of 200 or 300 feet to the roaring river beneath. A short time previously the *détour* was not so difficult, for it was not then necessary to go so high up the stream to traverse it. Two snow-bridges had existed much lower down till a very short time before we came; but these having melted, and been carried away by the stream, we had to use a third, which, when we crossed it, looked as if it could not last many days, for it had already two large fissures running through it, one of which had been bridged by means of planks and stones, and the other we managed to avoid by making a slight round.

The march from Darcha to Patzio (eight miles) was plain easy work. From the former place we had considerably to increase the number of our coolies in order to carry grain for our horses, and wood for fuel. At Manāli we had already bought a supply of grain and rice for our servants, as we were told that they would be unable to procure any for themselves after a certain point; and at Kyelang we purchased five live sheep to be marched along with us, and killed as occasion required. At Patzio we also came upon a broken bridge, and were forced to make a long round in order to ford the main stream and its large tributary, and to follow for the most part of the way a track only, which was covered with large loose boulders, instead of using the ordinary path.

Zingzingbar, which lies at a height of nearly 15,000 feet, and is at the foot of the Bara Lacha Pass, was our next camping-place. Our tent was scarcely pitched at this spot before it began to pour with rain, which, at the end of twenty-four hours, turned to snow; and in a short space of time this covered the ground to the depth of six inches, and our tent was in some danger of falling from its weight, so that one night we were obliged to have men constantly at work knocking off the snow with long poles. On the fifth day of our imprisonment it began to clear, but our tents being too wet to move, we could not make a start till the following day.

During the interval of our forced detention at Zingzingbar, we had been compelled to renounce our intended journey into Ladakh—this route would necessarily have entailed our returning to India *viâ* Kashmir; but, from some newspapers which had followed us, we learnt that the British Government had issued orders closing all the passes into that country, on account of the famine then raging there, and that all the English who were then in Kashmir were to be required to leave it. We decided to retrace our steps, as it was impossible to proceed under those circumstances.

That the famine was a veritable one there is no doubt. But it was originally caused by, and its continuance may be attributed to, the conduct of a certain number of corrupt and grasping Hindú officials, who succeeded in making large purses for themselves in the following manner:—

The great cold which set in in Kashmir so early in the autumn of 1877 *did* destroy to a considerable extent the crops then ripening. The people, however, would still have had enough grain to have enabled them to get on till such time as they had sown and gathered in the spring crops of the following year; but the Hindú officials, or their emissaries, made a house to house visitation, and, ascertaining how much grain each man possessed, they seized it, paying the normal price,—the people having afterwards to buy back from them as much grain as they could afford to take (which was barely enough to support life), at the rate of 20 seers or 40 lb. to the rupee—a rate which would probably average nearly three times the price which these poor people had been paid for the grain thus forcibly taken from them.

It would seem that such tyrannical and barbarous

practices were once possible in Europe—as, for instance, in Italy, when its free cities had been deprived of their ancient liberties; for I recently came across an extract from an old book on geography, written by one Peter Heylyn in the early part of the reign of Charles I., or about 250 years ago, in which, speaking of Florence, he says: "The Duke useth here to buy up almost all the corne in the country at his own price, and sel it againe as deere as he list, forbidding any corne to be sold till his all be vented." Though by treaty the Maharajah of Kashmir acknowledges British supremacy, yet he has hitherto kept his subjects virtually in a state of slavery. If their means of subsistence fail them, they are not allowed to emigrate to India. Some few *do* escape—witness a small colony established at Nurpur not far from Dharmsala at the time of a famine which prevailed in Kashmir some forty years ago; and a few are also settled in Lahore; but, as a rule, I have been told it is the men alone who contrive to elude the strict watch which is kept over their movements, and that the wives and families remain behind.

During the summer of 1878 the famine seemed almost daily to increase; and a newspaper of 13th August states that "the skeletons of all the inhabitants of a pretty little village nestling at the foot of Gulmurg (twenty-eight miles from Srinagar and a favourite resort for summer visitors) had lately been discovered in a gorge above, where they had retreated in their endeavour to escape the Maharajah's *chuprassies* (or policemen), whose business it was to prevent emigration;" and also adds "that the Lolab valley was depopulated, and a large extent of the district beyond that become a desert." Such is the lamentable result of our having handed over this splendid and fertile country to the tender mercies of a Hindú bigot, with officials of the same faith as himself, the inhabitants of the country being Mohammedan. History shows us, in the case of our own Queen Mary, and also in that of Philip of Spain with regard to the Netherlands, that no rule is so cruel as that of a bigot over people of a faith differing from his own.[1]

We then returned to Kyelang, and remained some days, the weather being still very unsettled, and the idea of being caught in a snowstorm on the top of the Rotang seeming anything but agreeable. We left it on 7th September, and on the 11th went over the pass, having a glorious view of snowy peaks on the Koksir side of the mountain. The snow-field which it had taken us two hours to cross five weeks previously had entirely disappeared, so that we accomplished the same distance in a quarter of an hour. The wild flowers on both sides of the pass were still more numerous and varied than before, but, much to our regret, were not sufficiently advanced for us to procure their seed.

[1] Since the above was in the press, accounts of even worse atrocities in Kashmir have appeared in the newspapers. Whole boat-loads of starving people have been conveyed by the Maharajah's officials to the Woolar Lake, and there drowned. One man had strength to swim to shore, and informed an Englishman. This man, soon afterwards, died by poison. How long! how long! when will the supreme power rouse itself, which from the Himalayan Olympus dispassionately surveys the continent of India balancing in equal scales the legal privileges of the few and the natural rights of millions?

CHAPTER XX.

THE SOLANG VALLEY—ANNUAL FAIR AT SULTANPORE—MEETING OF THE GODS OF THE VARIOUS VILLAGES IN KULU—PARBUTI VALLEY—NOVEL MODE OF CROSSING A RIVER—HOT SPRINGS AT MANIKERN—BUBU PASS —RETURN TO KANGRA VALLEY—FORT AT KANGRA—JUWALA MUKI—ITS SACRED FIRES—SINGULAR ASPECT OF COUNTRY NEAR HOSHIARPORE—NATIVE CHRISTIAN MISSIONARY—JULLUNDER—RETURN TO LAHORE.

OUR friends at Manāli, hearing that we were about to return to the Kulu valley, wrote to invite us to visit them again, and we together made an excursion to the Solang valley, going up the right bank of the Beas. The entrance to this valley was about five miles from Manāli, at which distance we branched off to the left. The road to Rahla, and the Rotang Pass, on the top of which the Beas has its source, ascends steeply to the right on the opposite bank of the river. A large tract of ground at the mouth of the Solang valley is a mass of *débris* formed of enormous stones. Here and there are rugged-looking old deodaras, which look as if they had been buffeted and torn by the elements. As far as I could learn from those who had been to the upper end of this valley, there are no traces of there ever having been a lake which might have burst, and so spread devastation around; but this species of chaos has possibly owed its origin to an avalanche which may have dammed up the river for a time; and its waters, when released, would naturally rush down with resistless force.

On leaving Manāli we again stayed a few days at Raesun with our friend Mr M.; and on 11th October rode over with him to Sultanpore to see the last day of the fair, which had been carried on for a week, and takes place annually at that season. Each village in Kulu possesses its own particular god. The names of these deities appear to be local ones, as I have not seen them in any list of the Hindú Pantheon. The one belonging to Sultanpore is called Rugonath, and is said to have been stolen from Oudh more than 200 years ago. Rajah Juggut Sing, the then ruler of Kulu, had heard reports of the great wealth possessed by a Brahmin in the valley, and sent to demand money of him. The Brahmin refused to obey the rajah's command; and on a second messenger being sent to him he set fire to his house, whereby he and all his family were burnt to death. On this the rajah suddenly found himself attacked with leprosy; but in a dream he was informed that if he could only procure the idol Rugonath he would be cured. A messenger was accordingly sent to Oudh: he stole the god, was pursued, and overtaken; but Rugonath showed such a decided wish to go to Kulu, that the messenger was finally allowed to take him away, and as soon as he appeared in the valley the rajah became perfectly cured of his terrible disease.

At the time of this fair all the other gods in the valley are brought to Sultanpore to pay Rugonath a visit. Each temple has had certain lands granted to it rent free on condition that its god should be yearly taken to this fair. The funds arising from these lands are applied to the support of its attendants, and also supply food during their week's stay at Sultanpore to the people of the respective villages who have accompanied their idol thither.

The inferior gods are carried about in a species of palanquin, decorated with gay-coloured cloths and streamers, and adorned with flowers, which is borne on men's shoulders. Some are so small that they are carried by one man, who holds the shrine like a baby on his left arm. Rugonath, however, possesses a large car on wheels, which is dragged about by means of an enormous rope by two hundred or three hundred men.

The fair takes place on a raised plateau of some extent, which is situated to the south of the town. We were all seated near the young rajah, under an awning erected for the occasion in a commanding position, so that we could overlook all that was passing below. The ground formed a natural semicircle beneath and on either side of us, and there the women were seated, who were present as spectators only, dressed in all their silver ornaments and gayest clothes. Both men and women had wreaths of double marigolds round their heads. The former took an active part in the ceremonies, which commenced by their placing the palanquins containing the inferior gods on the ground, when they began dancing round them in a slow and regular measure, each with his left hand round his neighbour's waist, to the accompaniment of tom-toms and horns. After a time certain solo-dancers came forward, who moved in a rapid and animated manner. When the excitement was at its height, the attendants danced the gods up and down likewise, and made certain of them salaam to each other. Finally, the rajah himself went down and headed a procession of all the gods, taking hold of the rope attached to the car of Rugonath, and helping to drag it a considerable distance. When the car reached a certain point a large bonfire was lit, which seemed to be the conclusion of the festivities, for after that there was a general dispersion of the gods and their attendants to their respective homes.

On quitting our friend at Raesun we made an expedition to the Parbuti valley, the entrance to which is on the left bank of the Beas. About six miles below Sultanpore we had to cross the main stream on *mussocks*, as the inflated skins of oxen or sheep are called in the vernacular. For our convenience two of the larger skins were lashed together, and a *charpoy* (or native bedstead) fixed between them, on which we reclined. Two men on *mussocks* pulled and guided our little craft; whilst a third, also on this primitive contrivance, went in front of us and paddled. These skins are inflated with air, and then securely tied. When in the water the back of the animal is undermost, three legs stand upright, and the fourth is the place where the air is introduced. When about to enter the river the native pushes the skin a short distance away from him, and then throws himself upon it, holding a small paddle in his hands, with which he steers; and his legs, which hang in the water, assist him in advancing by means of the ordinary swimming motion.

That evening we encamped at the entrance of the Parbuti valley only, as it took a long time to get our tents and baggage across the river. The following day we made a double march, said to be only twelve miles, but over a very bad road, so that, although we started pretty early in the day, some of our servants who kept behind with the baggage did not come in till nearly midnight. Fortunately we were independent of our tents, there being a small forest officer's bungalow at Jerri, which was our halting-place. When about half-way thither we had a fine view before us of a mountain-chain averaging 20,000 feet above the sea, with many small glaciers on its summits.

In the Parbuti valley we found the *Pinus longifolia* in the lower part, and higher up the *P. excelsa* and deodaras; there were also wild olive, fig, and pear trees. Both in the Kulu and Parbuti valleys English fruit-trees seem to succeed wonderfully well; and it is not impossible that in time a great industry may spring up, and that district supply a great part of India with preserved fruits—for the climate is one that Europeans could live in all the year round—and, by proper management, the tinned fruits of Europe might be rivalled. Between Jerri and Manikern, twelve miles higher up the valley, there were a few tree rhododendrons.

About a mile before reaching the latter place there is a mountain view of singular grandeur and beauty. Seemingly towering to the sky, about 15,000 feet above where we were standing, and perhaps somewhere about fifteen miles distant from us as the crow flies, we saw, through an opening in the mountains, a great wall or chain of huge precipices terminating at their summits in finials and spires like a cathedral; and except that the colour of these rocks was mostly grey, with here and there a patch of glacier or snow, these points (to compare small things with great) had, to my mind, a great resemblance to Milan Cathedral, with its numberless tapering pinnacles. It struck us both that this peculiar effect might be due to the strata being perpendicular.

At Manikern there are hot springs bubbling up from

the earth in several spots. It is much visited by the Hindús as a place of pilgrimage. They also prize these springs on account of their great efficacy in rheumatic affections. This water is extremely hot—being nearly, if not quite, at boiling-point—so that the pilgrims and the inhabitants of the village are in the habit of boiling their rice and cakes of flour in it.

From Manikern we made an excursion to Phulga, the head of the Parbuti valley, and pitched our tents about 500 feet above the river. The road ascended considerably the whole way: much of the vegetation was of a deciduous character. Amongst other trees, there were some splendid specimens of the same variety of horse-chestnut as we had seen in Kashmir. I was informed by the head-man of the district that their fruit is used by the people as food. When fresh and uncooked, they are quite as bitter and hard as our English kind; but the natives, before using them, steep them seven days in water, and then, after pounding them, make the meal into cakes.

Our object in going to Phulga was to see a forest of deodaras, which, in the opinion of the chief forest official of the district, contains the finest grove of deodaras now remaining in the Himalayas. We were informed that the largest tree is 26 feet in circumference at five feet from the base, and 235 feet in height. A very large proportion were over 16 feet in girth, with a height hardly less than that of the colossus of the forest, which would, no doubt, have been considerably higher had it not, comparatively early in life, lost its leader and formed a double one.

After returning down the Parbuti valley, and spending one day at Sultanpore, on 4th November we started on our march into the Kangra valley. The first day was good and easy riding, the road being nowhere steep, but winding round the spurs of the mountains, which were clothed with jungle almost to their summits; but yet it was a continual ascent, so that we must have that day considerably diminished the height we had to reach in order to cross the Bubu Pass (10,000 feet) the following day. The road up to the summit was very fairly good, but is composed of steep zigzags. We had to ascend about 4000 feet in a distance of five miles. Near the top we saw only spruce-fir or *Abies Smithiana*, and silver firs or *Picea Webbiana;* but on descending on the other side there was an immediate and rapid change in the vegetation: tree rhododendrons and the evergreen oak were very abundant. The level space on the top of this pass is not larger than an ordinary dining-table. Behind us were the grand mountain-peaks to which I have alluded in describing the Parbuti valley; and the view in front of us was of almost unbounded extent, even down to the plains of India. In order to reach our halting-place at Budwani, we must have descended nearly as much as we had mounted on the other side: the gradient was even steeper. At the top of the pass we left English territory, and entered the native state of Mundi. The road from this point, though well made in the first instance, is now shamefully neglected.

From Budwani we rode to Jitingri, and from thence, for the next three marches, we followed the road we had passed over six months previously. At Palampore, however, we took a different line, and went to Kangra, the old capital of the district, which has a strong fort, and some interesting remains of temples, in its neighbourhood. This place was attacked by Mahmoud of Ghusnee, in the commencement of the eleventh century, but he did not take it. The present outer walls of the fort, and its inner gate, were built by Jehangir, who placed over the entrance a marble tablet of a very ancient date, on which was recorded that Alexander of Macedon married the daughter of the Rajah of Kangra. This tablet has been removed, nor could I ascertain where it now is (it is believed to be in some museum), but a very old native priest told a friend of ours that he well remembered it. About two hundred years ago Kangra was ruled by the rajahs of Chumba. After a time it was seized by another Rajput family, which in its turn was dispossessed by the Sikhs, from whom we took it at the end of the second Sikh war.

From Kangra our destination was Jullunder, about eight marches. We made a *détour*, which involved an extra march, in order to see Juwala Muki, which the Hindús esteem the most holy place in the Punjaub. Juwala Muki nestles close to a range of hills, about eight miles distant from the right bank of the river Beas. This town, as compared with others in India, had a medieval look. It is a mass of old buildings and temples, which, for the most part, are of hewn stone. The sanctity of the place is owing to the carburetted hydrogen gas which oozes out of the ground in many places, and is perpetually burning in more than one spot. There was no perceptible odour from it, nor any trace of smoke, and the flame had rather a bluish colour. The principal outlets for the gas were inside an ancient Hindú temple, which seemed in its pristine state within; but the exterior had been covered with modern designs in painted stucco in the time of Ranjit Singh, who also overlaid the roof with plates of gilt copper.

We were riding to Dhera, our next stopping-place,

when we saw a native running after us, gesticulating wildly, and at the same time saying something which we were too far off to hear. We waited for him to come up, and then saw that in one hand he held a *hookah,* or native pipe, and in the other the half of a large earthenware vessel, in which he carried some live embers. He began a long story, to the effect that he was just returning from Juwala Muki, whither he had gone very ill—had been quite cured there, and the embers he carried had been lit at the sacred fires. He was most pressing that we should accept some of them, even offering to take them to the bungalow for us. We declined, with thanks, when he begged us at least to take a pull at his *hookah.* The goddess Kali, and Baironath (another name for Shiva), seemed to be the favourite deities in that part. Under a sacred fig-tree, between Juwala Muki and Dhera, we saw his statue. From the branches of this tree were hung a number of small staves, no doubt native offerings to their spiritual police magistrate, as they consider him.

There was nothing particularly interesting on the next two marches, either in the way of scenery or of old monuments. But before reaching Bhurwein our road led through and round a succession of low hills of singular form, entirely composed of water-worn stones like a sea-beach, and very barren. Between Bhurwein and Gugrát these features were even more marked. On the north side of the hills there were a few *Pinus longifolia.* What soil there was seemed to be almost pure sand, except that in one or two spots there was a little cultivation where a tiny stream of water rendered a certain amount of irrigation possible, and a small village had consequently sprung up.

Our next march was to Hoshiarpore (eighteen miles), the first ten of which took us through the same style of scenery, after which we descended to the plains. The hills which I have just described occupy a considerable tract of country, and are not only barren in themselves, but the present state of things is doing much harm to the level country below, which, for some distance from them, is becoming unproductive from the gradual accumulation of sand on the surface, deposited upon it from above by the monsoon torrents. Possibly if wine-cultivation were attempted, or some trees planted on these barren hill-tracts—which, no doubt, were formerly covered with forests—the vegetation might in time form soil, and in the meantime their roots help to hold the sand together.

Hoshiarpore is a pretty little civil station, adjoining a native town of 13,000 souls, who are mostly Hindús. We called upon a native Christian missionary, who took a more hopeful view of the progress of Christianity as regarding Bengal (his native province) and the Punjaub, where he has lived seventeen years, than one commonly hears. He became a Christian at sixteen years of age. His mother, who is still alive, remains a Hindú. This missionary's wife has always been a Christian, her parents having been converted many years ago. They were, both of them, most simple and unaffected, but, at the same time, very intelligent people, and I regretted much that we had not more opportunities of conversing with them. They speak of themselves as natives; and Mrs C., a young woman with a large family, has the good sense to adopt the native *chuddar*, or thin veil, over the head and figure, though in their house and surroundings they live as Europeans.

Besides Hoshiarpore there are three other small Christian communities within a distance of twenty miles. Mr C.'s opinion was, that the uprising of the Sikh religion had, in some degree, unsettled people's minds in the Punjaub, and this more readily disposed them to listen to other teaching. He told us that he numbered more Mohammedans than Hindús amongst his converts, his congregations being composed principally of the *zemindari*, or land-holding class. We also gathered from him that in Bengal the educated natives, both Hindú and Mussulman, have a high opinion of the advantages of European civilisation; and, in particular, often lament the evil results of their system of early marriages. But the difficulties in the way of a reform in this respect are very great; for the custom of early engagements is so universal, that any youth who is not married at the age of sixteen is supposed to have something against him, and finds it very difficult to obtain a wife. From Hoshiarpore we drove to Jullunder, and went thence by rail to Lahore.

CHAPTER XXI.

LUCKNOW—ITS SAD ASSOCIATIONS—RESIDENCY—SKETCH OF THE HISTORY OF OUDH AND ITS RULERS—BUILDINGS AT LUCKNOW—CLAUDE MARTIN, THE FRENCH ADVENTURER—FYZABAD—TWO LARGE TOMBS—AJOUDHYA —CAWNPORE.

After staying a short time at Lahore we went direct to Lucknow, the present capital of Oudh—an intensely interesting place, from the stirring events which happened there in 1857 during the Mutiny. Before describing it, I will give a brief account of the colonisation of Oudh in Mohammedan times by both Rajputs and Mussulmans.

In the year A.D. 1193, Shahab-ud-din Ghori conquered and slew Rajah Prithora of Delhi. In the following year he also overthrew his great rival Rajah Jeichund of Kanouj, and made at different times vigorous attacks upon Mount Aboo, Gwalior, Benares, Gaya, and Ajmere, which were some of the centres of Rajput power and Hindú devotion. The Brahmin was contented to fold his hands and curse the barbarian. The Rajput, whose tradition it was that his race should be lords of the land in which they dwelt, could not bear to see his rajah bow beneath the Mohammedan yoke; but, only roused to a sense of his danger when too late for action, his resource was flight. Thus the Rajputs wandered southwards, northwards, and eastwards. This last direction led them to Oudh, their old seat of empire, from whence they had been driven out by the Bhurs. The second great class which helped to colonise that province comprises those who settled there after the Mohammedan power was firmly established, and had either had grants of land given them, or a special permission from the Moghul Court to emigrate thither. Some of these were Rajputs who had taken service with the conqueror. The Mohammedan armies contained numbers of such, especially during the reigns of Jehangir and Shah Jehan, who had both of them Rajput mothers. The earliest date of such grants of land was in 1527, in the time of the Emperor Baber, who conferred an estate in Oudh on Sheikh Bayazeed, an Afghan leader who had come and given in his submission to that prince. From that period till the end of the seventeenth century their numbers slowly increased; but since that time no new colonies have been planted.

Ajoudhya, the ancient capital of Oudh, is said to have covered an area of 48 *kos* (the *kos* varies from a mile and a quarter to a mile and a half in length). The origin of this city is connected with the mythic history of Oudh. Tradition says that for security's sake it was founded, not on the transitory earth, but on the chariot-wheel of the great Creator himself. The first rulers were of the so-called Solar race. On the fall or death of Rama, the last of these, Ajoudhya became a wilderness, the royal race was dispersed; and from its different members, who were thus scattered, the present rajahs of Jeypore, Oodypore, and others claim to descend. Little or nothing is really known of the history of Ajoudhya until it came under Mohammedan rule, except that we may gather, from the height and size of the mounds which still exist, that it must have for a long period been the site of an important city.

To Bikramajit, a strong supporter of the Brahminical revival, is attributed the rediscovery of Ajoudhya, after it had long been concealed by the growth of the jungle. Tradition enumerates more: that one dynasty ruled that province, some members of which were Buddhists or Jains, who are supposed to have built some old *deoharas,* or places of worship, belonging to those religions, which are still to be seen, but with modern restorations. Ajoudhya after this fell under the power of the rajahs of Kanouj, and at the time of the Mohammedan conquest contained three important Hindú shrines, which had, however, very few attendants attached to them.

In A.D. 1528 the Emperor Baber built a mosque on the site of one of these, Aurungzebe utilised another; and between the years 1658 and 1707, either he or one of his predecessors did the same with a third.

In the year 1855 there was a collision between the Hindús and Mussulmans. These last charged up the steps of one of the Hindú temples, but were driven back with considerable loss. The Hindús followed up their success and took the Jamamasthan—the enclosure where Baber had erected his mosque. Several of the king's regiments were looking on at the struggle, but they had strict orders not to interfere. It is said that up to that time both Hindús and Mohammedans used to worship in this mosque-temple, but now, since it came under British rule, a railing has been put up. The Mohammedans pray within the mosque; and in the outer court the Hindús have made a shrine where they bring their offerings.

Sadut Khan was the first of the Nawabs, or rulers in Oudh, who were originally viziers appointed by the King of Delhi, but gradually threw off even the semblance of allegiance. His successor was Safdar Jung, whose tomb I have already mentioned when describing the monuments near Delhi.

The period of the Nawab rule begins in 1723, and ends in 1856 with the deposition of Wajid Ali Shah, the ninth in succession from Sadut Khan. The title of king was conferred on the Nawabs by the British Government in 1819, because the then ruler, Gheis-ud-din Hyder, had complained of feeling himself aggrieved on more than one occasion when, on meeting in the street some descendants of the old kings of Delhi, the elephant on which he was riding had been compelled to kneel till they had passed by. The bestowal of this title upon him enabled him to dispense with what he considered a lowering of his dignity in the eyes of his people, though the province in general did not approve of this change of appellation, partly because it was done at the recommendation of the East India Company, and also because they considered it (the Mussulman portion of the population at least) an insult to the Delhi throne, in that they make no distinction between the words king and emperor, having only one word for the two; and so held that the Nawab, by being styled king, was putting himself on an equality with the great head of the Mohammedans in India.

The British Government deposed Wajid Ali Shah in 1856, on his refusal to sign the treaty which was to provide for the better government of his kingdom—whose rulers had latterly been given up to avarice, intemperance, and effeminate indulgences—and annexed the province that same year.

Lucknow, which had become the capital of Oudh only from the time of Ausuf-ud-dowla, A.D. 1775, is situated on the river Goomtee, which is navigable for some miles above the town, and also down to where it flows into the Ganges. Many of the buildings at Lucknow are pretty as seen in a photograph, but are extremely disappointing in reality; for, as contrasted with the Moghul architecture, there is as much inferiority as between a genuine old Gothic cathedral and a building of the time of the Georges.

The architectural unities have been totally disregarded. All is plaster and stucco, with great incongruities of design; and yet, with all this, the style is preferable to that of any ordinary modern English house, for there is at least some individuality about it.

The chief interest of the place for us English people must always centre in the Residency, which was built about the year 1800 by the Nawab Sadut Ali Khan for the use of the British Resident at his court. It is situated on a piece of ground which is slightly elevated above the plain; and up to the year 1857 was quite in the midst of a part of the native city, which has since that time been razed to the ground.

The history of the siege of Lucknow is too well known to need recapitulation here. The little cemetery in the grounds of the Residency tells a sad tale of officers and men who were killed under fire, and of helpless women and children who sank under the privations of a siege. I was much struck with the inscription over Sir Henry Lawrence's grave—it is so terse, and expresses so well what a good soldier of God and of his country should feel: "Here lies Henry Lawrence, who tried to do his duty;" the date; and below this, the words, "The Lord have mercy on his soul."

The siege began the end of June, and may be said to have been at an end the 25th of September. Many of the women and children had to remain in the *tykhana*, or underground rooms, during the whole of that period.

During the time of the earlier rulers of Oudh, who were only styled Soubadars and Nawabs, European architecture had crept in, modified, however, to a certain extent, with fantastic native additions, giving the buildings a quaintness of design. The foreign element was introduced by Claude Martin, a French soldier of fortune, who was born at Lyons in 1735, and died in Lucknow in 1800. He arrived in India in 1758, and served under Count Lally, who came in command of an armament which had been fitted out with the intention of extinguishing British commerce in India.

It is said that Martin deserted from Lally's force at the siege of Pondicherry, in consequence of his commander's severity; but it is more probable that he came over as a prisoner of war on the surrender of that garrison in 1761. He afterwards entered the English army, and rose to the rank of captain. Later on, he was employed to survey the estates of the Nawab of Oudh, and then became an adventurer in his service, having given up his pay in the East India Company's army, though still retaining his military rank. Martin then settled down in Lucknow, turned banker, and speculated largely and with great success. Between the years 1775 and 1797 he built houses, planted parks, and introduced a certain amount of Western civilisation. He made gunpowder, coined money, and imported European goods for his patron. In a short time he amassed an immense fortune, the greater part of which he devoted to founding educational institutions at Lyons, Calcutta, and Lucknow, where the Martinière College still perpetuates his name, and has separate departments for Europeans and natives; and a school for girls is also supported out of its funds. Claude Martin became a general before his death, which took place in the Turrad Buksh, which was the royal palace from the time of Sadut Ali Khan to that of Wajid Ali. According to the instructions which he had given some time previously, Martin's body was taken to the Martinière and buried there, as he feared that, at some time or other, that building might be confiscated by a native ruler, who would be deterred from doing so by the fact of its being a tomb.

The great Imambara, called the House of the Prophet, is by far the finest building in Lucknow, though a considerable portion of the European element has been introduced into the mosque, and various gateways near it. The large hall was built during the time of Ausuf-ud-dowla: its date has been variously given as 1783 and 1797. This building consists of a large central hall, 162 feet long by 53 feet 6 inches wide; it has verandahs on two sides of it, and at each end there is an octagonal chamber. The roof is made of a coarse kind of concrete, some feet in thickness, which has been formed upon a centring of bricks and mud, and then allowed to stand to dry. At the end of a year or two the centring could be removed, and the roofing was complete, being all in one piece. This building is now used as an arsenal. The mosque, which has been turned into barracks, has a deep cornice of acanthus-leaves the whole length of its frontage. This group of building is said to have been begun during a year of famine, in order to give employment to the starving population.

The Hoseinabad Imambara was erected by Mahomed Ali Shah, the third king of Oudh. The principal building contains his tomb and that of his mother. The interior is filled with chandeliers and globes of coloured glass. A general cleaning and renovation was going on when we saw it, in preparation for the Mohammedan festival of the Moharrum, when the gardens attached to it, as well as the principal chambers, would be illuminated with myriads of lamps. Its endowment, which is a very wealthy one, the British Government has set apart for the maintenance of the ex-royal family, who are living in Calcutta.

From Lucknow we went to Fyzabad, which was the capital up to rather more than a century ago. The only buildings worthy of notice which we could discover there were one or two gateways, ornamented with raised stucco-work, and two tombs, each within a garden. One of these was said to be the tomb of Ausuf-ud-dowla, and the other that of his mother or his wife, for there seemed to be different opinions upon this point. There was also one quaint house in the native bazaar, evidently of Hindú work: it was covered with numbers of raised plaster figures and other designs along its whole frontage. The tombs must possess rich foundations. There are numbers of small houses within the walls of the enclosures, which all appeared to be occupied. The Begum's tomb is by far the finer building of the two. It is 175 feet square, and stands on a platform about 20 feet in height. The greater part, if not all, of this structure is of a greyish-coloured stone, which has been covered over with whitewash. There is a large dome in the centre, and a smaller one on each of the chambers, which project at the four corners, whilst the sides are ornamented at intervals with tiny pinnacles. There is a good deal of raised carving on the exterior of this building. The designs have somewhat of the renaissance style about them, though this tomb must have been erected at too early a date to have been affected by the Claude Martin school of Lucknow; and therefore the European element is not altogether offensive; for much of the Indian taste mixed with Western ideas prevails in the decorations. The Begum's tomb is in the large central hall; the enclosed colonnade surrounding this is divided into several vaulted chambers, all opening out of one another. The interior walls, tinted of a deep French grey colour, are very highly ornamented with raised stucco-work, in white, which has been dusted over with minute fragments of mica, and give them a silvery appearance. The general character of this ornamental work reminded me much of the wall-decorations in some of the apartments at Versailles or in the Louvre.

From Fyzabad we drove over to Ajoudhya, about four miles distant. The present city covers a very large extent of ground, and contains a great number of Hindú temples, which appeared to be all more or less connected with the worship of Vishnu. Of the ancient city nothing remains; but in all directions there are enormous mounds, upon many of which modern buildings have been erected. It is most probable that the original city was built before the age of stone or fire-burnt bricks, and that all its temples and palaces were of sun-dried bricks or wood, else they could hardly have so completely vanished.

On first entering the modern Ajoudhya there is a large mass of masonry on the left hand, which resembles a fort. After mounting to the top of this by a long flight of steps, we reached a temple of comparatively modern date, placed in the centre of a courtyard, with chambers all round it for the attendants. The temple itself is on a raised platform, about three feet in height. The verandah which encircles it is supported on columns, and painted in bright colours. In the interior there is a statue of Hanuman, or the monkey-god. The lintel and side-posts of the principal doorway of the temple are of silver, in rich raised Arabesque work, about four inches in width.

Monkeys seem to be especially venerated in Ajoudhya. Nowhere else have I ever seen those animals so bold or in such numbers: they would come and steal from the store of a grain merchant even when the owner was seated there, though they appeared to distrust white people, and kept at a more respectful distance from us.

We also visited Cawnpore, which has sadder reminiscences than any other place in India. It possesses no fine buildings, either native or European, but is becoming a great centre of commerce. Two large cotton-mills are in full operation, and the Government have a large leather manufactory. The chief interest for strangers in that place is the tragic well, where so many bodies of dead and dying European women and children were thrown. Over this well has been placed a marble statue by Baron Marochetti; the inscription round the base of this was supplied by Lord Canning, and runs thus: "Sacred to the perpetual memory of a great company of Christian people, chiefly women and children, who, near this spot, were cruelly massacred by the followers of the rebel Nana Dhoodopunt of Bithoor, and cast—the dying with the dead—into the well below, on the 15th day of July 1857." The whole is surrounded by a high railing, within which no native is allowed to pass. This well is in the middle of a large, well-kept garden, in which are two or three enclosures full of the graves of those whose bodies were cast into the well, and of others who perished at that time. The Memorial Church, erected by the English Government, is a large building, which has, externally, not much architectural beauty. The effect of the interior is pleasing to the eye, and its proportions are good.

CHAPTER XXII.

CAWNPORE TO POONA—ROCK-HEWN TEMPLES AT POONA—HYDERÁBAD IN THE DEKHAN—SHORT HISTORICAL SKETCH OF THE PRESENT REIGNING FAMILY—THE NATIVE CITY—ITS VARIED AND TURBULENT POPULATION —A BREAKFAST AT SIR SALÁR JUNG'S—CONCLUSION.

FROM Cawnpore we made a rapid journey to Poona. On this our second visit we heard that within a couple of miles of that place there are two very ancient stone temples, or rather, a temple and a rock-hewn temple, excavated in a similar manner to the one at Karlee, only much smaller. Both of them are below the level of the ground, and are therefore effectually concealed till you are close upon them, which would account for their appearing to be known to few of the European residents of Poona. The rock is of a basaltic character. The entrance to these temples is through an archway cut in the rock; an area has been formed by removing the stone to the depth of perhaps fourteen feet, and in the centre of this enclosed space is a temple open on all sides, and supported on many pillars formed by the intervening stone having been removed: the roof has simply been formed by that portion of the rock being left *in statu quo*. Apparently the superincumbent weight was too great for its supports, consequently the roof has split in half, owing to the giving way of the pillars beneath that portion.

On the side of the enclosure facing the entrance there is another temple, made on the plan of that at Karlee, being on the reverse principle to the one I have just described; for the rock in this case is only cut away sufficiently to leave the necessary space for the worshippers—the walls, pillars, and roof being of the living rock; and, as at Karlee, the temple is only lighted from the entrance. The day we visited it was a gala-day. Numbers of natives—chiefly Brahmins and their wives and families — were performing their devotions there. We were not allowed to enter the innermost shrine. On the walls were some very spirited figures of nearly life-size; and also some sketches in black and white, which had a great deal of character in them. Both these temples are now dedicated to the worship of Shiva. From their form one would judge that they could never have been Buddhist.

On quitting Poona we went on a visit to the British Resident at Hyderabad, in the Dekhan. From the time of the Persian invasion of India under Nadir Shah, in 1738-39, the Moghul provinces became more and more independent of Delhi. The Nizam of the Dekhan began to rule as a sovereign prince, and treated the Nawab of Arcot as his feudatory. The Nizam of Hyderabad (under which name he is better known) had served in the army of Aurungzebe, and filled important posts at the Court of Delhi, which had appointed him governor of all its possessions in the Dekhan: he had been engaged in frequent wars with the Mahrattas of the Dekhan and those of Berar. The Nawab of Arcot was originally his deputy, but by degrees that appointment was becoming hereditary, though it was in the gift of the Nizam, who received a yearly tribute.

About the year 1740 there were troubles in the Carnatic. A kinsman of the Nawab, named Chunda Sahib, got possession of Trichinopoly, which enraged him; and the Nizam also was much displeased because the Nawab would not pay his accustomed tribute. The Nawab being killed in a battle against the Mahrattas, he was succeeded by his son, who took possession of the province without any reference to the Nizam, who was more indignant than ever at being thus defied, and demanded that the arrears of tribute should be immediately paid up, and threatened to oust him in case of refusal. On this the Nawab moved into the fort at Velore, where he was murdered at the instigation of a kinsman, who was himself proclaimed Nawab; but on finding that the treasures of the murdered man would not be given up to him, and his troops being clamorous for pay, he made his escape disguised as a woman, and Sayid Muhummed, the son of the former Nawab, was proclaimed in his stead. In 1743, the whole Carnatic being in a state of anarchy, the Nizam marched to Arcot, with an army of 80,000 horse and 200,000 foot, and named one of his own generals governor. This man being poisoned, he sent another; but the people insisted upon having some member of the old ruling family over them. The Nizam yielded, and gave out that Sayid Muhummed was the real Nawab, and the general, Anwar-ud-din, his guardian only. The following year the young Nawab was murdered on the occasion of a wedding, and being the last of his dynasty, Anwar-ud-din was then appointed Nawab. The Nizam dying in 1748, a war of succession ensued between three candidates. These were, the eldest and the second sons of the late Nizam, and one of his grandsons, named Musafir Jung.

Duplaix, the French governor of Pondicherry, espoused the cause of this last, and hoped to place rulers both at Hyderabad and at Arcot. He succeeded in establishing Chunda Sahib at Arcot; but when Anwar-ud-din was slain in battle, his son Muhammad Ali escaped to the south, and became known as the English Nawab of Arcot, Chunda Sahib being styled the French Nawab. Duplaix then wanted to create a French Nizam also, but the British Government had taken up the cause of Muhammad Ali, who was holding out at Trichinopoly.

The French urged Chunda Sahib to attack Trichinopoly, the possession of which, by their own nominee, was a matter of great importance to them, as it would enable their combined forces to march into the Dekhan, and place a French Nizam on the throne of Hyderabad. The want of money was a great obstacle to this scheme. Neither of the French candidates possessed any, so operations had to be delayed till they could try and squeeze some out of the Hindú rajahs; but in the meantime news came that Nazir Jung, the second son of the old Nizam, and uncle to the French candidate, had established himself on the throne of Hyderabad, and was marching into the Carnatic at the head of a large army, after having gained over to his cause all the so-called rajahs and Nawabs of that province. Both the English and the French Nawab supported him, though he is best known as the English Nizam.

The French took the field with their allies, but their cause was hopeless. Some of the French officers broke out into open mutiny, and the French Nizam was forced to surrender, his uncle promising, on the Koran, not to hurt him; but he nevertheless placed him in irons. In this manner it came about that an English Nizam was placed at Hyderabad, and an English Nawab at Arcot, the French Nizam being a prisoner in the ruler's hands, and the French Nawab being obliged to fly to Pondicherry. Very shortly after this, three Afghan chieftains who belonged to the Nizam's camp rebelled against him. He galloped to the spot, and was shot dead, when the French Nizam, being released from prison, was placed on the throne. He confirmed Chunda Sahib in his government at Arcot, but gave Duplaix the charge of the Carnatic country south of the Kistna.

Another revolution occurred in 1751, on the Nizam's return from a short visit he had paid to Pondicherry. This, like the former disturbance, was headed by some turbulent Afghans, and in the uproar which ensued this Nizam was also killed. Bussy, the French general who had accompanied him on his return to his own states, then selected his successor from amongst several state prisoners who were detained at Hyderabad, set him free, and proclaimed him Nizam under the name of Salabat Jung. This man was of course devoted to the French interests.

At this period the fortunes of the French in India had reached their culminating point. The English had lost their footing in the Dekhan, and our power was also much shaken in the rest of the peninsula. Our nominee still held Trichinopoly; but that place was closely besieged by the French and their Nawab. At this critical moment Robert Clive, a young captain, came forward. He saw that the only chance for us was to relieve Trichinopoly, and thought the only way to accomplish this was to draw the enemy elsewhere. With this end in view he marched upon Arcot, when its garrison became alarmed and fled. He entered it, and occupied the fort.

The enemy did exactly what he had calculated upon, and sent an army of 10,000 men to try and recover Arcot. Clive held out for fifty days with only 120 Europeans and 200 sepoys, resisting all assaults, filling up each breach as soon as made, and sallying out at night to attack the besiegers. The Mahrattas, struck with admiration at his brave defence, marched to his assistance. The commander of the opposing force tried threats and bribes, but in vain; he was obliged to leave Arcot in Clive's possession. This was the turning-point of the war. Though the French were still all-powerful in the Dekhan, and their Nizam was on the throne of Hyderabad, yet their cause was on the decline. They were compelled to raise the siege of Trichinopoly; their Nawab at Arcot surrendered to a Hindú rajah, was put to death, and Muhammad Ali, the English nominee, was placed there.

In 1754 peace was made between the English and French in India, and it was agreed that the then state of things should continue—that the French should keep their Nizam at Hyderabad, and we our Nawab at Arcot. Salabut Jung reigned as Nizam till 1761, when he was imprisoned and put to death two years later by his brother Ali, who ascended the throne. Ali was involved in wars with the Mahrattas during the greater part of his reign. In 1795 he took the field against Scindia, who had brought a large force, and obliged the Nizam to retreat to Kurdah, where, when his supplies fell short, he had to sign a convention, by which he resigned the fort and district of Dowlatabad to the Mahrattas; agreed also to pay three crores of rupees (equal at par to three millions of our money), and to deliver over his Prime Minister as a hostage.

At that time it was customary for the Nizams to

maintain two battalions of female sepoys, who were regularly trained to military exercises, mounted guard in the interior of the palace, and when the Nizam went out they carried him on their shoulders on a kind of palanquin. They were present at the battle of Kurdah, and were called *zuffer pultáns*, or victorious battalions. The pay of each individual was equal to about ten shillings per month of our money. I was told that the present Nizam no longer maintains such female warriors, but that the Emir-i-Kebir (whose wife is the only surviving daughter of Secunder Jah, he himself being a relation of the young Nizam, and, during his minority, co-regent with Sir Salár Jung) has a small body of them. Nizam Ali dying in 1803, he was succeeded by his son Secunder Jah, who at first maintained amicable relations with the British Government; but he soon fell into the hands of some low designing persons, who endeavoured to persuade him to resist all proposals of whatever nature which might come from the British Government. This state of things could not long continue: either the provisions of our treaty must be upheld, or we must leave the province; for any troops which might be left there would have virtually remained in an enemy's country without means of communicating with British territory.

The Nizam, on being remonstrated with, speedily became alarmed, and came to terms, of which the chief conditions were, that he should dismiss his two principal ill advisers, make some provision for Asim-ul-Omrah, the former Prime Minister, separate the civil and military administrations in Berar from each other, and intrust such offices to persons in whom the English Government had confidence; and also that the English Resident should be admitted to an audience with him whenever he required it. These terms were ratified by the Nizam, subject to some slight modifications; but the reconciliation was a short-lived one, for, on the death in 1808 of Meer Allum, his Prime Minister, new difficulties sprang up, arising from the choice of a successor to his office. After much discussion this appointment was given to the late Minister's son, who would appear to have been most unfitted for the post, for he was a great intriguer, though not wanting in ability. He was a firm believer in signs and omens, and was much influenced by them in the concerns of his daily life.

About this time the Nizam began to show symptoms of insanity. In 1811 this had reached to such a pitch that he distrusted every one, and would eat no food except what he had prepared with his own hands; and also ceased to appear in public. His feelings, too, towards the English Government seemed to experience a change. In 1815 his sons collected round them a host of the vagabonds who at that time swarmed in the city, and committed the greatest excesses, ending by seizing an attendant belonging to the Residency in order to extort money. The young princes were finally taken captive and removed to the fortress of Golconda, though not without bloodshed and the death of a British officer who was with the escort. In 1818 the Nizam emerged from his voluntary seclusion for a few weeks only, and then seems to have again relapsed into his former apathy. Secunder Jah died in 1828, and was succeeded by Nazir-ud-dowlah. He was followed in 1857 by Afzul-ud-dowlah, who, dying in 1869, Nuboob Ali Khan, the present Nizam, came to the throne, being at that time a child of barely three years of age. During his minority the government is administered by two co-regents—Sir Salár Jung (who is also Prime Minister), and the Emir-i-Kebir, who is a near connection of the royal family.

The aspect of the country is very singular for some time before reaching Hyderabad from the Bombay side. Shortly before arriving at the railway station of Lingumphalli the whole ground is covered with colossal boulders of a species of granite, which in some instances are accurately poised three or four of them one above the other. They would seem much too large to have been ever placed in that position by the hand of man, and yet most of them are arranged with a certain regularity of line and disposition which staggers one at first sight.

The city of Hyderabad stands on the south side of the Musah river, which becomes a rapid stream during the rainy season, but is very shallow at other times. The city proper, which is about four miles in length by three in breadth, is enclosed by high walls, and is approached by an arched bridge over the river. The streets are narrow, crooked, and badly paved. The Nizam is a Mohammedan of the Sunni sect; Sir Salár Jung, being of Persian descent, belongs to the Shias; the general population of the country round is Hindú. The city of Hyderabad, formerly called Baugnugger, was founded about 1685 by Mahomed Cooly Cuttub Shah. In 1687 it was taken and plundered by the Moghul forces of Aurungzebe: its inhabitants had previously retired to the fortress of Golconda.

Aurungabad was at one time the capital of the Nizam's dominions, but it was abandoned as being too near the Mahratta frontier. The city of Hyderabad contains a great mixture of races and types: there are seen Arabs,

Afghans, Sikhs, Pathans, and also people from Oudh. Many of these originally entered the country in the character of mercenary levies. The Arabs are most turbulent and unruly members of the community, as are also the mixed race descended from the original settlers of that nation; so that an order has of late been issued that no more Arabs are to be allowed to enter the state —and should any one leave it, he will in future not be permitted to return to it.

In the Nizam's dominions there are numbers of petty chiefs who possess country estates, which they manage by deputy, as they themselves prefer to live in the city: each of these chiefs has his quota of armed attendants. In driving through the city, almost every other man one meets bears arms, and carries a sword, a matchlock, or a dagger, occasionally even all three. On the smallest cause of offence weapons are drawn. Beyond the city is a lake of considerable size, which has been formed by a dam. This piece of water is of such extent that a small steamer is kept upon it, on board of which we steamed about for some time. There is also another lake between Hyderabad and Secunderabad, which last is the British military station, and about seven miles distant from the former place.

We also drove to Golconda, about six miles to the west of Hyderabad, where there are numerous domed tombs clustered together. These have a fine effect when seen at a little distance; but a nearer view of them is very disappointing when one has seen monuments of a like nature far superior in the more northern parts of India. No one—not even the Prime Minister—is permitted to enter the fortress at Golconda unless the Nizam be residing there. The reason for this prohibition does not clearly appear; but I heard of cases in which persons who had ventured to approach too near had been fired upon by the guard.

During our stay we were invited to breakfast with Sir Salár Jung. The meat was served in the regular European manner, with the addition of two or three native dishes. After breakfast the minister showed us over his house, which contains a great many suites of rooms fitted up in European style; and he afterwards took us to see his own private apartments—his business room, with only a writing-table and a couple of chairs in it. Opening out of this is a tiny ante-room, where he sits on cushions on the ground during his hours of relaxation, and takes his meals in regular native fashion. His palace covers an enormous extent of ground. We did not see the ladies' apartments, which are quite at the back; but we were shown one room, fitted up, as far as I can remember, by Sir Salár's father, the walls of which are decorated in a singular manner, being entirely covered with cups, saucers, and plates of china, mortared into their places. Some of these are good specimens of porcelain, but the majority are very poor examples of inferior English ware.

I must here conclude our tour in Central and Northern India; but we hope, at no distant date, to visit its southern part, where many fine temples and other objects of interest are to be found, which I may write about at some future time, if I have not already exhausted the patience of my readers.